Delaware Saengerbund

Delaware Saengerbund

1853–2003

Hilde Cox and Trudy Gilgenast

Wilmington, DE
2002

Published by Cedar Tree Books, Ltd.
Nine Germay Drive
Wilmington, DE 19804, USA

ISBN: 1-892142-16-3

Title: Delaware Saengerbund 1853–2003
Authors: Hilde Cox and Trudy Gilgenast
Typography: Angela Werner of Michael Höhne Design
Publishing Director: Nicholas Cerchio

Library of Congress Cataloging-in-Publication Data

Cox, Hilde.
    Delaware Saengerbund : 1853-2003 / Hilde Cox and Trudy Gilgenast.
        p. cm.
Includes bibliographical references (p.   ) and index.
    ISBN 1-892142-16-3 (alk. paper)
    1. Delaware Saengerbund--History.   I. Gilgenast, Trudy. II. Title.
    ML27.U5 D44 2002
    782.5'06'0751--dc21

                                                            2002014095

Printed in the United States of America on 60# archival, acid-free paper by Sheridan Books of Ann Arbor, Michigan.

Contents

List of Illustrations

COLOR PLATES

This book is dedicated to the

Delaware Saengerbund presidents and officers

who showed courage and determination, sacrifice, and wisdom

to establish and nurture a German society in Delaware

Acknowledgements

We are grateful to the many people who have contributed their time and talents to bring this project to fruition. We thank the Board of Directors and members of the Delaware Saengerbund for their support. We thank Ruth Olivier for her sincere interest in the history of the organization, reading the handwritten minutes, and teaching the script to Hilde Cox; Heidi Valiante, Wilhelmine O'Shea, for reading and translating early minutes; Andy Olivier, for his research in newspapers and his oral history; Ed Brandenberger, for research in newspapers; Lloyd Maier, for research into Christian Krauch and Daniel Maier; Gus Teipelke, Cliff Weber, and Joe Pouser, for photographs of artifacts, places and people; Alfred Escheu, Simon Schock, Dr. Iris Busch, Erika and Heinz Ambrosch, for viewpoint interviews; and Paul Heinemann for an accurate account of the early Ogletown years.

We appreciate the help we received from the research libraries. We would like to thank especially William Thomas for his detailed research in newspapers and records at the Historical Society of Delaware; the staff of the Historical Society of Delaware, for their help in research; Hagley Museum and Library, for providing newspaper and records research; the Balch Institute, for newspaper research and photographs; Joseph Neville, for reference material, and also the German Society of Pennsylvania. During the many hours we spent at the University of Delaware's Morris Library, we found the students in the microfilm section to be always kind and helpful in assisting us, and they deserve our special thanks.

Our sincere appreciation goes to Dr. Carol Hoffecker for providing helpful suggestions in the early stages of the book and writing the perceptive foreword to the finished product. We thank above all our editor Karen Druliner for her expertise, patience, humor, and skillful guidance in writing the manuscript.

Finally we express our heartfelt thanks to our families: to Bill Cox for his encouragement to write down the Saengerbund's history for future generations; to children Stephanie, Daniel, and Anne, who have fond memories of times spent at the Delaware Saengerbund; and to the entire Gilgenast family for sharing a love of customs and traditions and for their interest in preserving their heritage. *Herzlichen Dank!*

Foreword

It takes an enormous commitment from generations of people to sustain an organization for 150 years the midst of America's fast-moving society. The survival of Wilmington Delaware's Saengerbund, originally an all-male German singing society, is particularly remarkable. German immigration to America, including the Wilmington area, peaked in the mid- to late nineteenth century. In the twentieth century, while the immigrant community matured beyond most members' remembrance of their ancestors' homeland, America's relationship with Germany underwent dramatic swings from bitter enmity to close friendship. Through it all, while other of Delaware's German ethnic organizations have declined and died, the Saengerbund has endured and thrived. Today it retains an important role in the local community, both for those who have a German heritage, and those who do not.

This volume makes the reason for the Saengerbund's success clear: The organization has adapted itself to changing times. After 110 years as a German-speaking, all-male club, in 1963 the membership made the life-saving decisions to switch to English and to admit women. Both were crucial to the group's survival. Otherwise, it would be impossible to contemplate the creation of the book that you hold in your hand: researched and written in the English language by two highly-committed and capable women. It would also be impossible to imagine that the organization could have moved forward to build its present suburban complex in Ogletown, Delaware, and to develop Oktoberfest and similar events that introduce aspects of German culture to new generations of German Americans, as well as to people of other ethnic backgrounds.

Although the authors never lose sight of their focus on the Saengerbund, this volume offers a valuable introduction to the history of Delaware's German immigrant community as a whole. Its authors carefully place the establishment of that community into the context of German political, cultural, and social history, and they set the Wilmington immigrants into a broader picture of German immigration to the United States. They also chronicle the histories of other German American organizations that once flourished, then disappeared from the Wilmington area. They have made excellent use of the Saengerbund's surviving minute books and have filled in the gaps with reference to the newspaper coverage that the organization regularly received a century ago.

As early as 1890, when some of the children of immigrants of the 1840s were already grandparents, members of the community were asking one another, "Who will teach the German language to the next generation?" This is the perennial question that eventually confronts every immigrant community, and it has no simple answer. Grandparents' recollections of the homeland are but memories, while cousins who remained behind have experienced many changes that occurred after the immigrants' leaving. Grandchildren cannot be expected to experience the world of their grandparents. And yet we know that people who forget the past of their family and society are left in a confusing cultural limbo. The authors of this book have provided a valuable resource that will bring back memories to some, but, more importantly, will instruct the next generation in those ways of their ancestors that have enduring value for their future and for the future of the United States as a "Nation of Immigrants."

Carol E. Hoffecker
Richards Professor of History
University of Delaware

Introduction

On March 17, 2003, the Delaware Saengerbund will celebrate its 150th *Stiftungsfest*, the anniversary of its founding day. Although the anniversary was not celebrated regularly in the early years, it became one of the society's traditional events after 1900. Some years the Stiftungsfest was an elegant evening affair with a banquet and grand ball attended by hundreds of members and guests. In other years, only a few members gathered to hold on to the dream of continuing the tradition of the German singing society here in Delaware. More recently, the Stiftungsfest has opened with a reception and an exhibit called *Ein Blick zurück—Looking back*—that showcased memorabilia from the Saengerbund's archives to acquaint members with the society's history. These exhibits provided the background for this book. The information was drawn mostly from the Saengerbund's minutes, which begin in 1853 and extend to the present, with a gap from 1889 to 1913 due to missing record books. Because the proceedings of the early years were handwritten in old German script, which few members are able to read, it has been necessary to transliterate them into modern German writing and then translate them into English.

The Saengerbund material was augmented by other sources, mainly the newspaper files housed at the University of Delaware, Hagley Museum and Library, the Balch Institute, as well as materials in the Delaware Historical Society's library. The newspaper accounts bring concerts, picnics, and festivals to life, especially for the period of the missing minutes. The *Alte Herren*, the men in charge of the club business, are more than names in a record book when we see them in old photographs. Some are included here, as are photos of artifacts rescued from the old German Hall in Wilmington. For the Ogletown years, current members shared firsthand information through interviews.

The full record yields a colorful picture of 150 years of Delaware history created by German immigrants and their descendants. The primary audience of this book is intended to be the members of the Delaware Saengerbund, for many younger and new members know little of the society's early history. Readers who are interested in regional history also may find this book of interest, while others may be inspired to start their own research for more information about relatives mentioned in the society's records.

The material is arranged in two parts: the Wilmington years, 1853–1966, and the Ogletown years, 1967–present. The first part is organized chronologically; the second part follows the order of committee reports at a general membership meeting and provides an historical description of each group, committee, or event.

The appendix includes lists of music directors and officers, chorus members of 1853 and 1903, current chorus, Ladies, and Enzian Volkstanzgruppe members, and members and students who have received awards. A selected glossary of German terms provides aid in understanding the context.

Finally, this book answers frequently asked questions: How did the Saengerbund begin? When was the *Damen-Verein*—the Ladies Auxiliary—founded? When did the society's business language change from German to English? When did the Delaware Saengerbund move from Wilmington to Newark? Has there always been an Oktoberfest?

Today, the history of the Delaware Saengerbund is still being written, as new names and events are discovered and added to the record. The customs and traditions celebrated throughout our history form a cultural link among the generations and contribute to the preservation of German ethnic identity and heritage. Although the roots of a proud heritage have been transplanted, they have taken well to the new soil.

Looking back today allows us to take pride in the Saengerbund of yesterday and today—and to hope for its future as a German American society where German cultural traditions are honored and shared.

Hilde Cox and Trudy Gilgenast
Newark, Delaware
2002

Delaware Saengerbund

1

Across the Wide, Wide Sea

Ein stolzes Schiff streift einsam durch die Wellen
und trägt uns unsre deutschen Brüder fort.
Die Fahne weht, die weissen Segel schwellen,
Amerika ist ihr Bestimmungsort.
Seht auf dem Verdeck sie stehen,
sich noch einmal umzusehen
ins Vaterland, ins heimatliche Grün,
seht, wie sie übers grosse Weltmeer ziehn.

Auswandererlied, Anfang 1800

Alone, a proud ship plows the waves
And carries off our German brothers.
The flag is waving, the white sails swell—
America is their destination.
See them standing there on deck,
gazing back once more
Towards the fatherland and the
green meadows of home,
See how they sail across the wide, wide sea.

Immigrant Song, early 19th century

- Emigration -

Nineteenth-century Germany was a kaleidoscope of monarchies, principalities, and small states, each imposing its own set of strict regulations upon its subjects' daily lives. Owning land, getting an education, choosing a profession or trade, marrying, and traveling out of state—these privileges were withheld from the vast majority. As a result, the people made many attempts to bring about reforms and to create constitutions that would establish and guarantee basic rights for everyone. This struggle for freedom and prosperity engulfed young men and women during the 1830s and 1840s. Inspired by the successful American revolution fifty years earlier, they hoped to accomplish a similar change and create a better life in their homeland. Letters from American relatives who described a more liberated way of life also kindled their desire to live without regulation and taxation.

In earlier years, farmers and rural workers had immigrated to America because of failed harvests and food shortages. Now failed German state governments and the resulting unrest caused many *Bürger*, the citizens of small towns and large cities, to embark on a new course of action. Since political assemblies were closely watched or prohibited, the singing societies and sport associations of every town provided safe places to gather. They were meeting grounds where information was exchanged and plans for the future were discussed. At *Sängerfeste* and *Turnfeste*—regional song festivals and athletic assemblies—the thousands of participants expressed their ideas and ideals through songs.

Newspapers that followed the movement closely and printed stories about the widespread unrest were quickly censored. Flyers with titles like "Demands of the People" were circulated in Baden and Württemberg, calling for *tatkräftiges Handeln,* or immediate action. Finally, in March 1848, the people of Berlin and Vienna took their demands into the streets.

Initially it seemed that the March Revolution might bring about the desired changes. The first parliamentary National Assembly was held in Frankfurt and charged with the dual task of drawing up a national constitution and creating a central government. By 1849, twenty-eight German states had recognized the new constitution that spelled out *The Fundamental Rights of the German People,* but it was a short-lived victory. Pressured by local demonstrations calling for implementation of the statutes, the authorities reacted by calling in the military to crush all uprisings. At the same time, members of the National Assembly proved unable to overcome their own conflicts of interest as represented by the political parties. After the National Assembly was dissolved, a reactionary backlash gripped the German states. Constitutions were revised and stricken, newspapers closed down. Political gatherings

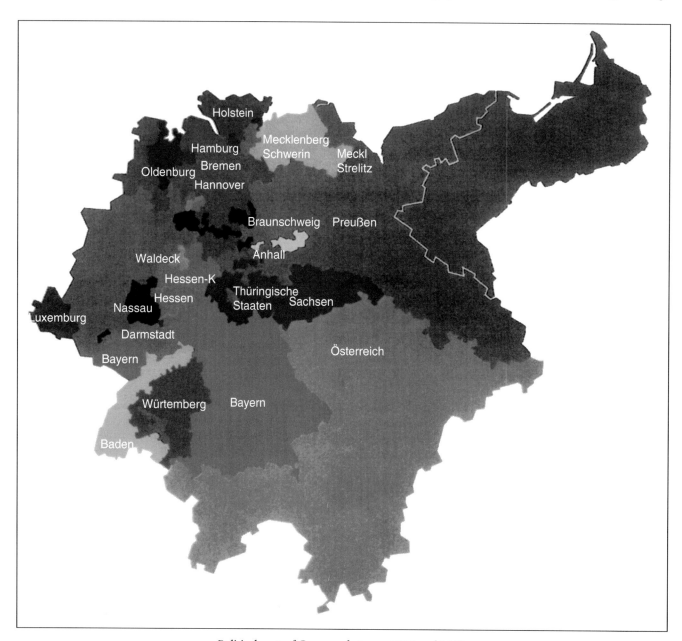

Political map of Germany between 1815 and 1848.

were prohibited, their spokesmen arrested. By 1851, the spirit of freedom had been enchained again by the ruling authorities. Many young people felt they had to choose between burying their hopes or leaving home to realize their dreams in another country. From the Grand Duchy of Baden alone, eighty thousand people—nearly one-sixth of the population—fled across the borders to Switzerland or Great Britain, while the majority of courageous exiles made their way to America.

-Immigration-

United States Census and Immigration reports from the years 1850–1855 registered the increasing numbers of immigrants from Germany and Austria.

1850	1851	1852	1853	1854	1855
78,896	72,482	145,918	141,946	215,009	71,918

The port cities of New York, Philadelphia, and Baltimore accommodated a large number of this new wave of German immigrants. German societies, established by immigrants who had arrived during the famines in the eighteenth century, were able to look after the newcomers' immediate needs and help them settle in the new country. Among such groups was The Philadelphia German Society, the oldest German society in America, chartered on December 26, 1764, for "the purpose of contributing to the relief of distressed Germans in Pennsylvania." The German Society of Maryland followed in 1783 to aid Germans in Maryland. In Delaware, Germans from the Baltic Sea region had come as settlers at the invitation of the Swedish crown as early as 1638 when the Swedes established Fort Christina. When sailing vessels could land anywhere along the Delaware and its tributary rivers, Fort Christina, New Castle, and Grubb's Landing developed into regular ports of call. German settlers who disembarked there worked the land along the Christina and Delaware Rivers. As members of Old Swedes Church, they were entitled to be buried in the church cemetery, and a German plot reserved for German Lutheran clergy is still marked in the church's records. Later, when New Castle lost its importance as a port, fewer Germans found their way to Delaware and there was no need for a German aid society.

In the 1850s, as the new group of immigrants from Germany, the "Forty-Eighters" as they became known, debarked at the three major harbor towns, Delaware and its largest city, Wilmington, came into focus again as a place where employment might be found. The first and now rare *Directory and Register of the Borough of Wilmington and Brandywine of 1814* (the Delaware Saengerbund owns one of only two known copies) described Wilmington's location in terms of its neighboring cities: "Wilmington is a flourishing borough, pleasantly situated, between Christiana and Brandywine Creeks, within about three miles of the river Delaware, in latitude 39° 54' 21" N. and longitude 1° 27' 31" E. from Washington City. Distant from Philadelphia twenty-eight miles and course nearly due S.W. from Baltimore seventy and an half miles, and from Washington City one hundred and twelve miles." In 1814, Wilmington was a small mill town of about 5,000 people, but early on its enterprising citizens recognized the need for industrial expansion. Development was advanced by the city's access to the Delaware River and the Christiana, or Christina River, as it is now called. By 1840, Wilmington's population was about 8,500. The number rose to 13,000 by 1847 and to 16,163 in 1853. During each decade between 1840 and 1890, the population increased by 45 percent. The seventh census of 1850 registered 3,513 Irish immigrants living in Delaware. Of that number 1,215 worked in Wilmington, making the Irish the largest ethnic group in the city. In contrast, only 343 Germans were registered in Delaware, and only 157 lived in Wilmington.

After 1850, the town grew rapidly and factories soon replaced the old flour mills. Contractors and industrialists actively sought workers for the new factories. Broadsides advertising jobs were posted in all three major harbor towns, and on occasion contractors personally sought out skilled workers on the wharves, even paying their fare to Wilmington.

In her 1982 book, *Wilmington—A Pictorial History,* historian and author Carol Hoffecker presents a bird's-eye view of Wilmington's industrial landscape: "The railroad provided the major impetus toward industrialization in Wilmington. The Philadelphia, Wilmington and Baltimore Railroad came through the city in 1837. The rails followed the west bank of the Delaware River from Philadelphia, crossed the Brandywine, and paralleled the Christina through Wilmington toward the Chesapeake. The narrow strip of land separating the rails from the river became prime industrial real estate for foundries and plants building railroad cars, boilers, steamboats, and yachts. By the 1860s Wilmington's largest employers were located there."

The Pusey and Jones foundry that manufactured all kinds of machinery, the Charles Bush foundry that specialized in railroad car wheels, and the large Harlan and Hollingsworth shipbuilding company were eager to employ the young German immigrants who arrived at a time when jobs were plentiful. Skilled workers could find immediate employment as basket weavers, blacksmiths, coopers, coppersmiths, cordwainers, leather workers, machinists, or trimmers. Establishing a business was an alternate choice, because tailors, clothing merchants, shoemakers, bakers, butchers, or painters did not lack for customers in the growing town. By 1860, Wilmington had a population of nearly 20,000. At the time, over 1,200 Germans were registered in Delaware, and about half of them lived and worked in Wilmington where they settled within walking distance of the factories, roughly in the area of Front and 8th Streets, and French and Poplar Streets. Records indicate that there were 266 from Prussia, 216 from Baden, 144 from Württemberg, 129 from Bavaria, 221 from Hesse, 3 from Nassau, and 395 from other areas. In time, the German states from which they had emigrated seemed far removed. From their new-world perspective, their different home states had merged into the unified *Vaterland* they had dreamed of, and they had become "the Germans."

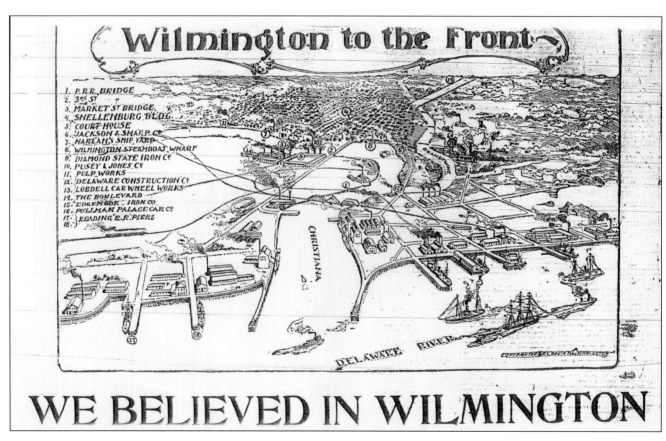

Map of Wilmington, 1906.

2

Awake, Ye Songs, Awake

Wacht auf, ihr Lieder! Wacht auf mit
*   Herz und Mund!*
Es gilt, ihr Brüder, dem Sängerbund!
Von Berges Höh' ins weite Land reicht des
*   Gesanges Zauberband.*
Er klingt, ihr Freunde, fern und nah, für euch
*   in tiefster Seele ja!*
Sei stark und gross, du Sängerbund!

*   -aus dem handgeschriebenen Liederbuch des Saengerbundes,*
*   1853*

Awake, ye songs, awake! Awake with
    heart and voice!
At stake, O brothers, is the singers' unity!
The song, like an enchanted ribbon, extends
    from mountain fields
So high to wide green meadows down
    below where it
Resounds deep in your souls, O friends near
    and far.
Be strong and great, O Saengerbund!

   -from the Saengerbund's handwritten song book, 1853

-The Founding of the Singing Society-

Young immigrants without relatives or friends in Wilmington looked for places to rent or took room and board at one of the hotels. On Sundays, they attended St. Mary's Catholic Church, Old Swedes Church, or the new German Lutheran Church that had been established in 1848. There were no local German societies to join, so the men socialized in the taverns, as they would have done in Germany, and the women visited each other in their homes or kept to themselves.

Christian Krauch was eager to welcome the men to his tavern on King Street and to hear news from the homeland that had endured so much turmoil. Krauch had left Germany in 1834. Since coming to Wilmington,

he had been successful as saloonkeeper, caterer, and brewer. Later he became proprietor of the Mount Vernon Hotel and Rosendale Pleasure Grounds, located near Lovering Avenue. It was a popular spot for picnics and parties and known as Wilmington's first outdoor park. In 1853, Krauch's new employee was a young man from Philadelphia, John Fehrenbach. He was born in Ettenheim, Baden, in 1831, and immigrated to the United States in 1849 at the age of eighteen. He learned the art of brewing while residing in Philadelphia and then moved on to Wilmington where he found employment with Christian Krauch.

John Fehrenbach loved to sing. He was aware that the German singing societies of the northeastern Atlantic region would gather for the fourth song festival in Philadelphia in June of that year. Wilmington did

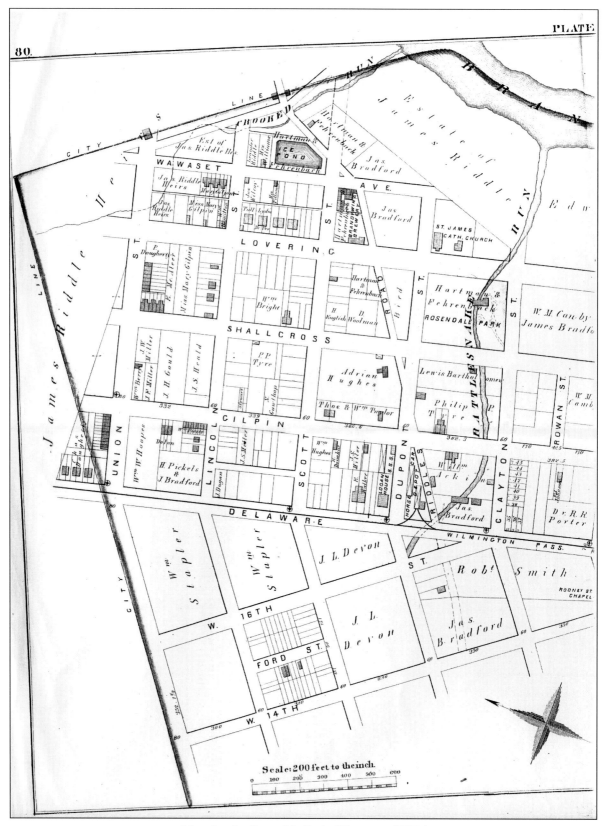

Map showing Rosendale Park. (Courtesy of HSD)

not have a German singing society, and so he wondered if there would be enough interest and good voices to form a *Männerchor,* a men's chorus. Those gathered on March 17, 1853, at their favorite *Stammtisch*—the table that was reserved for them each week in Krauch's tavern—were enthusiastic about the idea and agreed to organize formally.

John H. Mühlhausen, a tailor who first lived at 68 French Street and later at 210 East 5th Street, was appointed to work out a constitution and bring it to the next meeting on March 21. According to the minutes, the first order of business at that meeting was the discussion and acceptance of the constitution. As specified in the first article of the first constitution, the name of the organization was Sängerbund, also spelled as Saengerbund. The German word *Bund* is used for an association, alliance, league, or society that is "bound" together for a common purpose, in this case for the purpose of singing, as the second article of the constitution stated: "The Saengerbund's purpose is practice in singing and the training and development of voices." The constitution also specified that the organization was to consist of active, passive, and honorary members. Active members were classified as those who sang in the chorus; they were the *Sänger,* or singers. They could vote and hold office. Passive members—those who did not sing—could attend meetings, but had no voting rights and could not be elected to an office. Both were able to sponsor new members. Singing practice was held once a week. Business was conducted after each session and at a monthly general meeting. An initiation fee of 50 cents per member was collected, as well as dues of 6 1/4 cents per week, an amount that seems odd today. Seven members constituted a quorum. As long as the organization had four members, it was considered to be in existence. In case of dissolution, the property and assets were to go to an organization similar in spirit and objectives. This last article could never be changed, but the other articles could be revised quarterly, and a majority could vote for temporary changes at any meeting. Officers were elected quarterly, and the details of the duties and rights of both officers and members were noted in the bylaws.

The second order of business was the election of officers. Those chosen to lead the new Saengerbund were: chorus director, G. Anton; president, William Papenmeyer, a draftsman at the railroad depot; vice president, Ludwig Grieb, a tailor residing at 504 Shipley Street. The secretary was John H. Mühlhausen. The treasurer was Henry Bleyer who owned a wicker basket business and manufactured cradles, chairs, coaches, and sleigh bodies at 319 West Front Street. The office of music librarian went to John Fehrenbach. The third order of business was the nomination of Christian Krauch as honorary member. The new Saengerbund adjourned, then reconvened the very next day, March 22.

A membership list bearing the signatures of sixteen men is part of the first record book. In later years, these sixteen men were thought to have founded the Saengerbund on March 17, 1853. However, a closer look at the minutes shows that not all sixteen were present in March, and that several others, who were present, did not sign the membership list at all. At the second meeting on March 22, the sum of eight dollars was collected as an initiation fee, which could mean that sixteen men were present at that meeting and each paid fifty cents. It is believed that the minutes provide the more accurate list of names. There may have been other singers as well, since immigrants often joined a society, but left again after a short stay. In the margins of the record books, the verb *abgereist,* which means "departed from town," appears next to many names. Another source of confusion is that the spelling of

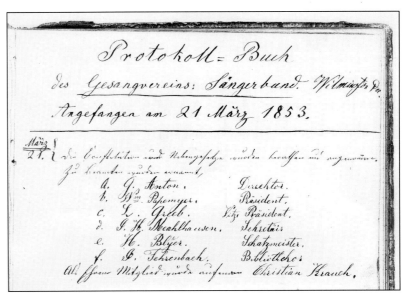

Record book of the Saengerbund, Wilmington, begun March 21, 1853, with roster of first officers.

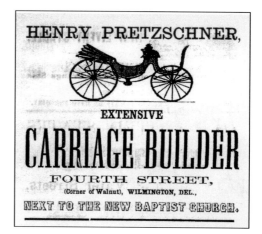
*Advertisements of members Bleyer, Mühlhausen, Hiller, Krauch, Prell, Pretzschner in the City Directory of 1857
(Courtesy of HSD), and Trustees' signatures of the Saengerbund No. 1.*

surnames is often inconsistent. As for first names, English frequently alternates with German so that *Johann* becomes *John*, who becomes *Tschon* when the English name is spelled the way it sounds in German. For the name Saengerbund, printed records show that the group used the *ae* spelling in its own name, but in the handwritten minutes, the choice of whether to use the *ae* or *ä* spelling was left up to the recording secretaries. This book uses the club's preferred spelling.

More men joined the chorus, and by June 1853, the Saengerbund had twenty-six active singers who met twice a week for rehearsals. Music director G. Anton copied the songs for the chorus by hand into individual songbooks. The songs addressed all themes of life, ranging from songs about the fatherland and leaving hearth and home to songs about war and peace. Sweet love songs, rousing drinking songs and march-like hiking songs were sung in four-part harmony, creating a bond of friendship among the members while also conjuring up memories of home. A solemn hymn, *Schäfers Sonntagslied: Das ist der Tag des Herrn* ("Shepherd's Sunday Song: This is the Day of the Lord") was reserved for special occasions. Over time it became the Delaware Saengerbund's signature song.

Many of the songs expressed a strong yearning for the simple folk life and the mysticism of its soul, typical of a German Männerchor's repertoire. They were also characteristic of the early nineteenth-century Romantic Movement—the time when the Brothers Grimm collected folktales, and Achim von Arnim and Clemens Brentano gathered songs that were published as a collection of old German folksongs in *Des Knaben Wunderhorn* in 1806. The book contained only words but no melodies and was a source of inspiration for composers like Friedrich Silcher, Conradin Kreutzer, and Carl Friedrich Zelter. Their compositions in the folksong style often gave the first tenor voice the melody and the three other voices—second tenor, first and second bass—the harmonies. These songs quickly became popular, and *Männer Gesangvereine*—men's singing societies—sprang up in every region, especially small villages. In contrast, the larger cities had a tradition of mixed choruses that devoted their time and skill to the classics and performed music by Bach, Mozart, or Beethoven in churches, opera houses, or music halls.

The young men who founded and joined the new singing societies enjoyed the camaraderie of these gatherings as much as the music. Each society had a *Vereinsfahne*, a flag that was carried in parades and displayed at regional festivals. Therefore, an important issue for the new Saengerbund in Wilmington was acquiring a flag that would identify the group in local parades and at the forthcoming regional song festival in Philadelphia. The committee responsible for its purchase consisted of director G. Anton and honorary member Christian Krauch. The fabric was purchased for $40, and $30 was paid for the design, an enormous amount for the fledgling society. Members raised the money by soliciting donations, and within two months they had collected a total of $92.78.

An outing planned for the Monday after Pentecost was the first social affair. By June, the society's inventory consisted of forty-three songbooks in two parts, a carrying case, an inkwell, sixteen hand-copied songbooks for the forthcoming Sängerfest, one music score, books of the recording secretary, one ballot box, and one brand new flag.

-Nordoestlicher Saengerbund-

German singing societies were established in nearly every American city where German immigrants settled. The larger cities—New York, Washington, Chicago—had mixed choruses as well as Männerchöre. From the beginning, these carried out the tradition of *Sänger-feste*—regional song festivals—as was the custom in Germany, where the first regional songfest had been held in Würzburg in 1845. Chicago hosted the first national song festival for the North American men's singing societies in 1849, and five choruses traveled there to participate.

The following year, 1850, Philadelphia hosted a song festival for the German Männerchöre of the northeastern states at which the umbrella organization, *Nordoestlicher Saengerbund,* or Northeastern Singers' Union of America, was founded. Coordinating song festivals was its main purpose. The Sängerfeste were held every year for a while, later at two-year and then three-year intervals. At the first Philadelphia Sängerfest, 400 singers representing fifteen societies participated. At the second festival, held in Baltimore in 1851, the number of participants increased to twenty-one societies and 500 singers. In 1852, at the third festival in New York City, thirty-one societies were represented by 800 singers. The choruses met for the fourth time in

Philadelphia, from June 25–28, 1853. Eight hundred and fifty voices representing thirty-five societies joined in song, with the Saengerbund of Wilmington among them for the first time.

Music Director G. Anton had obtained 54 badges for the singers and accompanying passive members. Tickets were reserved for the excursion steamboat that would carry the Saengerbund men's chorus from Wilmington to Philadelphia, and a brass band was hired to accompany them to the city wharf. On June 28, 1853, the *Delaware State Journal* reported: "About 40 Germans left this place for Philadelphia on Saturday to attend a musical celebration of the 'Saengerbund' of the Eastern and Middle States. They marched through our streets, accompanied by a band of music, prior to their departure. The Saengerbund of Wilmington was very handsomely represented in the great musical festival reception in Philadelphia on Saturday, June 25, 1853. We observe in the program that they were in the torch light procession and numbered 27 members under the direction of G. Anton."

The *Freie Presse* of Philadelphia also reported on June 28 that the Saengerbund from Wilmington participated with 30 singers. The report also noted that, "Das türkische Schenkenlied—'The Turkish Tavern Song'—was sung by the Philadelphia Glee Association who were so much applauded they had to sing it again. This group was among several others invited by the members of the 'Delaware Saengerbund' to attend their Flag Dedication ceremony in September." Invigorated, a young, proud chorus returned home, but its members were already disagreeing about the forthcoming flag-dedication ceremony.

-A House Divided-

The two-day festival was to be held on Monday, September 5 and Tuesday, September 6. The *Delaware Gazette* reported on Sept. 6: "Jubilee: - The Saengerbund Society of this city accompanied by a Society of the same name from Philadelphia paraded our streets yesterday. They marched under the stars and stripes to the thrilling strains produced by a well skilled band of performers. They were preceded by mounted marshals, and a number of juveniles carried a large national banner by the corners with care that betokens the reverence they have been taught by their parents … for the 'flag of the free and the brave.'" Nowhere in this

article is the Saengerbund's flag mentioned. In fact, so much controversy surrounded the flag dedication ceremony that Saengerbund records indicated it never took place.

Unable to solve their differences, the Saengerbund friends went their own ways. Attendance at rehearsals became sporadic. In November 1853, the society moved to a less expensive location rented from a Mr. McDonnell for $10 for three months, but many members did not come back. In February 1854, the remaining members resolved to pay future directors and requested that a director not be an active member of the society.

The first Stiftungsfest Anniversary Ball had been planned for March 21, 1854 and was to feature a six-man band. Two hundred tickets were to be printed in English, but there was no cause for celebration, because—on February 8, 1854—the minutes state that the music books were given to John Fehrenbach, the baton and other items to Solomon Prell for safekeeping. The flag was handed over to Christian Krauch. John Fehrenbach was named temporary president, John Betz treasurer and Valentin Walter librarian. As the last songs died away, the record book closed.

Luckily John Fehrenbach didn't give up so easily. He invited all former members and other men with an interest in singing to meet at John Betz's in April 1854. Baltimore was to host the fifth Sängerfest that June, and if the Wilmington Saengerbund was to participate, the singers had to get organized. A new constitution was worked out, and rehearsals were scheduled to begin three days later. John Fehrenbach was elected president, Ludwig Grieb vice president. The minutes show no

Handwritten song book cover for first bass, Saengerbund No.1.
(Courtesy of HSD)

further activity for the next few months, possibly because John Fehrenbach had returned to Philadelphia.

Ludwig Grieb, now in possession of the songbooks and music scores, brought about a revival of the dormant Saengerbund in 1856. Heinrich Albert from Saxony, a carriage maker by trade, became the new president and music director when he joined the society. He offered a room for rent in his house on 4th Street, and rehearsals were held there twice a week. The old constitution was revised and accepted. A May dance was the first social event.

That June, several members expressed their desire to amend the constitution in order to add a beneficial article and to institute a *Krankenkomitee*, a committee to visit the sick. Not everyone agreed. The dissidents argued that the Saengerbund had been chartered as a

social club, not a beneficial society. Several members resigned in protest. The few remaining suspended rehearsals during the hot summer. The flag, the Saengerbund's prize possession, was given to Ludwig Grieb for safekeeping.

-Saengerbund No. 1-

Not long afterwards, the former members of the original Saengerbund began meeting again. In October 1856, they instituted a new group and resolutely called it Saengerbund No. 1. Ludwig Grieb and Christian Krauch were approached by Saengerbund No.1 and asked to turn over the flag and music books to the new organization. Henry Bleyer was invited to become president, and a committee of trustees consisting of Bleyer, Augustus Hiller, and Christian Krauch was appointed to be the guardians of the club's flag and property. August Roebelen, choir director at the Deutsch-Lutherische Zionskirche, later called Zion Lutheran Church, agreed to take the singers of Saengerbund No. 1 under his baton. The chorus met in his restaurant at 43 King Street. The *Delaware Gazette* describes the first concert and a ball given on Easter Monday, April 13, 1857 at Odd Fellows Hall: "The saloon was festooned with our national bunting, and the stars and stripes never adorned the scene of a more

M. L. Lichtenstein, August Roebelen, and Henry Albert took turns as directors of the Saengerbund chorus. Henry Robelen, a son?, opened the piano and music store in 1871. (Courtesy of HSD)

merry and joyous company … Messrs. Lichtenstein and Triggs sang a number of handsome pieces." After the concert, the ball began with "the tripping of the light fantastic toe" to the music of the Harmonic Concert Band of Philadelphia.

Roebelen resigned after this successful concert, and Max L. Lichtenstein, whose dry goods business was located at 122 Market Street, was asked to become the new director. Membership records of the two societies show that several of the singers had remained friends and belonged to both choruses which were directed in turn by Roebelen, Lichtenstein, and Henry Albert. Also at this time, two American songs were added to the Saengerbund's handwritten song books, "Hail, Columbia" and "The Star-Spangled Banner."

Preparations now began for the seventh Sängerfest, to be held June 13-17, 1857, in Philadelphia. Of the two choruses, only Saengerbund No. 1 participated. Predictably, the members of the old Saengerbund took exception to the new club's manner of registering for the event, because they used the name Saengerbund without the distinguishing addition of No.1. The Philadelphia festivities ended on Tuesday with a picnic on Lemon Hill. To the amazement of the *Delaware Gazette* reporter, whose account appeared in print on June 19, 1857, "there were no visible signs of intoxication on the part of the 1,500 singers, despite the fact that 2,400 quarter casks of lager beer were consumed!" Following the Sängerfest, President Henry Bleyer presented Music Director Lichtenstein with a rosewood cane as a token of the chorus' gratitude. The cane's gold head was inscribed: "Presented by the Wilmington, Delaware, Saengerbund No. 1 to Mr. M. L. Lichtenstein."

In October of 1857, Wilmington's Zion Lutheran Church, then located at Fifth and Walnut Streets, planned a benefit concert to raise money for the new church building. Both Saengerbund choruses were invited to partcipate and, after the concert, the two small choruses realized that they would sound better in public performances if their voices were combined. First attempts towards reconciliation and reunion soon followed. For a time, each society stubbornly insisted on keeping its own name and statutes. After months of negotiating, a grand ball held on Pentecost Monday, May 24th, 1858, brought all the men together. Their wives, who had all remained friends over the years, presented the men with a floral wreath. The May 25 minutes of the Sängerbund state that, "From now on,

the two Sängerbund societies consider themselves as belonging to the Delaware Saengerbund which consists of the two Sängerbund societies of Wilmington." *Natürlich,* the first order of business was the writing of a new constitution by members of both societies for the new Delaware Saengerbund.

-Delaware Saengerbund-

Recording Secretary Ignaz Blank opened the pages of a new recording book on May 15, 1858. *The Delaware Saengerbund,* the name chosen unanimously for the new society, started out with a chorus of thirty-eight active voices. The society also had eighteen passive members, classified as nonsingers. In those days, members often switched back and forth from active to passive when they had less time available for social functions due to the increasing demands of their businesses. Only active members were eligible to hold office. Music directors Heinrich (Henry) Albert, August Roebelen, and Max L. Lichtenstein were named honorary members together with the first honorary member, Christian Krauch.

Club dues, still 25 cents each month, could be divided and paid weekly. New members were charged fifty cents as an initiation fee. If a member came late to rehearsals, he was fined 3 cents; if he missed a rehearsal he was charged a penalty of 6 cents; and if he failed to appear at a public performance, he was fined 25 cents. The general membership meeting was held on the last Saturday of each month.

The president appointed four standing committees and could appoint additional temporary committees as needed. The Finance Committee was in charge of bookkeeping and auditing. Because club officers saw it as their duty to keep excellent financial records, they balanced the books frequently and always knew exactly how much money was in the treasury. They were careful to keep the numbers in the black by always asking where the money to pay for anything would come from before they authorized any purchases. The Membership Committee was responsible for inquiring about proposed members, and the Music Committee sought the music director, selected songs, and determined public performances with the help of the director. The *Lokal-Komitee,* or Locality Committee, had the difficult job of finding a suitable room for rehearsals and performances, and keeping the rooms in good condition. In addition to these standing committees, the *Vergnügungs-Komitee*, the Entertainment Committee in charge of all the society's social events, was the most active temporary committee.

German taverns almost always had a *Nebenzimmer*, a quiet room off the main tavern room for banquets, which could also be used by groups and societies for their weekly or monthly meetings. The Delaware Saengerbund moved many times within Wilmington to find the right Nebenzimmer for rehearsals. Sometimes members cleaned and furnished the room to their liking, for example adding a stove and lights for winter rehearsals. Engaging an affordable room that did not cost too much money to heat in the winter was one way the society economized. When they rented a room in Mr. Bradford's Telegraph Building, at the NE Corner of 3rd and Market Streets, they paid $5.42 per month. At other times, rent was paid to Mr. John Lewis, dealer in coal and wood, justice of the peace, and real estate agent on Shipley Street.

Max L. Lichtenstein directed the new Delaware Saengerbund men's chorus, which had its own piano. Rehearsals were well attended, even during inclement

Advertisement of the Grand Concert that opened the way for a reunion of the two singing societies Saengerbund and Saengerbund No. 1. (Courtesy of UD)

weather. A well-received public concert in June of 1858 attested to the strength of the chorus.

The year 1859 opened with a ball to benefit singers planning to participate in the eighth Sängerfest of the Nordoestlicher Saengerbund, to be held July 11–16 in Baltimore. Thirty-five badges were ordered, the songbooks rebound, and the eagle topping the club's flagpole was given a new coat of gold paint. A June 17, 1859, report in the *Delaware Gazette* described the Saengerbund's flag as "… a blue banner with white wreath and harp on one side and the name on the other." This was the first time a description of the flag appeared in print.

That July, as planned, the group traveled to the Baltimore Sängerfest. It concluded with a picnic where old friendships were renewed, new ones were made; and invitations to visit each other were exchanged. Because of Wilmington's location between Philadelphia and Washington, DC, the Delaware Saengerbund developed equally close ties to the singing societies to the north and south. They were frequently host to or guests of Baltimore's Arion Gesangverein, the Philadelphia Saengerbund, and the Camden Männerchor.

In August, there was a picnic, something Saengerbund members loved. Like all Germans living in a city, they always looked forward to going out into the country and inhaling the fresh air of woods and meadows. Because Wilmington had no public parks, excursions often were made to a country estate or farm. A favorite spot for picnics, in addition to Rosendale Pleasure Grounds, was Jacob Alrichs' woods located in New Castle near the Bowerie. Minutes dated August 29, 1859, report every penny of the picnic's expenses and income, as can be seen in the translation of expenses that follows, while the *Delaware Gazette* presents the more picturesque side: "The Delaware Saengerbund passed our office yesterday morning in a procession preceded by a fine brass band. They were bound for the woods of Mr. Alrichs where they intended to spend the day on a picnic. They started from the corner of 4th and Market streets in four horse-drawn omnibuses about 10 o'clock.…"

The size of the dance platform, built for the occasion at the picnic grounds, was 60 x 40 feet. Joseph Stoeckle supplied the beer and the wine. The lemonade they served was mixed from water, twelve lemons, ten pounds of sugar, and one quart of brandy. The temperance stand served sarsaparilla, an herbal root beer. After paying all the bills, the club realized a profit of $78.66! The finance committee first proposed that $75.00 be deposited in a bank account, but then decided to invest the sum at 6% interest with member Henry Pretzschner who had a successful coach-making business at 4th and Walnut Streets.

A Christmas gathering brought the families of the chorus members together one more time. The year ended with Chorus Director Lichtenstein resigning for

EXPENSES

	Broken and borrowed glasses	$ 1.34
	Glasses from Ch. Buttner	4.75
	Lumberyard, for boards	8.33
	Deliver of boards	5.00
	Beer. etc. (see Stoeckle bill)	50.79
	Ross. to dig beer hole	1.62
	Police	14.62
	Music	1.08
	Meals for Musicians	.88
	Travel Expenses for Musicians	10.00
	Staging	.25
	1 dozen lemons	1.25
	10 pounds sugar	.25
	1 quart brandy	.20
	broken bottles	2.10
	3 boxes cigars	.37
	festival ribbons	9.92
	sarsaparilla	1.25
	Cakes from J. Stuck	1.80
	Cakes from F. Rapp	3.25
	7 pounds nails	.35
	Miscellaneous	.46
TOTAL EXPENSES		118.99

INCOME

	Festival Ribbons (F. Franke)	5.50
	Festival Ribbons (A. Dettling)	28.35
	Festival Ribbons (Chr. Spoerl)	1.35
	Beer and Lemonade tickets	112.15
	Beer bar income (Hartmann)	2.88
	Temperance Income (Gneb)	30.88
	Temperance Income (F. Weil)	9.88
	Temperance Income (W.Cloos)	3.42
	Festival Ribbons (A Kirn)	.25
	Leftover boards (Pretzschner)	4.60
TOTAL INCOME		197.65
EXPENSES		118.99
PROFIT		78.66

business reasons. Heinrich Albert, then proprietor of the Franklin House located on 4th Street near French Street, was hired to lead the chorus for an annual salary of $48. The treasury was sound, and all debts had been paid.

The new constitution served members well until December 1859. Following a proposal and agreement of the membership, the constitution and bylaws were then revised and amended to include a mutual beneficial article, the *Unterstützungs-Paragraph No. 2* which stated "The purpose of the society is practice in singing, mutual support in illness, death or other misfortune." This was the sick-fund article, meant to be implemented at times of illness and death in a member's family, which had caused acrimony and division two years earlier. This time the article was accepted, and the *Kranken-Komitee*, the committee to visit sick members and report on their health, became the fifth standing committee. Among other things, this amendment provided that a penalty of 50 cents would be collected for not attending a member's funeral.

In the spring of 1860, several members became sick. The Kranken-Komitee determined that two members had to visit the seriously ill brothers, Christian and Adolf Büttner, each day. Christian Büttner, who owned a saloon where the Turners started out, died, but Adolf, a nurseryman, recovered. One member continued to care for him. During his month-long illness he received $3.00 per week from the society's sick-fund, comparable to one week's earnings. For young men living alone, or families who suffered the sudden loss of the head of household's income, the *Sangesbrüder*—the brethren in song—proved to be their lifeline.

In November 1860, the constitution was rewritten again. This time Article 1 stated that "The name of the organization is *Delaware Saengerbund.*" Article 2 read, "The purpose of the organization is practice in singing to lead to a higher form of entertainment." The major revision was that the number of standing committees decreased from five to four: financial, membership, locality, and music. The Kranken-Komitee was dissolved because the beneficial clause had proven too cumbersome. Members preferred to help each other in an unregulated way or anonymously. But among German immigrants, the question of mutual assistance never went away. One reason that the Free Mason societies were so popular with Germans was that they offered sickness and death benefits to their members. Finally in 1869 the first German mutual beneficial society, the *Gegenseitiger Unterstützungs-Verein No. 1*, was chartered in Wilmington.

3

New Roots

In deinem Grund hab' Wurzeln ich geschlagen,
Und deine Stimme, Heimat, spricht in mir
Ich hab' dein Leid wie eignes Leid getragen
Und meine höchste Freude ruht in dir.

My roots sink deep, here in this ground,
Yet deep inside I hear the voice of home.
I bear your sorrows as I bear my own
And find my greatest joy at rest in you.

-Kriebel/Kröger, 17. Jahrhundert (17th century)

Even while the young men from Germany were putting down roots in Wilmington, they tried to live much as they had at home. No wonder, then, that so many German societies were chartered in Wilmington a few years after the Forty–Eighters arrived. Belonging to a society helped compensate for the friends and family they were unlikely to see ever again.

-Wilmington Turngemeinde-

The open space behind Christian Büttner's tavern at 326 French Street attracted the attention of the handful of men who had gathered inside on November 5, 1859, to organize a gymnastic society, the *Social-* *Demokratische Turngemeinde Wilmington Delaware,* better known as the *Wilmington Turners.* Proprietor Büttner agreed to pay half of the cost of setting up the sports equipment, furnish lights for evening training sessions, and provide a second-story room free of charge for meetings. John Stich was elected first speaker; Charles Knoblauch and Henry Feldmeier became the first gymnastic instructors. When musician Henry Albert joined a few months later, he was asked to lead a singing section, since the Turners had their own brand of songs and music.

Like the other singing societies, the Turner movement had its roots in the German Romantic period at the turn of the 19th century. Friedrich Jahn, called the *Turnvater* of the movement, developed a program for physical education that combined exercises in fresh air with the exercise of a free spirit. He opened the *Sportplatz Hasenheide,* the first outdoor field, near Berlin in 1811. The Turners' motto, "A sound mind in a sound body," echoed the spirit of the Greek Olympics. Those who joined believed that physical fitness through gymnastics would lead to a healthy mind. This idea eventually spread throughout the German states, and many *Turnvereine,* also called *Turngemeinden,* or Turners' societies, were founded.

The first *Turnerbund* was established in Hamburg in 1815. Members had to be eighteen years of age or older. The men most likely to be drawn to the physical exercises were workmen, skilled craftsmen, laborers, or independent businessmen. In time the social aspects of the Turnvereine became as important as the gymnastic training they offered, and Turner organizations developed a social calendar to include leisure-time events for families and friends.

The Turner movement sought to educate its members in citizenship so that they could live, not as mindless and willing subjects, but as advocates with a social conscience for all people. During the revolutionary years in Germany, the Turnvereine became strongholds for political dissenters against the monarchies. When open revolts began in 1848, many Turners took up arms to fight against monarchical troops. First in line were the Turners of Hesse. Only a few generations earlier, Hessian youth had been conscripted into the military by Friedrich II, Count of Hesse-Cassel, one of six German sovereigns who leased his troops to the English crown to fight against the American colonists in the War of Independence. This war left a deep impression on the Hessian soldiers. Of the 17,000 men conscripted from Hesse, over 6,000 decided to stay in America when their regiments were repatriated in 1784. Those who returned home to Hesse strongly advocated the democratic ideals of the young republic. In 1848 their grandchildren had a chance to live up to their grandfathers' dreams of succeeding in a revolution on home soil, but their efforts failed. Free-spirited gymnasts had no chance against a trained military assault. Faced with imprisonment or emigration, many Hessian Turners, like so many Germans in Baden and Württenberg, chose to immigrate to America, the country they had hoped to emulate. Here they were politically active and encouraged their members to learn English and become American citizens as soon as possible.

The leaders of the Turner movement settled in the larger cities, especially New York, Philadelphia, Cincinnati, and Baltimore, where they immediately founded German Turner societies. They maintained close contact with other clubs through a Turner newspaper. A regional organization, the North American Turner Society, was in charge of planning *Turnfeste,* the regional Turner festivals. The Wilmington Turners participated regularly and maintained close ties to the associations of Baltimore and Philadelphia. Dressed in white gym suits, black hats, and red scarves, the Wilmington Turners added color to every local parade.

In 1862, two years after Christian Büttner's death, the Turners moved their meetings to Jakob Baker's saloon. Member and carpenter Andreas Dettling (great grandfather of the dean of Delaware history, John Munroe) built a roof over the outdoor sports equipment behind the saloon. To celebrate the opening of this new *Sportplatz,* the Turners invited the Delaware Saengerbund members to share a keg of beer. From that day on, the Delaware Saengerbund and the Wilmington Turners maintained a close relationship, and many men belonged to both societies. They participated regularly in the social events, concerts, picnics, and festivals planned by either society for the next hundred years.

-Civil War Years-

Saengerbund friends enjoyed their regular get-togethers and started collecting typical club paraphernalia. On July 12, 1860, Christian Krauch presented the members with two drinking horns. Member Herting was commissioned to decorate the horns with silver mountings at a cost of $6 each. These horns were carried proudly in parades, along with the flag. That October, a harvest ball was held to help raise funds to finance the club's trip to New York for the ninth Sängerfest in 1861, but the song festival never took place. America had plunged into a Civil War that occupied everyone's thoughts and affected everyone's plans.

The New Year, with its disturbing news about the mobilization of troops, led to the formation of a new German society, the *deutsche Militärkompanie.* On April 19, 1861, a week after Fort Sumter had been fired upon, the *Delaware Gazette* reported that, "A meeting was held at Central Hall, First and King Streets, under management of the *Delaware Rifles*, a young German company of this city. The meeting was composed principally of our German citizens, and about 40 names were added to the roll. They proposed offering their services to the President." Eventually the deutsche Militärkompanie disbanded and its members were absorbed into other companies.

The Delaware Saengerbund had a brief connection to the Militärkompanie, because the two societies rented the Central Hall together and shared the costs, each paying $48 per year. It was not long before two windows, broken by the Delaware Rifles, had to be repaired by Saengerbund member Andreas Dettling. To make matters worse, the Militärkompanie was slow in paying its half of the expenses, forcing the Saengerbund to call on Wilmington's City Council for assistance in that matter.

After the ninth Sängerfest in Baltimore was cancelled, the only event that brought a little spark into the society's social calendar was the October harvest ball. In December 1861, the Saengerbund resolved to suspend rehearsals, due to the uncertainties caused by the war, and to call a general meeting every six months. Many Saengerbund members saw it as their duty to enlist, but not all names were recorded in the minutes.

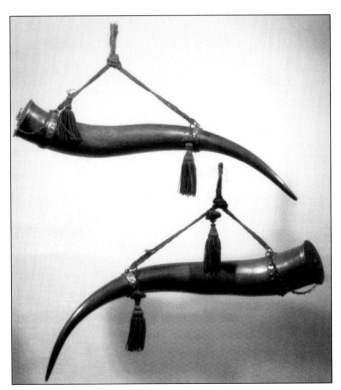

Christian Krauch presented two drinking horns to the Delaware Saengerbund in 1860. (Photo by Mike Ciosek)

Newspaper articles show that Music Director Henry Albert joined the Second Delaware Regiment; Andreas Grotz, Henry Feldmeier, and George Schellkopf returned from the battlefields; Corporal Jacob Pfeifer was listed as missing. Singing rehearsals resumed in 1863, but war still overshadowed the club's social gatherings. The war years felt like a prolonged Lenten season.

In Germany, it was customary to celebrate the renewal of life after the dark winter months. For that reason, a festive church service on Easter Sunday followed the solemnity and abstentions of Lent. On Easter Monday, everyone attended an *Oster-montagtanz*, an Easter Monday ball. This tradition was upheld in Wilmington by the German societies, and so the Delaware Saengerbund, the oldest German society, invited the others to an Easter Monday ball in April 1865. Also that year, a *Kränzchen*, or informal gathering with a dance, was held once a month to raise funds for the long trip to New York City for the ninth Sängerfest, finally scheduled after a hiatus of six years. From July 15 to July 19,1865, the Delaware Saengerbund's chorus was one of eighty-three participating in the event where 2,400 singers assembled to celebrate the end of the Civil War.

-Businessmen-

As the country regained its perspective, some of the Forty-Eighters who had fled their home states more than ten years earlier may have entertained the idea of returning to Germany, but nothing had changed there. The real changes had taken place here, in Wilmington. They had married, started families, and founded German societies. Some had already buried wives or infants or close friends. All who had started out as penniless immigrants worked hard, and several had established flourishing businesses. Many Saengerbund members owned bakeries: William Alsentzer, Jacob Balz, Jakob Kienle, John D. Kurtz, Henry Miller, Gottlieb Rehfuss, Frederick Stuck, Jakob Stuck, and William Weyl. Other members followed a wide variety of professions and trades, but most worked as brewers, carpenters, laborers, machinists, manufacturers, saloonkeepers, or tailors. In Germany, the breweries underwrote the furnishings for taverns and saloons when the owner contracted to sell only the beer from that brewery. Wilmington's brewers continued this practice, and that made it possible for German immigrants to open saloons. Saloon and tavern owners who belonged to the Delaware Saengerbund included Henry Blouth, John Fehrenbach, Henry Feldmeier, Henry Haar, Christian Krauch, Joseph Niedermaier, Christian Spoerl, and Joseph Stoeckle. By 1868, there were so many German businessmen in Wilmington that they decided to form a German Board of Trade. Little is known of this organization except that—on or shortly before July 26, 1870—sixty members of the German Board of Trade "arrived in Reading on a visit accompanied by sixteen members of the Franklin Cornet Band of Wilmington, all dressed in black pants and coat, dark blue fatigue cap, and gold trimmings and epaulets." According to the *Delaware Gazette's* account, Jacob Haenlen, who in 1868 had established Wilmington's first German newspaper, *Pionier*, was the group's spokesman.

The Delaware Saengerbund's active singers did their best to attend rehearsals faithfully, although their family and business responsibilities and their involvement in other societies made increasing demands on their time, as these brief sketches of the *alte Herren*, the founding members, show.

Henry Bleyer was involved in politics and urged fellow Saengerbund members to play an active role. In 1853, he was elected to City Council from the First Ward, and in 1856, he organized the *German Democratic Association*, a society that supported the Democratic Party ticket and evolved into the *Ostende-Deutsch-Demokratischer Club*—the German Democratic Club—located on the east side of Wilmington. He took great interest in city government, and was elected to the city council's standing committee, Street and Public Lamps Commission. He was also a second lieutenant in the Wilmington City Guard and first engineer of the Fire Department. In 1866, he chartered the *Germania Loan Association*.

Music Director Max L. Lichtenstein owned a fine dry-goods store and was a leading figure in musical events of the German societies, and president of the *Handel and Haydn Society* in 1864. He closely followed political developments in Germany and, as president of the *German Patriotic Club* in 1870, solicited contributions to aid German widows and orphans of the Franco-Prussian War. He used his business expertise to help charter a new beneficial society, the *Germania Loan Association No. 2* of 1873. In 1875, Lichtenstein served one term as city council president.

John Fehrenbach, who had been the driving force behind the first Saengerbund organization, returned from Philadelphia. He was married to Margaret Baker for twelve years and together they had seven children. In 1863 or 1864 he married Margaretta Pabst, and four children were born to this marriage. Fehrenbach bought the Franklin House on 4th Street from Henry Albert and started brewing beer there on a small scale. In 1865 his sister Theresa married Sangesbruder John Hartmann from Heidelsheim, Baden. The two brothers-in-law worked together to open a lager beer-brewing facility on Lovering Avenue. Incorporated in 1865 as the Hartmann & Fehrenbach Brewing Co., the brewery was enlarged several times and grew into one of the most successful businesses operating in Delaware.

Joseph Stoeckle from Buchau, Württemberg, joined the Saengerbund in 1855. He loved to play the cornet and was a charter member of the Wilmington City Cornet Band. He married Johanna Gropp of Philadelphia, and they had five children. Stoeckle owned Mechanic's Hall, a saloon on King Street and, like Krauch and Fehrenbach, began brewing his own beer. In 1875, he acquired the Bichta Brewery on Fifth and Adams Streets. Later known as the Diamond State Brewery, it became the brewery with the largest output of barrels in Delaware in the 1890s.

Many Saengerbund members were involved with other organizations, often as charter members or officers. A favorite society was the *Delaware Tribe No.1 of the Improved Order of Red Men,* which had a primarily German membership. The American Indian had always been a source of great fascination for Germans of all ages, and books of folklore and adventure were part of every library. Now that they lived in the land of the *Indianer*, they thought they could act like braves--at least in their leisure time. In 1857, Jakob Stuck was listed as Sachem of this group, and Christian Krauch as Senior Sachem. The *Hermann Loge Chapter No. 29*, a German Free Mason Lodge, was organized in July 1863, and counted John Fehrenbach, Andreas Dettling, and Christian Spoerl as active members and officers. A few years later, the Wilmington Germans organized another society present in almost all German towns, a *Schützen-Verein*, or marksmen's association.

-Schützen-Verein-

On August 31, 1868, members of three German societies were on the way to Christian Krauch's Rosendale Pleasure Park, according to the *Delaware Gazette*, September 1, 1868: "The Wilmington Saengerbund, the German Turners, and the Sharp Shooters of this city and several societies of Philadelphia and Camden, accompanied by two bands of music, paraded our streets about noon yesterday en route to Rosendale on the Brandywine where they spent the afternoon in a very pleasant picnic. They carried with them the American flag and a number of banners bearing appropriate mottoes." It was only natural that the local Germans had organized their own *Schützen-Verein*, often called the Sharp Shooting Society or Wilmington Rifle Club by the local newspapers. Seeing them reminded many parade-goers of their colorful counterparts present in nearly every German town.

Schützen-Vereine have a long tradition in Germany. Because the free cities were vulnerable to being overrun by greedy neighbors, they were often surrounded by high walls and *Schützengräben*—deep moats—dug out in front of the walls for added protection. There the men were trained as sharpshooters capable of defending the town and were registered in guilds. To keep up the marksmen's interest in training during peacetime, regional *Schützenfeste*—shooting festivals—featured target-shooting contests that offered valuable prizes. In 1433, for example, the city of Nürnberg hosted a festival at which sharpshooters from twenty-three cities, ranging in size from München to Neustadt an der Aisch, participated. Prizes included a horse, an ox, a crossbow, and a gold ring. To add fun and excitement to the contest, the marksman who came in last was awarded a pig—a custom that entered the German language as the idiom, *Da hast du gerade noch Schwein gehabt,* loosely translated as "you were lucky that you scraped by." When the guilds were no longer needed to train young men for military service, the men formed their own societies to practice target shooting. Attending regional shooting festivals, entering contests, and marching in colorful parades became routine activities for these societies, and the picturesque life of the marksman was even immortalized in Carl Maria von Weber's opera *Der Freischütz.*

Schützen-Verein advertisement of the upcoming Schützenfest – target shooting festival. (Courtesy of HSD)

Following the August picnic in Rosendale Park, the Wilmington Schützen-Verein held its first *Schützenfest,* or marksmanship competition, on November 10th. Again a reporter from the *Delaware Gazette* was there: "The Wilmington Sharp Shooting Society had a shooting match on the banks of the Brandywine, near Rosendale on Tuesday. The shooting commenced at 10 o'clock a.m. and was finished by … 1½ o'clock p.m., each contestant having twelve shots. After the match, the members of the society had a pleasant dinner. The society is not intended to be a distinctly German one, persons of any nativity being privileged to join it; neither is it at all military in its character." Nicholas Jenny, who was the society's first president, won first place, a silver buckle. The Schützenfest became an annual September event. In 1869, the Schützen-Verein held the contest at the Agricultural Society Fair Grounds west of Union Street, as reported by the *Delaware Gazette* on September 29, 1869:

Yesterday morning, about 10 o'clock, the club formed on King Street and marched out to the grounds in procession. There were about forty men carrying rifles; several carriages containing prominent citizens preceded by the Wilmington Cornet Band, and followed by several men bearing banners and about half a dozen carriages. Next came the Wilmington Saengerbund headed by a drum corps, followed by a handsome double carriage filled with little children. Those in the procession wore green badges and sprigs of green in their hats and all of them carried bouquets of flowers. The affair was quite a novelty and attracted much attention.

The club's headquarters were located on King Street. By 1871, the membership had grown to 230, half German and half American. Proceedings and accounts were kept in two languages, and shooting practice took place every Monday. The Wilmington Schützen competed in regional festivals in Philadelphia and Baltimore and returned with prizes, usually won by John Manz, Nicholas Jenny, and Joseph Stoeckle.

Grand Opening of the Schützen Park, formerly the Agricultural Grounds near Union Street, today Wawaset Park.
(Courtesy of HSD)

In May 1871, the fast-growing club arranged to purchase the fair grounds from the Agricultural Society of New Castle County. On September 25, 1871, the grand opening of the new Schützenpark began with a salute from a small cannon as described in the *Delaware Gazette*: "Yesterday was the commencement of the Schützenfest at the Wilmington Rifle Club Park. At ten o'clock the Philadelphia Society's ninety-five members arrived accompanied by the Liedertafel Brass Band. These men were clad in civilian's dress of black felt hat with green band and oak leaves, gray jackets and black pants, and carried rifles, the Wilmington Schützen in civilian's dress with feather in felt hat…." Following the festivities, dinner was served to 200 honored guests in the park's new refreshment hall that measured 180 by 50 feet. The club's *Schützenhaus*, located at the south end of the park, measured 35 by 70 feet and was 20 feet high with a ventilated roof that allowed the gunsmoke to escape. This annual festival became a popular Wilmington event that could draw 2,500 to 3,000 visitors.

The Schützen-Verein was a colorful addition to the social life of the Wilmington Germans, and the Schützenpark became a much-loved gathering place for other German groups' picnics and festivals. It was very important to the men that their families join them at festival events and that the children have a wonderful time playing games. Because these gatherings were such family affairs, club members always saw to it that no one became inebriated or behaved improperly. Festivals took place on weekdays, because Delaware's "blue laws" made Sunday entertainments illegal. Not even ice cream could be sold on a Sunday. The Schützen-Verein was active for about twenty years. After that membership declined due to a decreasing interest in target shooting and an increasing interest in *Kegeln*, bowling. The beloved Schützenpark became a famous racetrack, Wilmington Driving Park, and later still, Wawaset Park.

4

Intermezzo

Brüder, reicht die Hand zum Bunde!
Diese schöne Feierstunde
führ' uns hin zu lichten Höh'n.
Lasst, was irdisch ist, entfliehen!
Unsrer Freundschaft Harmonien
dauern ewig, fest und schön,
dauern ewig, fest und schön.

Brothers, let's join hands in unity!
May this sublime hour
Lead us to loftier heights
As we leave behind all earthbound notions.
The harmonies of our friendship
Shall last forever in firmness and beauty.
Shall last forever in firmness and beauty.

-Heintzsch/Mozart

During 1867 Saengerbund members kept busy rehearsing for the next song festival, visiting other singing societies, and planning the annual picnic, Kränzchen, and balls. The year's main event was to be the tenth Sängerfest, July 13–18 in Philadelphia. Because past directors Albert, Roebelen, and Lichtenstein were unavailable to direct the singers, President John Manz was chosen to lead the chorus.

John Manz had come to Wilmington to work as a machinist. He joined the Delaware Saengerbund in 1860 as a young man of 25, served on many committees, and was elected secretary, then president. In 1867, rehearsals were even held in his home. At Manz's request, Professor Leonhard of Philadelphia was asked to help the group study the music for the tenth Sängerfest. Due to his efforts, the chorus was well-prepared. Over 100 societies with 2,900 singers assembled at the Philadelphia festival headquarters, the National Guard Hall on Race Street. In honor of the occasion, the building was lavishly decorated with banners, greens, and flags, as were the streets through which the parade of singers wound its way. The *Delaware Gazette* later reported that, "under the leadership of Prof. John Manz, about 25 members of the Delaware Saengerbund left this city on board the *Eliza Hancox* for Philadelphia to participate in the great United National Festival." After the festival, members voted to present John Manz with a gift of $10 in appreciation of his hard work.

Manz returned to his business at the corner of Tatnall and Water Streets, improving machinery used to manufacture all kinds of agricultural implements. He also manufactured "a large lot of sausage cutters." The following year, John Manz opened a saloon at 17 East Second Street, "where will be found good accommodations for boarders by the meal, day, or week." Manz's brother Conrad was also a machinist and an outspoken and often critical member of the Delaware Saengerbund. He too opened a saloon that became known as Manz's Saenger Hall. John stayed involved with the Delaware Saengerbund, but Conrad did not, at least for a while.

-Liederkranz-

On March 19, 1868, Conrad Manz and nine other German men met to talk about forming a new singing society. This was not an unusual step; many German towns had more than one *Männerchor*, or men's choral group. Nearby Philadelphia had eighteen German singing societies that later formed the basis of the United Singers of Philadelphia. Because the range of choral music is broad—from sacred songs and classical harmonies to melodious folksongs and rousing drinking songs—singing societies often formed around the type of music the group preferred to study and perform, and men joined the group most in harmony with their own interests.

The name Conrad Manz and his friends chose for their group was *Liederkranz*, meaning "a wreath of songs." The first article of the Liederkranz constitution declared: "[Our] purpose shall be to live together harmoniously and sociably and to practice songs without affectation." These men were well aware that selecting music for the Saengerbund had often resulted in arguments among the singers. The Delaware Saengerbund chorus had participated in five of the previous Nordoestlicher Saengerbund's Sängerfeste and was used to hearing the larger choruses of Philadelphia, New York City, Baltimore, and Washington. Now Delaware's goal was to become good enough to enter the *Preissingen*—the singing contest—at the next festival. For a whole year the chorus would have to practice songs selected by the festival committee. Records for May 1868 show that the Saengerbund had already obtained the score and twelve songbooks for the 1869 Sängerfest in Baltimore. Looking back, it seems logical that members of the new Liederkranz just wanted to sing songs they enjoyed without the pressure of an impending

Preissingen. In fact, the Liederkranz minutes do not even mention the Baltimore Sängerfest.

The new Liederkranz had an active social calendar, much like that of the Saengerbund, with picnics, Kränzchen, and balls. Henry Albert was chosen as the Liederkranz's first music director; J. P. T. Fuekel was the second. The Delaware Saengerbund held no grudges against the new chorus and even invited the Liederkranzsingers to a Kränzchen in April. Moreover, because several Saengerbund members wanted to sing in both choruses, the Saengerbund's bylaws had to be amended: now active Saengerbund members could not become active members of another singing society, only passive. If they were singing in another chorus and registered there as active members, the Delaware Saengerbund could reclassify them as passive members without voting rights, but still allow them to sing.

J. P. T. Fuekel directed both the Delaware Saengerbund and the Liederkranz choruses. Born in 1842 in Trebur, Hesse, he attended the teacher's seminary in Wetterau. Because of his thorough musical training, Fuekel was in demand as both organist and choir leader. Part of his job as the Saengerbund's music director was to prepare the chorus for the 11th Sängerfest to be held July 10–16, 1869. That festival was a grand affair. Onlookers lined Baltimore's streets to witness the grand-opening procession from the railway station to Monument Square, "the entire line brilliant with Chinese lanterns and transparencies, and joyous with many bands of music." There were also fireworks reportedly enjoyed by over 200,000 people. For this occasion, the German ladies of Wilmington had presented the chorus with a new flag. Unfortunately no description appears in the minutes. The Saengerbund returned without a prize, but with renewed enthusiasm.

A grand concert and ball given by the society that December were much-talked-about events in the city, and on December 10, 1869, the *Delaware Gazette*'s reporter wished that, "before the winter closes, the Saengerbund will give us another concert, with one of those grand old choruses, only sung aright by the powerful and melodious voices from [the] Faderland. [sic]." But the *Vaterland* was in turmoil again. The Franco-Prussian War (1870–1871) occupied the minds of Wilmington Germans and, to express sympathy with their homeland, thirteen citizens met at the Atlantic Garden on King Street to form the *German Patriotic Club*. Max L. Lichtenstein became its president. The first item on the agenda was soliciting funds for widows and orphans in Germany. The small society then called upon the other Wilmington German clubs to participate in a grand concert on November 30 at Institute Hall, located at the northwest corner of Eighth and Market Streets. In a follow-up article December 21, 1870, the *Delaware Gazette* reported that, "The Saengerbund and Liederkranz, numbering about thirty persons, sang several choruses exceedingly well. The performers were loudly applauded, and in most instances [were] required to encore their pieces."

The two societies realized that it would be better to unite as one chorus—just as Saengerbund and Saengerbund No. 1 had done—so in December the Saengerbund officers appointed a committee consisting of Friedrich von Bourdon, Heinrich Müller (Henry Miller), and Jacob Haenlen to begin negotiating with the Liederkranz for a possible merger. At their December 31 meeting, the Liederkranz members resolved to join with the Delaware Saengerbund under the following conditions: Each society must relinquish its name, a new name must be agreed upon; and the inventories of both societies must be handed over to the new society.

-Delaware Harmonie-

Twenty-five Sangesbrüder met on January 10, 1871, at Hermann Ferry's house to organize the new singing society, *Delaware Harmonie*. This name was chosen almost unanimously, although the recording secretary inscribed "Delaware Saengerbund" in the minutes by habit and had to cross it out. The first officers were Ignaz Blank, president; Heinrich Müller (Henry Miller), vice president; Frederick von Bourdon, recording secretary; Leonhard Ritter, financial secretary; and August Hiller, treasurer. Music librarians were Franz Stuhlfeld and Joseph Sell; and trustees were Joseph Niedermaier, Hermann Ferry, and William Cloos. A constitution committee was appointed, as well as a music committee and a locality committee. The second meeting took place at the *Sänger und Schützen Halle* on King Street, and singing rehearsals were scheduled for Tuesdays and Thursdays. The music committee proposed that Frederick Becher be the music director, since he had already conducted the now-dissolved Liederkranz for a few months. Delaware Harmonie also joined the Nordoestlicher Saengerbund

and paid the registration fee of $10 for twenty members.

The Delaware Harmonie's constitution contained an important change. All members, active, passive, and honorary, had the same voting rights and could hold office. Now only matters pertaining to singing had to be decided by the active singers in the chorus. Dues remained 25 cents per month.

The locality committee recommended that the most appropriate place to practice would be the third floor of Saville's building at the southeast corner of 6th and Market Streets. The rent there was $265 per year, or $22.50 per month. Delaware Harmonie quickly agreed to split the rent with the Turners. A month later, the two groups presented an evening's entertainment for the benefit of one of their members.

Then good news arrived from Germany: the Franco-Prussian war was over. Wilmington's German citizens were elated and organized a great peace jubilee. Although steeped in democratic principles as German Forty-Eighters and Delawareans, most still felt a strong kinship with the land of their birth and wanted to hail the Kaiser. The *Delaware Gazette* reported in detail the great parade on May 1, 1871, providing a good account of the city's German societies. According to the paper, the procession formed on King Street at nine o'clock, and countermarched up Fourth and Market Streets. The half-mile-long parade was led by a group of policemen, the City Cornet Band, Chief Marshal Henry Feldmeier and his aides on horseback, followed by a large wagon filled with boys and decorated with evergreens and German and American flags. Next came the Delaware Harmonie Singing Society; the German Sunday School, the girls all in white with bouquets; the German Day School carrying a large German flag; wagons filled with little girls dressed in white; German carpenters preceded by a wagon trimmed with long shavings; German blacksmiths in a wagon; horsemen, German bakers in a wagon; more horsemen, wearing white caps and shirts and blue scarves; a wagon full of little girls; the Schützen-Verein, and many citizens of Wilmington not belonging to any German organization. And that was only the first half of the parade!

In the second half, the United Cornet Band, and the Turner Association were followed by a wagon bearing an inscription and carrying little girls. Marchers carrying pictures of Bismarck and Napoleon, Germany and France were next. The mayor and city council members followed in carriages, and after them, an open barouche drawn by four large black horses with red plumes and containing representatives of the Imperial Family. John Wallschmidt, in regimentals representing the Emperor, and J. H. Muehlhausen, representing the prince were next. They were followed by a group of German butchers on horseback; a car carrying little girls and Miss Liberty; and members representing many organizations including the German Lodge of Odd Fellows, German Red Men, German Aid Association, the Turners, and German shoemakers. A cluster of carriages and a large, painted wooden cannon brought up the rear.

This long, colorful procession was not equaled for many years. It attracted a large number of viewers and ended at the Agricultural Fairgrounds where August Roebelen delivered an oration. The rest of the day everyone enjoyed sporting exercises. A few months later, the fairgrounds were purchased by the Schützen-Verein and renamed *Schützen Park*.

The 12th Sängerfest took place in New York from July 25 to 29, 1871. Neither the minutes nor the newspapers mention whether Delaware Harmonie traveled to New York to join the seventy-two societies and 2,600 singers who participated. In the same year, Music Director Frederick Becher opened a *Singschule*, a singing school for women and girls, with the financial support of the Delaware Harmonie. Members of the women's chorus were required to participate in the society's public concerts. The men's chorus was not yet ready to form a mixed chorus with the women, but some of the men did enjoy working with the women on the theater productions that became part of the entertainment at Kränzchen evenings.

In the 1870s, there were so many German societies in Wilmington that the Delaware Harmonie no longer functioned as a "home away from home," as the old Delaware Saengerbund had done. Other societies, like the Turners and the Democratic Club, had their own *Gesangsektion*, singing sections. Everyone held the traditional balls at Christmas, on Easter Monday or Pentecost Monday, and the clubs competed with each other to rent the best hall. As early as July, for example, members of the *Vereinigte Bäcker-Gesellschaft*—the United Baker's

Association—invited the Delaware Harmonie to their December 24th Christmas Ball.

By this time, many older Harmonie members had become passive members, and it was increasingly difficult for younger members and officers to maintain their interest in rehearsals and concerts. In 1872, Delaware Harmonie did not purchase songbooks for the next Sängerfest, because the Nordoestlicher Saengerbund scheduled no Sängerfeste between 1873 and 1882, partly as a result of inefficient leadership and

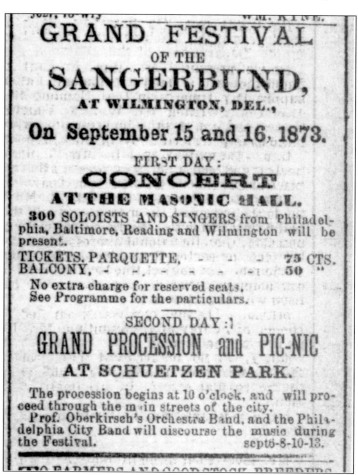

The Delaware Harmonie invited singing societies to a grand song festival under the name of Saengerbund. (Courtesy of HSD)

irreconcilable differences among the participating societies, and partly because of a greater interest in celebrating the American Centennial of 1876.

Down to five active singers and three passive members in 1873, the Delaware Harmonie moved to Eberhard Freye's saloon on French Street where members could rent a small room on the second floor for only $1 per month. The club's theater stage, tables, benches, and chairs were sold. J. P. T. Fuekel continued as music director, and a few members returned. These dire circumstances did not prevent Delaware Harmonie from planning a festival the former Saengerbund had never attempted—a Sängerfest in Wilmington. In August 1873, President Henry Miller proposed that several societies be invited to a Sängerfest that September. Because only $3.37 remained in the treasury, preliminary costs were covered by donations from the members. Some of the best northeastern choruses were invited to Wilmington, among them the Philadelphia Harmonie, the Damen Sektion des Philadelphia Sängerbundes, and the Camden Männerchor. Local singing societies were invited as well, and the orchestra Oberkirch played for everyone's enjoyment during the two-day festival. On September 12, 1873, the *Delaware Gazette* announced, "A Great Musical Entertainment: A grand concert of the United Singers is to be given at the Masonic Hall, in this city on Monday evening, September 15th. As about 400 singers are to come here from Philadelphia on this occasion, we presume it will be the grandest concert ever given in this city." The Sängerfest was considered a great success socially, but not financially. It is interesting to note that the grand festival was advertised in the *Delaware Gazette* under the name "Saengerbund" rather than "Delaware Harmonie." Wilmingtonians never paid any attention to the name changes. To them, the stately German men's chorus was always "the Saengerbund."

That the Harmonie did not have the momentum to continue much longer is clear in the 1874 minutes, which close with a sad, strange undertaking. The society was trying to recover the old Delaware Saengerbund flag from a pawnshop in Wilmington. Why or when it had been taken there was not recorded. Records do show that honorary member and trustee, Christian Krauch, who had always cared for the Delaware Saengerbund's belongings, had died four years earlier, in November 1870. So, when the Delaware Harmonie decided to suspend rehearsals, members took precautions. In September 1874, one year after the great Wilmington Sängerfest, they gave all of the society's remaining possessions to Daniel Maier for safekeeping against a security deposit of $75.

No minutes were recorded for the years 1875 and 1876, probably because President Heinrich Müller and Secretary Frederick von Bourdon were busy with a new endeavor, *Verehrer deutscher Classiker*, the German Literary Society.

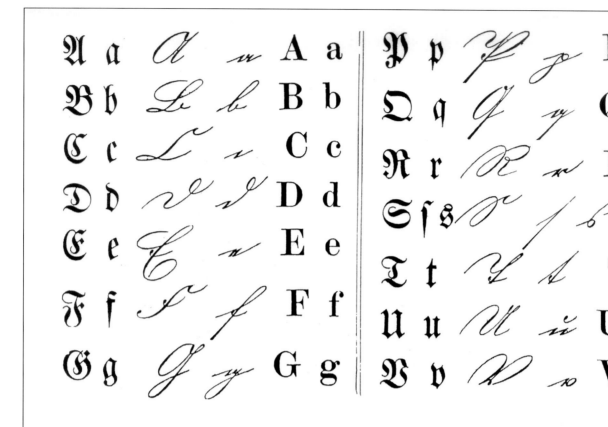

The German alphabet, printed in Witter's Deutsch-Englische Lesefibel, 1881.

5

Treasuring the German Language

Ich weiss nicht was soll es bedeuten,	I know not what it presages
Dass ich so traurig bin,	That I am so sad today;
Ein Märchen aus uralten Zeiten,	A legend of former ages
Das kommt mir nicht aus dem Sinn.	Will not from my thoughts away.
Die Luft ist kühl und es dunkelt,	The air is cool and it darkles
Und ruhig fließt der Rhein.	The Rhine flows calmly on.
Der Gipfel des Berges funkelt	The peak of the mountain sparkles
Im Abendsonnenschein.	In the glow of the evening sun.

—Heine/Silcher

-German Literary Society
—
German Library Association-

On March 9, 1873, the reading group Verehrer deutscher Classiker (VDC), Venerators of Classic German Literature, called a business meeting to formalize their occasional get-togethers and become a full-fledged German literary society. For several months they had been meeting in private homes to read and discuss German literature. The group started one evening, when Heinrich Müller was enjoying his Abendschoppen, or glass of wine, in Andreas Wilhelm's tavern at 411 Shipley Street. Müller spoke enthusiastically of his love for Heinrich Heine's poetry and invited his friends, who had been listening with interest, to his house the following Sunday. He wanted them to hear Heine's Die Harzreise, a description of a journey through the Harz mountains. After that, the friends met regularly in private homes to read and discuss German literature. One of their goals was to establish a library of classic German books in Wilmington.

It was not unusual for private citizens in Germany to own a library and share its treasures with their friends. For example, in 1834 Johann Caspar Engelhardt established a circulating library in the small town of Neustadt an der Aisch. Engelhardt was a rope maker by profession, but he also owned a publishing house and bookstore. He became mayor of the town and later was a cofounder of the singing society, *Liedertafel*. His library contained more than 1,000 editions of authors widely read in his time, including Kleist, Schiller, Goethe, Heine, Kotzebue, and Gotthelf, as well as Shakespeare, Dumas, Hugo, Dickens, and Scott in translation. The almost completely-preserved library of these slender, pocketsized volumes is now housed in the city's historical museum.

Heinrich Müller was a baker who had come to Wilmington from Chur-Hesse in 1859. He joined the Delaware Saengerbund and was a charter member of the Wilmington Turners. He was widely read, could recite Goethe's *Faust* by heart, and must have wondered where the books to slake his insatiable thirst for German literature would come from and who would share his love for the classics. He soon found friends who agreed that Wilmington needed a German library. They elected him president of the new organization, VDC. Clemens Meves served as vice president; Sebastian Burkhart as librarian; Andreas Wilhelm as treasurer; and Frederick von Bourdon as secretary. The other charter members were Anton Hauber, Casimir Abberger, John Manz, John Stoecklein, and Hermann Rau, editor of Wilmington's German newspaper, *Pionier*. The organization's purpose was stated in Article 2 of its constitution: "[To cultivate] the German language and literature and [in another handwriting] institution and maintenance of a German library."

The men diligently collected books, accepted donations, and ordered volumes from publishing houses in Philadelphia and Germany. Sometimes a shipment arrived in such lamentable shape that the books had to be rebound or returned to the publisher. Because they were every bit as frugal as the Delaware Saengerbund's officers, the society would not pay for anything that could not be used. By 1875, the library was ready to open. A notice in the *Delaware Gazette* on December 9, 1875, informed readers of this important event:

A German Library

What our German Citizens are doing in a Literary Direction

A library has opened at No. 411 Shipley Street. The library is the result of much labor on the part of several very intelligent German citizens, and it is really a very valuable addition to the literature of our city. The library at pre-

sent contains over 600 volumes and will be increased during the next three weeks to about 1,000 volumes.

The slender volumes looked exactly like those that graced Engelhardt's library in Neustadt. The complete works of Goethe, Schiller, Wieland, Herder, Boerne, Heine, Richter, Lessing, Thümel, Seymes, and Zschoke were there, as well as translations of Shakespeare, Paine, Scott, Dickens, and Cooper's complete works, including *Der letzte Mohikaner* (*The Last of the Mohicans*), and the *Brockhaus*, a sixteen-volume encyclopedia purchased for $33. The set was a gift from honorary member James Killgore. John Greiner donated a few rare, antique volumes from the sixteenth and seventeenth centuries. The article went on to say that the library was "open daily and all German citizens, and all of our people who are able to read German, can freely avail themselves of its privileges, as no charge is made."

Literary meetings of the VDC continued on Monday evenings or Sunday mornings with readings, lectures and discussions. The subjects ranged from humanism and socialism to revelation and reason. Members also closely studied the writings of Thomas Paine. That these lectures were in no way "dry" is suggested by one entry in the minutes "not to pay for the beer since it was spoiled." The VDC also had a social calendar similar to other German societies and often arranged picnics, fairs, and outings with other clubs. A delightful *Ostermontagstanz*—Easter Monday Dance—became the society's annual Stiftungfest celebration during the fifty years of its existence.

VDC Secretary Frederick von Bourdon, called "Fritz" or "Fred" by his friends, and Joseph Stoeckle were both from Buchau. Born in 1828, von Bourdon immigrated at age 21 to the United States. After residing in Pennsylvania, he came to Wilmington where he made the German Library his personal domain. He saw to it that the collection was continually enlarged, catalogued, and well cared-for. He served as secretary or librarian until his death in 1899.

On January 20, 1881, the society was incorporated as the *Deutscher Bibliothek Verein*, The German Library Association (DBV). As the association's library grew, it required more space, so the books were moved to the Herdman Building located on 4 East 4th Street. Needing another group to share the monthly rental cost, DBV officers approached the Delaware Saengerbund.

The library's letterhead decorated its honorary membership diploma. (Courtesy of HSD)

-Rebirth of the Delaware Saengerbund-

Daniel Maier had been entrusted with the belongings of the Delaware Harmonie. For more than two years, there were no rehearsals, and no Sängerfeste, but that did not mean the singing had stopped. Whenever the old Sangesbrüder got together for a glass of beer or wine at Conrad Manz's tavern, they usually broke out in harmony. Maier sang first tenor; Christoph Bauer, second tenor; Francis Scheu, the new editor of the *Pionier*, first bass; and Manz, second bass. Soon word got around that there was a new *Gesangverein*, singing society, in Conrad Manz's tavern, which soon was referred to as Manz's *Sänger Halle*. More and more friends came to join the quartet. The room was so small that one group had to wait downstairs until another one finished upstairs. In May of 1877, Maier, Bauer, Manz, Hertzler, Francis and Gustav Scheu, and Georg Sharp decided to reactivate the constitution of the Delaware Saengerbund. They elected officers, and Daniel Maier became president; Georg Sharp, treasurer; Francis Scheu, secretary; and M. Hertzler, music librarian.

The Delaware Harmonie came out of retirement one last time. Then, on August 18, 1877, William Cloos, vice president, announced that the Delaware Harmonie would be dissolved and all its belongings given to the new society. At a combined meeting on August 24th, Daniel Maier—simultaneously treasurer of the Delaware Harmonie and first president of the reactivated Delaware Saengerbund—proposed that the Saengerbund accept all members of the Delaware Harmonie, active or passive, without a ballot or dues, into the new society. The proposal was accepted. United and happy, the Sangesbrüder moved all the belongings from Maier's home to the Delaware Saengerbund's new location at Conrad Manz's tavern. First Julius Hess, then J. P. T. Fuekel served as music directors, and once again rehearsals were held regularly.

Soon a larger meeting place was needed. In December 1879, the hall in the Herdman Building on 4th Street became available for $288 per year. About this time, the VDC officers approached the Delaware Saengerbund and suggested that they share the hall and rental fee. A joint board of trustees was formed, and numerous events were planned for the hall, often referred to as the German Hall. The move was celebrated with a grand ball on New Year's Eve. Members of both societies also attended the library's Easter Monday ball, and a special two-week-long fair was held in October. The fair's main attraction was the chancing-off of numerous prizes donated by members and friends, including the grand prize, a 130-piece set of porcelain.

-German Language Schools-

The Delaware Saengerbund and the German Library Association's common bond was the German language. Morris Faber, rabbi of Ohabe Shalom Synagogue and a member of the library, proposed in 1881 that the two societies open a German language school on Saturdays. The vote was in favor of the school, provided that eight children of poor families would be instructed without paying. A separate school committee was formed consisting of Morris Faber, Daniel Maier, Henry Miller, Francis Scheu, Eberhard Freye, Friedrich Becher, and Anton Hauber. Miss Anna Radnitzki was hired as the teacher at a salary of $5 per month. Books and slates were purchased. A year later, the two societies turned over all teaching materials to the *Deutsche Schulverein*—school committee—which was in charge of the German American school, established on April 1, 1882.

A fifty-year span of census reports shows an increasing number of German immigrants to the State of Delaware and the city of Wilmington.

YEAR	DELAWARE	WILMINGTON
1860	1,263	603
1870	1,142	684
1880	1,310	773

1890	2,469	1,944
1900	2,523	1,924
1910	3,564	2,798

The 1890 census shows 61,431 people living in Wilmington. At the same time, the number of foreign-born citizens was 9,085. Almost half were from Ireland, and close to 2,000 had come from Germany. Thomas Scharf, in his *History of Delaware* (1888), estimated that the German-speaking population of Wilmington at that time was three times higher or 6,000, but his estimate included the second and third generation of Germans living in Wilmington and their influence on the make-up of the city. The city also exerted its influence on the German neighborhood: "English ways" were easily accepted, especially by the younger generation. This was no small matter of concern, and the question, "Who will teach the German language to the next generation?" was asked frequently. German parents wanted their children to continue speaking, reading, and writing the language that was their direct connection to the homeland. In order to follow as closely as possible their cherished traditions, they had formed clubs, founded churches, established businesses, and celebrated festivals. The German language prevailed in songs and association meeting records, in liturgies and sermons, and in social get-togethers. Pressure was added by relatives overseas who expected their grandchildren, nieces, and nephews to be able to read and write letters in German.

The children of the Forty-Eighters had come of school age in the early 1860s. At that time, the Rev. Heinrich Weicksel of Zion Lutheran Church saw the need for language instruction and on August 23, 1864, he placed an ad in the *Delaware* Gazette offering lessons in the German language. By 1865, members of the Zion Lutheran congregation—many Saengerbund members among them—were eager to establish a weekday school where the children could learn German vocabulary, grammar, and script, which had letters and strokes similar to the old German *Fraktur*, or calligraphy.

On October 27, 1865, the *Delaware Gazette* reported receiving a communication "from a committee in charge of the German and English school, in which they offered $4,500 for the building at the corner of Sixth and French Streets." In this communication, Rev. Weicksel stated that "the school had relieved the Board of Education from the charge of

about 100 scholars, and if they should be able to purchase said house they would be able to accommodate many more." Rev. Weicksel's con-gregation did purchase the building, and the *Wochenschule*, or daily school, located in the lower room, boasted an enrollment of 100 to 130 children. The school was supported wholeheartedly by the German societies. The *Delaware Gazette* of September 9, 1866, noted that "The German Turners of this city gave a picnic at Rosendale yesterday for the benefit of the German and English School. They marched up Market street about nine o'clock, with a fine band of music, the 'stars and stripes,' and the flag of the Saengerbund. The company were all dressed in linen, and presented a uniform, cool and pleasant appearance." The second anniversary of the German and English school was held in Odd Fellows Hall, on Friday evening, June 8, 1866. When Pastor Weicksel resigned in 1867, the school lost a competent leader. It also became independent of the Zion Lutheran Church and had to struggle for survival.

The German Catholic community followed by establishing its own school. By the 1870s, there were upwards of 600 German Catholics in the city. *Herz Jesu Kirche*—Sacred Heart Church—had been built in 1874 as a place of worship for German-speaking Catholics. On July 24, 1874, the *Delaware Gazette* reported that, "The German Catholics of our city have heretofore been worshipping in common with all others, but after the completion of this church they will have the truth proclaimed to them in their own language, and have their children instructed in the various branches of study in their native language."

The Dedication Mass was held in the completed basement on April 25, 1875. The Reverend Father Wendelin Mayer, O.S.B., came from Germany as the first pastor. He established a German school in the parish and built a convent for the Benedictine nuns who taught there. Support for the teaching of German was so great that on November 17, 1895, the *Sunday Morning Star* announced that "Father Prior Sylvester … will give one hour every day to any child, no matter what denomination or nationality for the study of the German language, free of charge." Sacred Heart became known as a school where the teaching of German was a great factor in contributing to the students' excellence. This fact was noted twenty years later, in a 1906 article in the *Sunday Morning Star*: "Lots of men of affairs have gained their lead in life through the Sacred Heart Parish School. Some entered the field of law, others the ministry, and many became well established businessmen. The knowledge of German is a great help for success."

The German Baptist church, located on Walnut Street, conducted German language services from the time of its founding in 1856. Whether a German school was connected with the church is not known. The Jewish community in Wilmington was relatively small and did not have a synagogue until 1880 when Ohabe Shalom synagogue was dedicated on March 19. Rabbi Morris Faber served there from 1880 until 1887. The German Jewish families of the Moses Montefiore Society opened a night school where Hebrew and German were taught during the week to the children of the congregation. An 1881 German school census published by C. Witter in St. Louis, Missouri, showed that Delaware had one private German school with one teacher for 60 pupils and one Catholic German school with three teachers for 75 pupils.

-German Newspapers-

The fondness of the Germans for their language, their *Muttersprache*, or mother tongue, also made it possible for a weekly German newspaper, *Pionier*, to flourish among the daily newspapers published in Wilmington. Jakob Haenlen, *Pionier's* publisher, had joined the Delaware Saengerbund in 1869 as an active singer. When he realized the feasibility of a German newspaper, he started one. On Oct. 25, 1869, the minutes of the Delaware Saengerbund recorded "… that an announcement about the next concert and ball was to be placed into the '*Pionier.*'" Two years later in 1871, when Haenlen left the city to become editor of the *Staats Journal* in Trenton, New Jersey, he was presented with a fine gold watch for his services to the German community here.

Hermann Rau from Richmond, Virginia, took over the *Pionier* in September 1871. He joined the Delaware Harmonie and became a charter member of the literary society, VDC. On May 3, 1874, several German men met in his office to debate the steps involved in establishing a Delaware Lodge of the German Order of the Harugari, a Masonic group. In July 1875, Rau and Colonel Henry Buxbaum started the German Military Company for the purpose of participating in the Centennial celebrations in Philadelphia. After Rau died

in 1876, Franz (Francis) Scheu became *Pionier's* next publisher.

Scheu had been born in Württemberg and, after immigrating, first resided at Egg Harbor, New Jersey. There he served a term as mayor and superintendent of the Atlantic County public schools. He published the *Atlantic Beacon* in English and the *Egg Harbor Pilot* in German. For several years he edited the *Philadelphia Sonntagsblatt*, a Sunday German language paper. In 1876 he moved to Wilmington and took over the *Pionier*; in 1881 he changed the paper's name to *Wilmington Freie Presse* and published it as a daily morning paper. Scheu also became very active in the Delaware Saengerbund and the German Library Association, helping to write the constitution. He was the first to suggest that the two societies should merge, but he was ahead of his time and his proposal was rejected. Scheu was also one of the organizers and chief supporters of the German American School. He strongly believed in educating German children in their mother tongue and also in continuing to observe German customs. He and his wife had eight sons and two daughters. After he died in 1886, his sons continued the *Freie Presse* until it was taken over by A. J. Kooch, at that time the only German notary in Wilmington. Later, in 1901, Max Goetz acquired the newspaper, and the *Freie Presse* became the *Wilmington Lokal-Anzeiger und Freie Presse.*

All five publishers contributed to the cohesiveness of the German community. They were conscientious about reporting the news, announcing forthcoming events, and following-up afterward with colorful descriptions. This was a good way of keeping the language alive and and it was also good business. Today only several bound volumes of the *Wilmington Lokal=Anzeiger* survive. They were donated to the Balch Institute by the Turners.

-Volksfeste-

In 1882 when teacher Fritz Schaefer of the *Deutsche Schulverein*—the German school board—called on all German societies to participate in a festival for the benefit of the German American school, the response was positive. Newspaper publisher Francis Scheu served as chairman of the festival committee that included Peter Ebner, Conrad Manz, Henry Miller, Joseph Stoeckle, Frederick von Bourdon, and John Wagner.

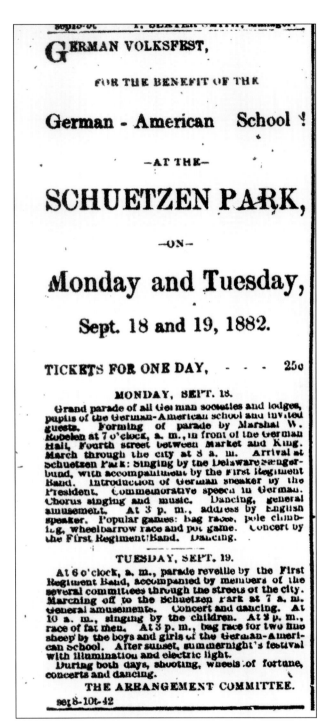

GERMAN VOLKSFEST,

FOR THE BENEFIT OF THE

German - American   School !

—AT THE—

SCHUETZEN PARK,

—ON—

Monday and Tuesday,

Sept. 18 and 19, 1882.

TICKETS FOR ONE DAY, - - -   25c

MONDAY, SEPT. 18.

Grand parade of all German societies and lodges, pupils of the German-American school and invited guests. Forming of parade by Marshal W. Kubelen at 7 o'clock, a. m., in front of the German Hall, Fourth street between Market and King. March through the city at 8 a. m. Arrival at Schuetzen Park: Singing by the Delaware Saengerbund, with accompaniment by the First Regiment Band. Introduction of German speaker by the President. Commemorative speech in German. Chorus singing and music. Dancing, general amusement. At 3 p. m., address by English speaker. Popular games: bag race, pole climbing, wheelbarrow race and pot game. Concert by the First Regiment Band. Dancing.

TUESDAY, SEPT. 19.

At 6 o'clock, a. m., parade reveille by the First Regiment Band, accompanied by members of the several committees through the streets of the city. Marching off to the Schuetzen Park at 7 a. m. General amusements. Concert and dancing. At 10 a. m., singing by the children. At 3 p. m., race of fat men. At 3 p. m., bag race for two fine sheep by the boys and girls of the German-American school. After sunset, summernight's festival with illumination and electric light.

During both days, shooting, wheels of fortune, concerts and dancing.

THE ARRANGEMENT COMMITTEE.

sep 8-10t-42

The first Volksfest was held in Schützen Park in 1882 and advertised in the Every Evening. *(Courtesy of UD)*

The *Volksfest*—or folk festival—was held on Monday and Tuesday, September 18 and 19. *Every Evening* reported, with amazement on September 18, 1882, that all the German businesses were closed during the festival:

The German's Festtag—A Big Time at Schuetzen Park—The German Volksfest—This is a gala day among the German residents of Wilmington, and business is suspended, in a measure, among the Teuton tradespeople, and all seem devoting the best efforts to make the German Volksfest, which began this morning at Schuetzen Park, a success. The fest is given for the benefit of the German-American school of this city, and the cause being a worthy one, and the nature of the fest being enjoyable will undoubtedly serve to make the occasion pleasant as well as beneficial to the school.

The festival parade began on Monday morning at 8 o'clock, after everyone had assembled in front of the German Hall in the Herdman Building on 4th Street, between King and Market. The parade was led by a wagon "gaily festooned with flag buntings, evergreens and flowers, conveying about thirty female pupils of the German-American school, dressed in white carrying bouquets and flags." The Wilmington Turners followed, and after them a wagon carrying the boys of the school who were seated among flowers and flags. The newspaper also described the Delaware Saengerbund's wagon pulled by four horses:

In the center of the vehicle a shrine of flowers rose out of a bed of evergreens. On the throne sat a fair-haired German girl, clad in white, with bands of gold about her head and wearing a small coronet. She carried a small lyre in her hands in impersonation of the goddess of music. About her feet were four small girls, representing the seasons, each proffering her offering of fruit. Another young miss clad in the costume of the Germans with the red, orange, and black flag woven around her head represented Germany. By her side rode a lady impersonating the goddess of liberty wearing the flag of the United States about her. The typical Uncle Sam rode majestically in the midst of the fair goddesses, whose presence did not induce him to abandon a cigar!

Saengerbund President Peter Ebner, Secretary Daniel Maier, and several members followed in carriages, as did members of the city council and board of education. Representatives of other German societies, bands, and a brewery wagon added to the colorful parade that was watched by hundreds of people. The parade arrived at Schützen Park, which was decorated with flags and flowers, at eleven o'clock. *Every Evening*'s reporter continued: "The speaker's stand had been erected at the north end of the hall, and the south end is used for dispensing liquid refreshments in the shape of beer. To the south of the main building is the restaurant where sauerkraut is dished out for the hungry. Everything is in readiness for the amusements this afternoon, which will consist of foot races, bag races, pole climbing, and other national amusements."

The First Regimental Band played, school children and the German choruses of Wilmington sang selected German folksongs, and dancing lasted until late in the evening. The first Volksfest was such a success that it was decided to hold another one the following year, and to make it three days long. *Every Evening*, the daily Wilmington paper, was well-prepared to describe the 1883 festival:

The Volksfest by Telegraph--- In furtherance of Every Evening's efforts to report the Volksfest fully and satisfactory, arrangements have been made with the Western Union Telegraph Company to connect *Every Evening*'s office by wire with the Schuetzen Park during continuance of the Volksfest. A telegraph operator will be stationed at Schuetzen Park and the doings of each day will be telegraphed as fast as they take place.

Every Evening's special Volksfest edition for September 17–19 thoroughly covered the three-day festival:

"Our German friends with the hearty co-operation of citizens without regard to nationality, today opened auspiciously the three days' rejoicing of the Volksfest. The *Freie Presse*'s timely plea for moderation in the use of the good things of the time is likely to be heeded by the Germans who are not given to excess, and we hope none that join in this Teutonic festival will bring discredit upon the Germans, the responsible hosts of the occasion."

Every Evening's reporter interviewed a well-read German, whose name was not given, but who could have been Henry Miller, about the history and meaning of a Volksfest. He connected it to the tradition of clan and family gatherings and the custom of whole villages and towns turning out for celebrations marking an historic event or special season. Asked about the Volksfest in Wilmington, he replied:

"The Volksfest in America is dear to us. Here we are foreigners. It is our duty to make ourselves good citizens of the land of our adoption, but it is also our duty to keep up the same connections we have learned to value in our native land and to educate our children to the same heritage of family hood, and by this mingling to develop and broaden the good there is in us and to weed out the evil; to maintain the standard of membership in the German family high enough and if we can, to make each member resolve to do nothing to dishonor it. And so you will see," said the speaker coming down to less ethereal regions, "that what the German wants in his Volksfest is not only sauerkraut and beer, but he has a higher principle: He wants everybody to be happy and to be better for being happy."

Mayor Wales, Governor Stockley, and Senator Bayard were at the head of the 1883 parade, led by Chief Marshall C. B. Rhoads, music director of the Delaware Saengerbund. Hundreds of industrial displays divided into ten divisions took over one-half hour to pass the corner of Fifth and Market Streets. The festivities continued at the Schützen Park with amusements, games, speeches, dancing, and good food and drink, under the watchful eyes of 17 city policemen, who were hired to "promptly expel all obstreperous patrons." The invited speaker, Senator Thomas Bayard, welcomed the opportunity the Volksfest provided for all people to get to know each other:

It has become a common saying that "one half of the world does not know how the other half lives," which plainly means that wrapped in our personal pursuits and intent only on our individual objects we do not give ourselves the trouble to find out how it fares with our fellow-sojourner. Trace the history of nations or individuals, and there can scarcely be found a public war or private quarrel which was not the result of a mutual misunderstanding. Ignorance of each other leads to misunderstanding and from this to a blind and bitter conflict. The Volksfest is intended to let the people know each other. Therefore I view this festival as having important public functions and containing in its simple and pleasant observances the germs for high usefulness in the solution of the difficult problems that confront civilized governments everywhere. Senator Bayard was a great favorite among German Americans. His democratic ways and liberal ideas had earned him their sincere friendship, and the Delaware Saengerbund made him a lifetime honorary member.

Concerts, songs and music, and performances by the Turners entertained the thousands who attended the festival. Games, wheelbarrow races, sack races, and greased pole climbs amused the younger people. In the evening, seven Paris-made Arnoux electric lights swinging from high poles illuminated the park grounds and the throng of merry-makers. There were few disturbances on the festival grounds and "the police on duty had but few unruly persons to take in charge. Streams of young lads poured into the park over the fence, and many of those caught in the act were led to the front gate and through the turnstile." A sheep escaped. Eight-year-old Andrea Beyerlein had won it in the children's sack race and was anxious for its return. Everyone was awaiting the next Volksfest, which took place the following year.

The Delaware Saengerbund men looked "cool and spiffy" in the 1884 parade. They were dressed in white fishermen's hats, carried Chinese umbrellas, and wore blue badges with the name Delaware Saengerbund embossed in gold letters. However, subsequent festivals were never quite as large and elaborate as the one in 1883 had been. Perhaps Saengerbund organizers were following the advice of the *Every Evening* reporter who commented on September 20, 1883, "if the Volksfest is to be an annual thing, we sincerely hope it may not take on the features of costly and extravagant displays that are likely to doom the Baltimore Oriole to an early death. It should be born in mind throughout the three festival days that the serious object is the advancement of education."

What brought the Volksfeste to an early end was the fact that expenses exceeded income, and the German societies began looking into other ways to raise funds for the German American school. Still, the Volksfeste had brought Wilmington's German organizations closer together. Now, owning a center of their own for meetings and social affairs became the Saengerbund's goal.

6

German Hall

Das ist der Tag des Herrn!	This is the day of the Lord!
Das ist der Tag des Herrn!	This is the day of the Lord!
Ich bin allein auf weiter Flur,	I am alone on the meadow lea,
nah eine Morgenglocke nur,	A morning bell the only sound,
nur Stille nah und fern,	And silence all around.
das ist der Tag des Herrn!	This is the day of the Lord!

-Kücken

After thirty years of struggle, the Delaware Saengerbund entered a new phase. The long-held dream of Wilmington's German societies—owning their own home—moved nearer to reality when Francis Scheu noticed an appropriate building for sale. *Every Evening*, December 22, 1881, revealed the Saengerbund's plans: "The committee appointed to consider the advisability of purchasing the large building on 6th Street near French, adjoining Wesleyan College and formerly a portion of that institute, reported that the owner, Wilmington Savings Fund Society had not yet agreed on a price. There is every likelihood that the building will be purchased by the German societies."

After two years of mulling over the prospect, the German Library Association and the Delaware Saengerbund, at a joint meeting in December 1883, resolved to buy the property at 205 East 6th Street to establish a German Hall. The price was $7,500. Of this amount, they paid $1,500 in cash and mortgaged the rest. President Heinrich Müller and Secretary Eberhard Freye of the Library Association, and President Daniel Maier and Secretary George Metzner of the Delaware Saengerbund signed the $6,000 mortgage. Six hundred certificates at $5 each, at 6% interest payable in three years, were made available to members and friends by each society. General Henry du Pont was one of the first to subscribe as a stockholder, a fact that gave members a great deal of confidence. Payment of the bonds would be guaranteed through a second mortgage on the building, to be repaid at a time to be decided by the board of directors.

The building on 205 East Sixth Street was part of the Wesleyan Female College. It was purchased by the Delaware Saengerbund and the German Library Association and became known as German Hall. (Courtesy of Hagley Museum)

Managing the German Hall was the responsibility of the *Verwaltungsrat*—a Board of Trustees—a system that had proven useful during the stay at Herdman's Hall. The board was composed of an equal number of members from each society. In later years the number included six members from the Saengerbund and six from the Library Association, with a thirteenth member chosen by the twelve in case a deciding vote had to be cast.

The Delaware Saengerbund and the German Library Association each owned shares in the German Hall and were assessed a yearly rental fee that entitled each club to use the hall one evening per week. The four-story building had a small kitchen, a large dining room, and a bar on the first floor. The large hall used for rehearsals and balls was on the second floor. A stage for theater productions and entertainment stretched across one end of this room, and the ornate, black grand piano was kept there. The third story housed the library and several *Logen Zimmer*, or meeting rooms. A small apartment in the upper story was rented to the caretaker of the house. Other German and Wilmington societies could rent the hall when it was not being used by the Saengerbund or the Library Association, and the income from the rentals was equally shared by the two

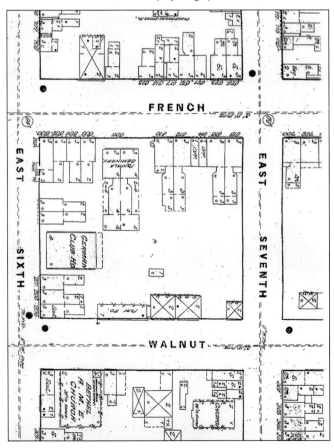

Map with location of German Hall. (Courtesy of HSD)

societies after the Verwaltungsrat had paid the bills. The building, referred to by Wilmingtonians as the German Hall, became the new center for all activities of the German societies.

Through purchasing shares, the Wilmington Turner Association became co-owner of the German Hall in 1885 and 1886. However, the Turners' need to use and store gymnastic equipment and the noise caused by their exercises led to difficulties. When the Saengerbund's piano was constantly out of tune and broken from being moved too many times, the Turners were charged $10 for repairs. At this point, the Turners, who also resented the fact that the other two societies had not legalized their part ownership on the property title decided to move out *unter Sang und Klang*—with song and music—and resolved to build their own *Turnhalle*. Their plan was finally realized in 1894, when the property of David Bush at 802–808 French Street went up for sale. The Turners had the two-story dwellings torn down and replaced with a large brick edifice that included a basement for their exercise equipment and a main floor auditorium for assemblies and entertainments. Wilmington Germans were pleased to have a second hall available for their many social events.

Now that they owned the German Hall at 205 East Sixth Street, there were increased responsibilities for the Saengerbund. The dedicated group of men—Daniel Maier, Peter Ebner, Anton Hauber, Charles Yetter, Harry Zimmermann, and Joseph Sell—who had been the driving force behind purchasing the building soon took over the leadership in all affairs. With their guidance, the Saengerbund reached new prosperity and visibility. At the end of 1885, the society had 135 members (23 active singers and 112 passive members). A year later 106 members were registered (20 singers, 83 passive, and 3 honorary members). In 1888 the society grew to 159 members (23 active, 135 passive, and one honorary member), the result of an increased number of immigrants.

During the 1880s and into the 1890s, almost one and one-half million Germans entered the United States, the largest wave of German immigrants. Germany was still a coalition of sovereign states. The north German states had created a confederation in 1866 with a ruling parliament called the *Reichstag*. After 1871 the Reichstag was dominated by Prussia and Chancellor Otto von Bismarck. He was suspicious of anyone who did not favor the official parties of the

German Hall was home to the German societies until 1965.

Reichstag and especially targeted Catholics politically involved with the Catholic *Zentrum Partei*—the Center Party. Anyone belonging to the various Social Democratic parties and movements was also suspect, as in the time of the March Revolution forty years earlier. When the Reichstag passed the Anti-Socialist Law in 1878, many workers who were actively involved and threatened with imprisonment sought a safe haven elsewhere. Some fled to Switzerland and England. Those with relatives in the United States who could vouch for them braved the still-hazardous journey across the Atlantic.

Between 1880 and 1900, Wilmington's German population almost tripled. Due to the many new immigrants, two new organizations were formed. One was the *Arbeiterverein Labor Lyceum*, a German workers organization that promptly formed the *Arbeiter-Gesangverein*, a workers' singing society. The Labor Lyceum bought an old fire hall at Second and Jackson Streets as its headquarters, and when that building became too small, relocated to 5th and DuPont Streets. The Labor Lyceum Hall became the third meeting center for German societies, mainly for the German Bakers and Brewers unions. The Labor Lyceum also opened a German school and English night school, but found them too expensive to run and closed both after three years. A second new organization, the *Arbeiter Kranken und Sterbekasse*, was incorporated in 1893. It was a beneficial society offering sickness and death benefits to its members.

-Calvin B. Rhoads-

Calvin B. Rhoads, well-known in Wilmington's German circles, was the Saengerbund's colorful music director from 1882 to 1894. After coming from Reading in 1873, he first worked as an assistant clerk in the Schützen Park. His musical abilities were soon discovered, and his baritone voice made him an instant success in the city's choirs. At various times he led the choirs at Old Swede's, Trinity, St. Peter's, Calvary, Grace, Second Baptist, and St. Stephen's, as well as the Old Choral Club, Millard Club, and the Delaware Saengerbund.

Professor Rhoads's relationship with the chorus was colorful, as noted in the minutes. During a special meeting on March 29, 1883, his resignation was read into the record, but not accepted. At that same meeting, it was resolved that no member could visit the bar during rehearsals without permission of the director or president. The minutes also indicate that starting rehearsals late and taking time out for a smoke bothered some of the more punctual members, but not the jovial Calvin Rhoads. The minutes of July 10, 1884, reflect continuing problems, especially when President Daniel Maier was asked to confer with Rhoads about keeping order during rehearsals. That August, Rhoads again turned in his resignation, but he was persuaded to stay on. After all, the 14th Sängerfest was to take place the following July in Brooklyn, and preparations had to be made. Twelve singers were ready to sign up: Christian Bacher, Raymond Beyerlein, Peter Ebner, Gustav George, Anton Hauber, Daniel Maier, George B. Metzner, A. Steinke, Gustav Steinke, Fred Weil, Charles Yetter, Harry Zimmermann. They did participate, but without their director.

Another special meeting was called in August 1885. This time the Saengerbund was determined to cancel Rhoads's contract as director, since he "often did not appear for public performances of the chorus."

Apparently the demands of the public office Mr. Rhoads held that year (he was mayor of Wilmington) left him little time for his musical responsibilities. In September, there was an election for a new director. The four names on the ballot were C. B. Rhoads, Frederick Becher, J. P. T. Fuekel, and Julius Hess. By majority vote, C. B. Rhoads was reelected. The singers then surprised him on his birthday by giving him a baton. He remained their director until his sudden death in 1894 at age 58. The Saengerbund chorus sang a touching farewell at the funeral service and gave floral offerings in the design of lyres and harps, each with a broken string.

-Fundraising-

Raising the funds needed to maintain the German Hall continued to be a major focus of the Saengerbund's trustees and officers. The minutes show that the 1885 Volksfest organized by the German American School ended with a loss of $4.65. Since Saengerbund officers, Harry Zimmermann, Daniel Maier, Peter Ebner, and Anton Hauber, were all successful businessmen, they considered other ways to raise money for the German Hall. At the time steamboat excursions were popular so, in June of 1886, they rented the *Republic* for $550 for an excursion to Cape May. The excursion was advertised in all the Wilmington papers, the *Freie Presse, Every Evening, Morning News, Republican*, and *Sunday Morning Star* and was a great success. The total income was $902.86 and the expenses only $737.50; thus leaving an *Ueberschuss*—a profit—of $165.36 in the treasury.

At a meeting in 1887, Harry Zimmermann proposed another excursion, but after a long discussion, the majority voted against it. The idea of an excursion came up again in 1888. In a meeting that lasted until 2 a.m., those with happy memories of the first excursion won out over members who feared a financial disaster. Charles Yetter proposed selling tickets by subscription for $1 per person, children free. That seemed too high, so the ticket price was decreased to 75 cents. Finally the men agreed on 85 cents. *Schatzmeister*—treasurer— Harry Zimmermann was authorized to rent the *Republic* for the excursion to Cape May. This meeting finally ended when Secretary Anton Hauber got up from his seat and went home.

The *Republic* was the finest pleasure boat then navigating the Delaware River and Bay. It had fourteen staterooms that rented for $2.50 each and two parlors, available for $5.00 each. Each newspaper was given six complimentary tickets, each active singer two. A delegation from Reading quickly made reservations.

The Saengerbund hired a fifteen-man band for the occasion. New for this excursion was a refreshment concession consisting of an oyster bar and an ice cream stand. The total income was $1,683.74, and the total expenses, $1,049.35. After also subtracting the $100 deposit that had been paid to the boat company beforehand, the total Ueberschuss was $534.39. At the very next meeting, Saengerbund members made a donation to the Deutsche Schulverein, the committee in charge of the German American school.

The Saengerbund chorus's next major event was the Nordoestlicher Saengerbund's 15th Sängerfest, held in Baltimore from June 30 to July 4, 1888. The following October, at the invitation of the Turners, the Saengerbund and several other choruses participated in the Wilmington Fair. A concert and ball on December 11 crowned a successful year.

-The Saengerbund's Fortieth Anniversary-

The Delaware Saengerbund's minutes for 1889 through 1914 have been lost. Those years were undoubtedly active ones for the society, so it is fortunate that some of the highlights were recorded in Wilmington's newspapers. In 1893, for example, the club could look back at the first ten years in its own home *and* proudly celebrate its 40th Stiftungsfest. On this occasion, President Daniel Maier celebrated his 25th anniversary as an active singer and also his tenth anniversary as president of the society. In recognition of "his long, arduous and unselfish labors in behalf of the organization," he was presented with a handsome bronze clock. Honorary members who received framed diplomas included Joseph Niedermaier (whose diploma is preserved at the Delaware Saengerbund), W. M. S. Brown, Henry Feldmeier, Andrew Grotz, Mrs. Hertel, Georg Hirzel, John D. Kurtz, John Maier, Henry Miller, Georg Schellkopf, Joseph Stoeckle, Christian Spoerl, and Frederick Weil. Special guests included the Aurora Saengerbund of Newark, New Jersey, and two local singing societies, the Gesangssektion of the Wilmington Turngemeinde, directed by Gerhard Schirmer, and the Arbeiter Gesangverein, directed by Frederick Becher.

Details about the 40th anniversary were included in *History of Wilmington* published by the *Every Evening* newspaper in 1894. This book also contains the 1890 census information and one chapter devoted to Wilmington's German community, including the history of the Delaware Saengerbund and the German Library Association, and a few biographical sketches of older and younger Germans. Among them are the brewer Joseph Stoeckle and his son Harry; the brewers John Fehrenbach and John Hartmann, with an outline of the growth of their breweries; Peter Ebner, Daniel Maier, and Anton Hauber, who were all officers of the Delaware Saengerbund; as well as Morris Grubb, Frederick Kleitz, Hermann Erb, and John Seidel, representative young businessmen. Wilmington was proud of its German citizens, as the article clearly indicates: "It may be truthfully said that of the German-American population throughout this country, no city is more fortunate in active business men and in loyal citizens than Wilmington."

-First Prize!-

The year 1897 brought the long-awaited fulfillment of another dream. Following the short tenure of Gerhard Schirmer, Carl A. Hartmann became the Saengerbund's new music director. Hartmann was an excellent musician who knew how to motivate the singers. Rehearsals were attended faithfully and, at the 18th Sängerfest in Philadelphia in June 1897, the singers harvested the fruits of their labors: a First Prize! With the song *Abendfeier*—"Evening Celebration" by Attenhofer—the Saengerbund received 139 out of 150

Emblem of the Nordoestlicher Saengerbund.

possible points. This placed the Wilmington group eleven points ahead of the other seventeen choruses competing in the singing contest's third class. The men returned home in triumph and were greeted at the train station by their wives and children and the happy tunes of a brass band. Now the Saengerbund could look forward to a new century with pride and confidence.

-The Alte Herren-

Despite the joy of having arrived at its fortieth anniversary and having placed first in the Preissingen, there was the sadness of knowing that some of the founding members had already passed from the scene. John Feherenbach had died in 1887; John Hartmann in 1890. Joseph Stoeckle, a man admired by all who knew him for his never-ending energy, did not live to see his name in print. He died in December 1893 during the influenza epidemic that devastated Wilmington. All the men who had pushed for the purchase of the German Hall were drivers in their personal lives as well. Many were successful businessmen, belonged to more than one German society, and were active in their churches.

Caspar Conrad worked at J. P. T. Fuekel's sauerkraut factory and was known as Caspar the Yodeler. He and Peter Ebner, Frederick Kleitz, and Harry Zimmermann formed the Tyrolean Quartet. Saloon owners Harry Schnepf and Christoph Bauer accompanied the quartet on the zither. After Caspar Conrad inherited a farm in Germany from an uncle, he returned there to manage it.

Peter Ebner, born in Memel, Prussia, in 1852, went to sea for ten years, long enough to see all of the Mediterranean countries including Spain, Italy, and Turkey. He also sailed to Egypt, Denmark, Norway, Sweden, the East and West Indies and part of Africa. He was shipwrecked three times, once surviving three weeks adrift in a small boat. Ebner arrived in America in 1868 and settled in Wilmington in 1877. He first owned a restaurant, then started a bottling business at the corner of 4th and Union Streets. By 1890 the bottling plant employed twenty-six workers. The Saengerbund ordered Ebner's *soft stoff*, nonalcoholic drinks, for picnics and festivals. In 1888 Ebner received a special pin from the DSB in honor of his services.

Anton Hauber, a carriage builder by trade, was born in 1845 in Ellwangen, Württemberg. He emigrated in 1868 and came to Wilmington in 1870.

After first working in his profession, he decided to go into the restaurant business. At one time he owned the Cosmopolitan Café at 510 Market Street. He joined the Delaware Saengerbund in 1870 and became a charter member of the VDC, the German Library Association. In 1885 he was president of the Saengerbund, the German Library Association, and the Wilmington Turners all at the same time.

Daniel Maier, born in 1845 in Bissingen, Württemberg, came to Wilmington at age 22. His uncle, John Maier, owned a bakery business. Daniel Maier soon opened his own bakery. He married Wilhelmina Hartmann, and five sons and two daughters were born to them. He joined the Liederkranz in 1868. Using his powers of conciliation, Maier was able to convince the Saengerbund and Liederkranz to unite. Once, after he returned to Germany for a home visit, an extremely rare undertaking, the Saengerbund welcomed him back at a special luncheon. Maier served as Saengerbund president for more than ten years and sang in the Zion Lutheran Church choir for over thirty years.

Joseph Niedermaier, from Buchau, Württemberg, was born on December 8, 1824. He joined the Saengerbund in 1854, the year he is first listed in the *Wilmington City Directory*. He worked as a laborer until 1869, then opened a saloon at 413 King Street. In 1877 he owned a saloon at 119 Shipley Street. When he died on October 31, 1900, the obituary in *Every Evening* called him "one of the oldest and most highly respected German citizens of Wilmington who was esteemed by all who knew him for his integrity and uprightness of character."

Joseph Sell joined the Liederkranz in 1870. He was a carpenter and staircase maker. When his tools were destroyed in the city fire of 1881, the Saengerbund gave him $15 to help buy replacements. He served as the Saengerbund's president from 1898 to 1899 and again from 1906 to 1907. He owned a small farm on Delaware Avenue where he cultivated peach trees and raised rabbit dogs.

Joseph Stoeckle, founder of Stoeckle's Brewery, was a man of unusual popularity. Tatkräftiges Handeln had characterized him throughout his life, as his obituary in the December 24, 1983, *Sunday Morning Star* shows: "Starting life at the very foot of the ladder, he amassed within a comparatively short time an estate that will approximate a half-million dollars. This was the result of his own energy, pluck, and hard work. He did not know the meaning of rest or the ordinary acceptation of that word. His was a tireless energy that swept along with all the restless force of a Niagara." Stoeckle never forgot his own poor beginnings and responded generously to anyone in need. He was a member of the Zion Lutheran Church and almost all the German societies in Wilmington.

Charles Yetter came to Wilmington in 1876 and opened a bakery in a three-story building at 11 East 4th Street. He advertised "Mother's Home Made Bread," ice cream, biscuits, and fancy cakes for all occasions. His bakery employed thirteen workers and required three large wagons to deliver the freshly baked bread and pastries around the city. He sang in the Sacred Heart Church choir for many, many years.

Heinrich Zimmerman arrived in Wilmington in 1880. He joined the Saengerbund and sang first bass. He lived at the northwest corner of 4th and Tatnall Streets where his successful catering business was also located. On August 12, 1906, his obituary in the *Sunday Morning Star* said that, "As a caterer he had no equal in this city. In fact, he was really the pioneer of the catering art in Wilmington."

-The Founding of the Damen-Verein-

German women preferred to remain in the background, letting the men lead in decision-making and public appearances, but when called upon out of necessity the women proved as *tatkräftig,* or strong, as their husbands. When Wilhelmina Dettling, grandmother of Delaware historian John A. Munroe, was left to care for five children after her husband Andreas's death in 1898 at the young age of 39, she opened a general store in her small home on Walnut Street to make ends meet. Munroe, writing in *Delaware History* Volume XXIX, Number 2, noted that the little store prospered because of her "ingenuity, hard work, and great prudence." These same characteristics applied to other German women who unexpectedly became heads of households.

Widows Elizabeth Manz and Barbara Manz continued to keep the family taverns open after their husbands, John and Conrad, passed away. Johanna Stoeckle developed into a keen businesswoman when she took over the Diamond State brewery after the death of her husband Joseph. Mary Stuck continued the bakery business of her husband Jacob, as did Rosa Yetter when Charles Yetter died. Catherine Ebner presided over the Peter Ebner's bottling plant after his death until their sons could take over the business.

These women and others like them who succeeded in business were also willing to take on a larger, more independent role in society in order to bring about changes. This became apparent when, on March 18, 1896, several women met in the home of Mrs. Peter Ebner to establish the *Damen-Verein*—Ladies of the Delaware Saengerbund—as an auxiliary to the Delaware Saengerbund. The ladies auxiliary was organized along the lines of the Saengerbund with a constitution and bylaws and its own treasury. Monthly meetings were held to discuss upcoming events. Coffee and cake were served after the business meeting adjourned.

Because minutes of these early years have not survived, all available information comes from newspaper articles or sparse Saengerbund minutes. The women were recognized for the first time in the minutes of April 30, 1858. *Die Frauen Wilmingtons—* the women of Wilmington—had presented a wreath of flowers on the occasion of the reunion of the two Saengerbund choruses. In 1868, the Saengerbund appointed an arrangements committee to work out "ways and means for the best of the club and the well being of all members." This committee was charged with "working with the ladies." Even then the women may have been meeting often enough to be considered a committee by the men. In 1869, when the chorus boarded the train to Baltimore for the Sängerfest, the women presented the chorus with a new flag to carry in the opening parade. When the singers returned from a festival or an outing, the women and children met them with flowers at the railroad station. Each year the women helped with the Saengerbund's Christmas tree party and wrapped boxes of chocolates for the children. All this was acknowledged gratefully by the Saengerbund's recording secretary.

After their official charter as Ladies of the Delaware Saengerbund, their activities increased and included cooking dinners for club functions and catering weddings, birthday parties, or anniversaries. One of the favorite dishes they served was *Frikadellen,* meat patties made the old-fashioned way with cooked meat. The recipe found its way into *Every Evening's* cookery column on December 31, 1900: "Mix 1-lb. chopped veal or other cooked meat with 2 beaten eggs. Add some butter together with 1- cup breadcrumbs. Add 1 chopped onion and moisten with warm water or the broth of the stewed meat. Season with salt and pepper. Form into small balls and fry until brown."

A newspaper article dated May 13, 1906, described one special event the Damen-Verein had planned to celebrate their 10th anniversary: "A novelty of the newest kind will be the May Tree Ball arranged by the Ladies Club of the Delaware Saengerbund for tomorrow night to take place at the German Hall. The

An advertisement for the Ladies' 10th anniversary welcomes everybody to a May Tree Ball in 1906.

financial result of the ball … will be handed over to the treasurer of the Saengerbund for the purpose of defraying some of the expenses of the trip to the Sängerfest to be held in Newark, N.J. next month." The columnist attended the ball and reported:

> The May Pole Ball … was one of the most enjoyable social functions given this past winter. The German Hall was literally filled with ladies in fancy gowns, accompanied by their gentlemen escorts. The Hall was beautifully decorated with plants and flowers, and the evening was spent in great enjoyment. The Ball opened with a fancy dance by eight young ladies dressed in white, wearing apple blossom bouquets, and other floral decorations, around the May pole, which was erected in the large dance hall. It was a beautiful sight and the applause was generous.

Over time, the Ladies' reputation for excellence and efficiency grew. Originally food preparations for fairs, picnics, and larger Saengerbund festivities had been in the hands of caterers like Christian Krauch or Harry Zimmermann. When the society began holding its annual Volksfest in 1903, the Ladies of the Delaware Saengerbund helped Zimmermann prepare food in the German Kitchen. After he passed away in 1906, they were able to take charge of the German Kitchen themselves. A reporter noted in 1912, "The visitors need not provide themselves with luncheons, because

the necessities of the inner man will be amply supplied at the German Kitchen, over which the Ladies Club of the Delaware Saengerbund will swing its scepter…. This fact alone will give the assurance of something real good to eat." The article did not mention that, because the women always were concerned that the food they prepared be affordable to large families, they never charged too much for the dinners. Nor did they amass a huge treasury. Most of the money they earned was used to support the work of the Saengerbund chorus and to help pay bills for the upkeep of the German Hall.

The Ladies also showed their concern for the disadvantaged by contributing some of their treasury to charities of their own choosing, as the *Sunday Morning Star* reported on May 15, 1908: "On Thursday afternoon, a large delegation of the Ladies' Club of the Delaware Saengerbund went on a noble visit of charity. Usually every year this organization saves up a pretty good sum, which is devoted to charitable purposes. On Thursday they visited the office of the Delaware Anti-Tuberculosis Society [at] No. 602 West Street, the Home of Friendless Children, and the Home For Incurables. At each place they left substantial gifts for the good of those institutions."

These women who enjoyed working together also planned many social get-togethers and outings. Picnics and trips to the nearby beaches became annual events of the Damen-Verein. When Mrs. Rosa Yetter was president in 1911 and 1912, the ladies celebrated her fifty-fourth birthday in the German Hall with a "huge birthday cake in the center of the table and a bouquet of carnations on either side, extending the entire length of the table."

Following the example of the Damen-Verein, other German societies chartered their own women's auxiliaries. The Ladies of the Golden Eagle were associated with the Liberty Lodge No. 10; the Wilmington Turngemeinde had a *Damensektion*; Martha Lodge No. 184 was a ladies' branch of the Harugari Lodge, and the Labor Lyceum had a Ladies Aid society. German churches also benefited from the work of their ladies auxiliaries or *Frauenvereine*, as they were also called.

Most of the German women's societies were not politically active, just as most of the men's organizations were not.

Saengerbund men were slow in recognizing the official 1896 charter of the Ladies of the Delaware Saengerbund, although they appreciated the work and support they received from that organization. The program notes of the 50th Stiftungsfest in 1903 include a toast given by J. P. T. Fuekel to *Die Frauen*—The Ladies. Once again the women had planned ahead: The president of the Damen-Verein presented the Saengerbund officers with a silver fiftieth anniversary plaque in the form of an open song book engraved with the names of all active singers of 1903. It was placed in an ornate golden frame and hung on the wall in the German Hall.

The Ladies of the Delaware Saengerbund presented a golden wreath with the inscription Delaware Saengerbund and an open book inscribed with the names of the chorus members to the Delaware Saengerbund at the occasion of the 50th Stiftungsfest in 1903.
(Photo by Mike Ciosek)

7

The Days of Roses

Noch ist die blühende, goldene Zeit,
O du schöne Welt, wie bist du so weit!
Und so weit ist mein Herz, und so blau wie der Tag,
wie die Lüfte durchjubelt von Lerchenschlag!
Ihr Fröhlichen singt, weil das Leben noch mait
Noch ist ja die schöne, die blühende Zeit,
noch sind die Tage der Rosen,
     die Tage der Rosen!

It is the golden time of blossoms still,
And the world is wide and beautiful.
So wide is my heart, and as blue as the day,
As the air is filled with the song of the lark.
Sing, sing, be merry and gay,
As long as life, as young as the May.
It is the beautiful blossoming time,
     The time of the roses, the roses.

-Roquette/Baumgartner

The new century began with the remarkable 19th Sängerfest in June 1900. That year was also the golden anniversary of the Nordoestlicher Saengerbund, and 6,000 singers, representing 174 singing societies assembled in New York City. For this occasion, the German Emperor Wilhelm II donated an ornate silver statue of a *Minnesänger*—a troubadour—as a contest prize. It later was won by the Philadelphia Junger Männerchor after that chorus placed first in three consecutive Sängerfeste.

The year 1903 opened with a New Year's Eve concert by the Delaware Saengerbund for the benefit of the Associated Charities. Frederick Becher directed the chorus, and John D. Kurtz Jr. accompanied. The program began with the march from Wagner's *Tannhaüser* played by Becher's orchestra. The chorus followed with "Die Ehre Gottes" by Beethoven and "Spring Song" by Silcher. Then the Saengerbund's double quartet sang an original poem—"The Old Shellpot Mill"—written by member Ludwig Melchior and set to music by Frederick Becher. Also on the program were soloists Mrs. A. J. Kooch and Charles Yetter and coronetist Daniel Maier. The Wilmington Mandolin Club played several selections including Strauss's "Blue Danube Waltz." Rossini's "Martinelli" closed the program which—according the *Sunday Morning Star*'s announcement of the concert on December 24, 1902—was "followed by a hop."

-The Fiftieth Anniversary-

The concert was an auspicious beginning to the Saengerbund's golden anniversary year. The society had been newly incorporated as Delaware Saengerbund, Inc., and the constitution had been revised. Members were now classified as active, passive, contributing, lifetime, and honorary. *Active members* had to be respectable men 21 or older who had been living for at least six months in Delaware. They had to have an understanding of the German language and some musical talent. After attending three probationary rehearsals they could be accepted into the chorus as active members by the music director. Once they paid the initiation fee of one dollar, they owed no further dues. *Passive members* had to have some knowledge of German, which made them eligible to vote and hold office, since all business was conducted in German. Any other respectable citizen of Delaware could become a *contributing member* without voting rights. Passive or contributing members could apply for lifetime membership without dues if they had medical or financial hardships.

There were now fifty-five voices in the chorus: fourteen first tenors, fourteen second tenors, sixteen first basses, and eleven second basses. One hundred and thirty men were passive or contributing members, and fifteen were on the honorary roll.

The men's songbook for four-part harmony, *Beliebte Chöre für vierstimmigen Männergesang*, published by Gebrüder Hug & Co. (Leipzig und Zürich, 1903), included a dedication to the Delaware Saengerbund that was printed at the top of each page. The words, *Gesang hält jung!*—"Singing keeps you young"—had been written by Dr. William Forgo, the author of the Saengerbund's 50th anniversary booklet, and the men proved it when they posed for anniversary photographs included in the Saengerbund's 50th anniversary booklet. Rare photographs of officers and chairmen of the festival, as well as the list of active singers, honorary, passive, and contributing members included in the booklet make the only surviving copy a treasure. On March 14, 1903, the *Wilmington Lokal=Anzeiger* printed a commemorative edition complete with portraits of the officers and the history of the society on the front page, framed in red and gold.

The 50th Stiftungsfest was celebrated in grand style with a banquet and ball on Wednesday, March 18, 1903.

Hampel's orchestra opened the evening's festivities with an overture, and President Harry Zimmermann welcomed the guests. The chorus sang *Noch sind die Tage der Rosen*—"It is the Time of Roses"—followed by the keynote speaker, Carl Kuhl. Toastmaster William F. Kurtz introduced the toasts: Heinrich Müller, "Our Society;" Music Director C. A. Hartmann, "The German Song;" Honorary President Daniel Maier, "Our Honorary Members;" Wilmington Mayor George Fisher, "Our City;" Henry Detreux, "Our Guests;" J. P. T. Fuekel, "The Ladies;" and Dr. Jacobson, "The Press."

The banquet menu consisted of cold meats (ham, tongue, roast pork, roast veal); a main course of roast turkey with cranberry sauce, mashed potatoes and French peas; salads of chicken, potato, and lobster served with mayonnaise; condiments of celery, gherkins, olives, onions, mixed pickles, red beets; assorted fruits, bread, butter, and biscuits. Swiss cheesecake and coffee were served for dessert. Deidesheimer wine, chosen after a wine-tasting visit to Bogner & Co. wine merchants in Philadelphia, completed the menu. The grand ball afterwards added to the elation felt by all Saengerbund members.

In June, the Saengerbund participated in the 20th festival of the Nordoestlicher Saengerbund. The June 14, 1903 *Sunday Morning Star* wished the more than sixty singers a successful journey to Baltimore and announced that, "The members of the local Saengerbund will leave German Hall at 7:15 … this morning and will parade to Delaware Avenue Station over the following route: Sixth Street to Market to Ninth to Delaware Avenue to the station. Herman Gossen will be chief marshal of the parade, which will be headed by the Philharmonic band of thirty-five pieces." Although Delaware's Saengerbund did not qualify for a prize in the second-class competition, it was a memorable event, because President Theodore Roosevelt was in the audience.

A greater reward came four years later when the city of Wilmington invited the chorus to participate at the unveiling of the Thomas F. Bayard monument in Rockford Park. On June 22, 1907, the *Sunday Morning Star* reported that the Saengerbund's participation was particularly significant since Mr. Bayard had always taken an active interest in the society, and his democratic ways and liberal ideas earned him the sincere friendship of Delaware Germans. In 1883 they had invited him to deliver the opening address at the German Volksfest, and he was a lifetime, honorary

CHARITY CONCERT

of Delaware Saengerbund for the flood sufferers, to be given on
SUNDAY EVENING, MAY 25, at the

GARRICK THEATRE

MANY NEW CHORUSES will be rendered. Soloists of the best reputation
will be heard. Box seats, $1.00; other tickets from 25 cents to 50 cents. Tickets
at Robelen Piano Company, No. 710 Market street.

GRAND COMPLIMENTARY CONCERT

Given by the Delaware Saengerbund, at the

GRAND OPERA HOUSE, MONDAY EVE., APRIL 27, 08.

For the benefit of the Delaware Anti-Tuberculosis Society
Soloists : Miss Isabelle Wales and Mr. Joseph Pistor

RESERVED SEATS, 15c, 25c and 50c, AT THE ROBELEN PIANO
STORE, ON AND AFTER APRIL 24, 9. A. M.

Grand Testimonial Concert

In Memory of the Late

N. Du Shane Cloward

Dockstader's Theatre   **Garrick**   This Afternoon at 3

Auspices of the
Combined Musical Organizations of Wilmington

PARTICIPANTS

Wilmington Choral Society
60 voices......................T. Leslie Carpenter, Director.

Delaware Saengerbund
60 voices......................Otto Wenzel, Director.

Philharmonic Chorus
65 voices......................Jacob T. Clymer, Director.

Wilmington Orchestra
50 pieces......................Charles M. Banks, Director.

Soloists—Miss Isabelle B. Wales, Mrs. Leonard E. Wales,
Mr. Frederick W. Wyatt, Mr. Frank H. Mason, Mr. Herman
Gossen, Mr. J. Frank Ayers, Mr. E. Roscoe Shrader, Violoncello.

Elks Quartette—Messrs. Albert Bothman, David Snellenburg,
Jos. E. McCullen, Jas. W. Gillespie.

General Director, T. Leslie Carpenter.
Business Manager, J. Leonard Johnson.

Seats Now Selling at Theatre, Box Office

PRICES-- Box Seats and Orchestra......................$1.00
Balcony......................75c and 50c

*The Saengerbund participated in many benefit concerts.
(Courtesy of UD)*

Saengerbund member. This event was also a wonderful finale to Music Director Carl Hartmann's years of work with the chorus.

Rehearsals now continued with Otto Wenzel as the new director. The Saengerbund prepared its spring concert as a benefit for the Delaware Anti-Tuberculosis Society and rented the Grand Opera House in anticipation of a large audience. They were disappointed despite a well-rendered musical program for a good cause. A follow-up report in the *Sunday Morning Star* on May 3, 1908, quoted a guest as saying, "Wilmington is a baseball city. If a game of ball instead of a concert was in progress no doubt nearly all the seats would be reserved." Fortunately the Saengerbund was never deterred by the size of the audience. The men loved to sing and perform, and the now sixty-member chorus was seen and heard in many parts of the city, from the Brandywine Springs Park to Ocean Beach Park in New Castle. Often several Wilmington choruses took part in the same event. The *Sunday Morning Star* of November 27, 1910, describes a concert given for the benefit of the family of N. Du Shane Cloward after his sudden death. He was a well-known singer, and had founded and directed the Wilmington Choral Club. "Many of the best musicians are represented … including the Delaware Saengerbund. This male singing society is unquestionably the best of its class in the East, and the prizes won by it at festivals bespeak the high degree of excellence that it has been brought to by its conductor, Mr. Otto Wenzel." Cloward had been a frequent guest at the Delaware Saengerbund and the promoter of events at Brandywine Springs Park where the Saengerbund held its annual Volksfest since 1903.

-Delaware Saengerbund Volksfeste-

By 1903, the Delaware Saengerbund had owned the German Hall for twenty years. The building was getting older and the cost of repairs continually depleted the society's treasury. Partly for this reason, and partly to continue the 50th anniversary celebration, President Harry Zimmermann suggested that his Sangesbrüder revive the Volksfest tradition that had been so well received by the people of Wilmington in the 1880s. If all went well, the profit from the festival could help pay for German Hall expenses. Rather then organizing one Volksfest for all German societies and sharing the profit, the Saengerbund decided to go it alone and invite the other societies as guests. The Turners liked this arrangement and decided to hold their own festival to help pay for the expenses of the Turnhalle. Also there was a precedent for these festivals. In 1892 Sacred Heart parish had begun celebrating a *Kirmes*, or *Kirchweih*, an annual celebration of the founding of the parish church, to help pay off the church's mortgage and support the school. Germans, with their love for outdoor festivals, enjoyed the opportunity to attend all the festivals.

The first Volksfest had been held in Schützen Park, but Schützen Park had changed hands and had become Wawaset Driving Park in the 1890s. That meant that the Delaware Saengerbund had to look for another place to hold its first, independent Volksfest. Possible locations included Shellpot Park and the Bavarian Park, favorite places for picnics and outings. Further out of town, Brandywine Springs Park, which had opened in 1886, was a popular place for a day in the country. Bordered by Newport Gap Pike, Faulkland Road, and the Red Clay Creek, the park had developed into a large amusement park that could be reached by railroad or trolley-car line. In 1902, when the Peoples Railway Company added a second track and more trolley cars, the park became even more accessible and the Saengerbund decided to hold its first Volksfest there on Monday and Tuesday, September 21–22, 1903. Sunday amusements were still illegal in Delaware. Harry Zimmermann oversaw the food preparation, assisted by the Damen-Verein.

Entertainment at the Saengerbund's first Volksfest included reenactments of a peasant wedding with performers costumed in colorful *Tracht*, the traditional attire of southern Germany. There were also performances by the chorus and band concerts. Children were entertained with games popular at the time like sack races, greased pole-climbing contests, pie-eating contests, and *Wurstschnappen*—a contest in which sausages were fastened to a string slightly above

Vaudeville acts performed by members of the Saengerbund were added to the annual Volksfest in 1905.
The Volksfest Committee met in Hermann Schechinger's Tremont House in preparation for the Volksfest.
(Courtesy of UD)

the children's heads, and the goal was to be the first to eat an entire sausage without using the hands. A grand masked ball concluded the day's festivities. The first Volksfest was such a success that it became an annual event.

At the second, 1904 Volksfest, the Wilmington Turners presented a gymnastic exhibition, the Reading Liederkranz was the special guest chorus, and Gatti's band played for everyone's listening and dancing pleasure. In 1905, the *Sunday Morning Star* reported that an encampment of the Union Veterans Legion of Wilmington would be the special guest of the Volksfest. The Volksfest committee, always looking for ways to improve the festival, stationed three small German bands throughout the park and added vaudeville acts. A visitor remarked, "This is a jolly crowd and there is music everywhere." But not everyone was happy. The weather was "unsettled," causing one person to complain "it was really foolish to arrange ... an outdoor festival when the moon was about to change." Each year, Saengerbund members wondered if the weather would be favorable, but regardless of the weather, the organizers gave it their all.

Harry Zimmermann had been in charge of catering the first three festivals. Then, while visiting his brother in Germany in August 1906, he suffered a heart attack and died, just a few weeks before the 4th annual Volksfest. But the Ladies of the Delaware Saengerbund had been well-trained and were able to take over the German Kitchen. The event was again a success.

Each year, the Volksfest was well-publicized. Large posters, flyers, and newspaper ads advertised the event. An August 19, 1906, announcement in the *Sunday Morning Star* instructed readers to, "Watch for the Decorated Car, Which Will Run Over the People's Line Saturday Evening, August 25, With Its Real German Band and Its Hundreds of Quarts of Sauerkraut, Distributed Free to All." The sauerkraut was handed out on wooden plates. There could be no doubt that it was fresh, for the *Star* had reported on August 5, 1906, that : "The cutting and preparing of about 1,000 gallons of fresh sauerkraut for the Volksfest of the Delaware Saengerbund will begin this week at J .P. T. Fuekel's factory at Fifth and Monroe streets. The work will take up nearly the entire week. The cabbage for this big order has been carefully selected from Delaware and New Jersey farms, and the quality is considered the very best."

A follow-up article in the *Sunday Morning Star* on September 2, 1906, reported that, as in previous years, the festival had included traditional peasant scenes including the reenactment of a peasant wedding and christening. A more comical attraction was the *Altweibermühle*, the old women's mill. Men dressed as old, feeble women were "placed in the top of the mill, and young and smiling they … came out of the other end and … [were] proudly led away by some handsome peasant swain." On the final day, "At every corner quartets, quintets, and double quartets could be heard, and never before was the German *Lied* [song] so honored. Everyone seemed to be in musical humor, and even our American friends joined in the spirit of song by rendering impromptu glees." Despite the bad weather, the Volksfest committee was able to say with confidence, "no deficit will be the result and dollar for dollar the expenses will be paid …" To show their appreciation to the ladies for their uncountable work hours that year, the September 2, *Sunday Morning Star* also reported that the men planned an outing to Conly's farm, "located about one-half mile from Harvey Station on the B. & O. Railroad."

Following the 1907 Volksfest, the Saengerbund invited Richard W. Crook, general manager of the Peoples Railroad and Brandywine Springs Park and several other officials of that corporation to dine at the Clayton House as a way of thanking them for the "many courtesies shown the committee during the festival." The *Sunday Morning Star* of September 29, 1907, elaborated:

When the cigars were lighted speeches began by silver-tongued orators, both in German and English. There sat modest Mr. Crook smiling and satisfied with himself, one care removed from his broad shoulders, namely the park season was over and not even the slightest accident had occurred. There was President Sell of the Saengerbund, always philosophic and congenial, but stern when the occasion offers itself. Bernard Kleitz, the treasurer … who says but little but thinks a great deal, and Harry Schnepf, the popular secretary of the foremost singing society of this state, smiling and good natured as usual and about twelve other members of the Volksfest committee…. During the smoking intermezzo, Mr. Crook was presented with a rare gift, a diploma as honorary member of the Delaware

Saengerbund for life.... To be an honorary member of the Delaware Saengerbund Association, which has promoted music and sociability for nearly sixty years ... is the highest gift awarded by German-American Societies in this city to anyone. Mr. Crook was greatly pleased....

Each year, the committee responsible for organizing the Volksfest had to work hard. Members met regularly to plan special attractions. On July 24, 1910, the *Sunday Morning Star* reported one such meeting at John Fehl's tavern at 4th and Tatnall that lasted until 10:30 p.m. The committee finally decided to go home, but Fehl had a surprise waiting and commanded them to stay. Moments later,

> Two large steaming pans, one of onions, and the other of peach pie, were brought in along with some fine snapper soup on the side. It must be noted that Mr. Fehl is an experienced pastry baker, and his brother cultivates snappers at Delaware City. Usually, Germans care but little for pie, but the onions smelled mighty inviting, and no true citizen of Delaware can deny the supremacy and delicious flavor of the peach, therefore the committee thoroughly enjoyed the feast of onion pie, peach pie, and snapper soup. The next meeting of the committee will take place at Schnepf's, and the menu will likely be regular German Leberknödel. Schnepf is not a pastry cook, but an old-line butcher who understands what a good piece of liver is. If the Volksfest committee can meet regularly every week and withstand acute indigestion as a result of all the good things its hosts furnish, it should be appointed for at least 99 years without being replaced.

The Saengerbund's Volksfest was an annual event from 1903 to 1914. The number of visitors at the last one, Tuesday and Wednesday, September 1–2, 1914, was "no less than 15,000," according to the *Sunday Morning Star* on September 6, 1914. "There was only one drawback," the reporter complained, "and that was an agent of the Law and Order Society who objected to the selling of beer. For this one particular reason the Volksfest of 1914 will go down in history as something entirely new and piquant, the 'beerless' Volksfest ...."

Dance cards for the winter balls. Waltzes were very popular.

The committee will be able to pay all the bills, and will still have a good little sum left which will be used for the relief fund of the war sufferers in Germany." The following year, the Delaware Saengerbund decided to suspend the Volksfest "on account of existing conditions."

-Days of Roses-

During the winter season, German Hall was alive with festivities. After the *Sylvester* (New Year's Eve) Ball, *Fasching* (the masked ball before the beginning of Lent) was the next major dance. On February 27, 1900, Wilmington's *Every Evening* described how 700 guests crowded into the German Hall for *Vier Jahreszeiten*— the four seasons ball, the theme that year. Five dollar gold pieces were awarded to the best-dressed individuals and groups. One hundred-fifty costumed couples marched in the grand carnival parade. The masked ball became more elaborate each year, opened by a colorful tableau. *Every Evening*'s reporter described the scene on Monday, February 26, 1906:

> The opening scene, entitled "Kaiser Rothbart's Court", arranged by Ludwig Melchior, was ... superb. The scene was produced on the stage while the First Infantry Orchestra played some selections from Wagner's *Lohengrin*. Numerous colored lights were used while the group was presented. The large auditorium hall was filled with visitors and masqueraders, but not a sound could be heard during ... this beautiful scene, which

lasted about fifteen minutes. [Then] the signal of the grand march was given by three sounds of the bell, and the great group of Kaiser Rothbart, consisting of prince and princesses and other court dignitaries, came down from this splendidly decorated stage, and the two court couriers represented by Carl Kausel and George Scott led the grand march. John Fehl followed as Kaiser Rothbart, making a very dignified ruler. Then followed the prince and princess in costly robes, smiles on their faces and admired by all. The fanciful "Fussvolk," the loyal subjects, marched after the noble knights in armor and other court attaches ....

That year the Ladies of the Delaware Saengerbund arrived at the masked ball costumed as nurses and won the prize for best-dressed group.

Other balls seem to have been equally elaborate. In 1908 the American Indian took center stage: "The opening scene was splendidly arranged to represent an act of American history, when Pocahontas, the daughter of the Indian chieftain Powhatan rescued Captain Smith who was a prisoner held by the tribe ...." The *Sunday Morning Star* reporter, in an account dated March 8, 1908, counted seventy-five masked couples following the *Indianer* court in the grand march "through the brilliantly lighted and decorated hall." This time the Ladies of the Delaware Saengerbund came costumed as Quaker ladies and again won the prize for the best-dressed group. A contrast to the account of the 1908 ball was the *Star*'s description of the morning after.

Katzenjammer [a hangover] is a pretty bad feeling, and it left its tracks on Tuesday after the great masked ball of the Delaware Saengerbund held on Monday night. The Katzenjammer seems to have spread pretty generally because on Tuesday evening there was no rehearsal or meeting of the Saengerbund, and even the members of the old and respected Beneficial Society No. 1 could not muster up a quorum. The German Hall was literally deserted, the only living person in that building being Ludwig Melchior, the "Hausvater" and his dog. The Lenten season will bring some order out of this chaos, and before one week has passed everything will again run smoothly and in regular order.

At the beginning of the twentieth century, the Delaware Saengerbund and the German Library Association had their houses well in order. The German Library Association had accumulated over 5,000 German books and close to 1,000 English books, a total value of over $4,000. Due to the skillful leadership of their officers, both societies were financially sound. The trustees of the German Hall were in a position to pay off the mortgage, but decided to wait. When interviewed by the *Sunday Morning Star* on March 8,

Advertisements of the Grand Masked Ball in the Wilmington Lokal-Anzeiger and Sunday Star. (Courtesy of Balch Institute)

1908, one trustee explained their reasoning: "We don't propose to make it too easy for our successors. We bought this hall, improved it, and went in debt for it. We worked hard to cut down our liabilities and we are situated now very comfortably. The little money we [still] owe does not worry us, and before we burn the mortgage we want to see besides a solid and substantial balance in the bank to our credit." Financial reports of the time showed that income and expenses were closely balanced at about $3,000.

The mortgage burning was scheduled for Wednesday, January 4, 1911. The *Sunday Morning Star* again interviewed a trustee on December 26, 1910 about the forthcoming event:

> There will be no great style about the festivities—plain and to the point is our plan. No fancy speeches, no full dress uniforms. It will be just in the same style as when we started, poor and unnoticed with a load of debt on our shoulders some 20 years ago. Henry Miller will tell us in his characteristic way about our progress and achievements, while our friend Anton Hauber, who is always serious and somewhat pessimistic, will let us know what we shall do hereafter. Of course, I don't mean that Hauber will give us a funeral sermon, when I talk about the "hereafter". No, I mean that Mr. Hauber will show and demonstrate to us how to live and keep out of debt. This is really the greatest problem of all.

Despite this somber prediction, the mortgage burning turned into one of the most elaborate German affairs held in the city that winter and was reported in the *Sunday Morning Star* of January 8, 1911. "Nearly every family of 'old German stock' in Wilmington was represented, and about 500 people witnessed the burning of a document that had bothered the trustees of the German Hall for so long. Reuther's Orchestra and the Delaware Saengerbund furnished the music. After all, nothing can be done in German circles without music, whether it be a birthday celebration, a mortgage burning or even a funeral." President Arthur Heinel welcomed the guests and introduced the speakers. As predicted, Henry Miller, speaking in German, gave his account of the early years of the German Hall. He spoke of the men who had poured so much energy into the growth of the societies and the acquisition of their club house, but had passed away "to sing in heavenly choirs," including Frederick von Bourdon, Harry Zimmermann, Charles Yetter, Peter Ebner, and Daniel Maier, who had died just two weeks earlier on December 23. To bring the guests into a cheerful mood again, Henry Miller disclosed a slight impropriety, which occurred after the mortgage papers were signed on March 17, 1884:

> "After we had closed the deal on the hall building, we had $2.50 left, and my friend, the late Joseph Stoeckle, who was a member of the board, suggested spending the amount. Of course, all consented and we went to see Henry Blouth of the Grand Union Hotel, and Mr. Stoeckle said to him: 'Henry, we have some money to spend. We just bought the building on Sixth street near Walnut, can you let us have what we want?'"
>
> "Sure," said Mr. Blouth, "you can have wine, champagne, or anything I have in the place."
>
> "Hold on, not so fast," said Mr. Stoeckle, "our cash is limited. We only have $2.50."
>
> "Don't make any difference, gentlemen, what will it be?"

With laughter and applause, the trustees' indiscretion was forgiven. Then Anton Hauber spoke in English, cognizant that many honorary American guests were present. His remarks included praise for the German newspaper editors, the late Francis Scheu, A. J. Kooch, and Max Goetz who all did considerable work to help establish a meeting place for Germans. He also spoke with regret of the German School, which did not prosper and had to be discontinued.

Georg Kalmbacher, president of the German Library Association said: "My only wish is that we all work together hand in hand to preserve this home which is now entirely our own." The guest speaker that evening was Henry Liertz of Philadelphia, a member of the German American Alliance. He addressed the question, "What Shall We German-Americans Do in the Future?" After the mortgage was burned, a grand polonaise opened the dance. Refreshments were served free. At intervals, the chorus, directed by Professor Otto Wenzel, entertained the guests with its best selections.

The Saengerbund now owned the German Hall, debt free. There was only one drawback: it did not have an outdoor garden. Ever since the Schützen Park had changed hands, the desire for a new German park increased as revealed in the *Sunday Morning Star* on August 21, 1910:

That Wilmington will soon have a German park seems reasonably sure. It has been under discussion for the past twenty years. A majority of German-Americans believe the time has come when a summer home for the families and themselves should be established. The only question to be decided is "Will it pay?" One man said: 'I will make myself responsible for at least 50 new members who will join the proposed park company. It has become a necessity to have a place to go with your family on leisure days away from the hot city and business. German Halls are practical for men, but a resort in the country is what we need in summer, for not all of us can afford to enjoy the pleasure of the seashore for a week. What

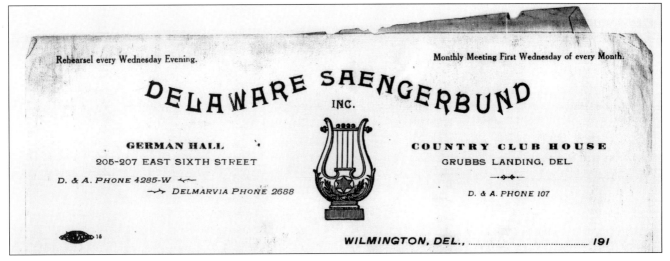

The Delaware Saengerbund's letterhead proudly annoucing its two properties. The summer home on the Delaware River was owned from 1912 to 1923. (Courtesy of Martha Schiek)

we want is a place where we can go by trolley or boat for a day or more, if we like, at moderate expense.

When the Taggart estate, a two-acre lot with a large stone house located at Grubb's Landing on the Delaware River went up for sale, Saengerbund officers bought it as a summer retreat for club members. The three-story house had twelve, high-ceilinged rooms, and the property was lined with trees and had direct access to the water. On the official opening day, June 24, 1911, six hundred people visited the property and stood under the trees listening to the Männerchor sing the Saengerbund's signature song, *Das ist der Tag des Herrn*, "This is the Day of the Lord".

Hundreds of people visited the new property. Picnics and parties, clam and shad bakes, and evening dances were held at this oasis away from the daily routine and hubbub of the city with its narrow streets and motorcar noises. Other clubs were invited to rent the facility, ensuring an income to help pay maintenance costs. Out-of-town choruses were frequent guests and greatly enjoyed a day in the country, as reported in the *Sunday Morning Star* on September 17, 1911: "Today the Camden, N. J. Männerchor will visit the summer home of the *Delaware Saengerbund* at Grubb's Landing. Harry F. Schnepf, secretary of the house committee of the Saengerbund home … received a letter [stating] that the Jerseyites would leave Darby this afternoon at about 1:00 p.m. in two special cars, and would leave Grubb's Landing for home at 9 p.m. …. The Saengerbund summer home is getting quite popular as a *Vergnügungsplatz* [a place for good times] for our German friends in Philadelphia and surrounding cities."

A proud Saengerbund showed off its summer home to the participants of the twenty-third Sängerfest, held in Philadelphia in 1912. Members commuted daily to Philadelphia where they joined the mass chorus of 6,000 singers. The concert was held in the new, temporary convention hall at Broad Street and Allegheny Avenue. The hall, which could seat 19,000 people, was dedicated during this festival.

Otto Wenzel, of Philadelphia, had been the Saengerbund's music director since 1908. He arrived in 1904 from Darmstadt where he had been educated as a teacher, organist, and pianist. *Leistet mehr*, try harder,

had been his advice to the Saengerbund chorus, if they wanted to compete in the highest category of the Nordoestlicher Saengerbund's song festivals, but in 1912 his advice fell on deaf ears. The chorus was too busy entertaining the sight-seers from Philadelphia who visited the country home to compete for a prize that year.

Later that summer, in August 1912, several hundred Saengerbund members hosted the singers of the Arion and Tioga Liedertafel of Philadelphia at the house on the river. The visitors, who had never before seen the Saengerbund's riverside home, loved its spaciousness and romantic view. On August 25, the *Sunday Morning Star* quoted one of the Arion singers: "We will be frequent visitors; this beats all my expectations."

The summer home also attracted new members. In 1912 the Saengerbund had 52 active singers and 720 passive and contributing members, but at one meeting in 1913, a line of 66 people applied for membership in the society, which soon increased to over 1,000 members. Also in 1913, when only a few members subscribed to the sixtieth Stiftungsfest ball in the German Hall, it was decided to hold the celebration at the summer home. The response was immediate. The *Sunday Morning Star* thought it noteworthy that the Ladies of the Delaware Saengerbund gave the club a substantial cash donation at the anniversary celebration that year.

The following year, the *Sunday Morning Star* reported on March 22, 1914, that at the sixty-first Stiftungsfest, honorary diplomas were presented to J. P.T. Fuekel, Henry Miller, and Raymond Beyerlein, and Joseph Sell was made honorary president. J. P. and W. L. Dockstadter, well-known proprietors of the Garrick Theater in Wilmington, were awarded honorary lifetime memberships. The Saengerbund gave concerts at the Garrick when the German Hall was too small.

Mayor Harrison W. Howell was the honored guest at this Stiftungsfest. In his address, he commended the Delaware Saengerbund's participation at the city's first Christmas celebration on the Court House lawn the previous year, as well as for its appearances at benefit concerts in the past. "Our city is justly proud of your organization," said the Mayor as he closed his remarks.

The years between 1903 and 1914 were indeed *die Tage der Rosen*, the days of roses, but the cold winds of change had begun scattering the blooms.

8

Winds of Change

Es geht eine dunkle Wolk' herein
mich deucht, es wird ein Regen sein,
ein Regen aus den Wolken
wohl in das grüne Gras.
Und scheinst du, liebe Sonn' nit bald,
so weset alls im grünen Wald;
und all die müden Blumen,
die haben müden Tod.

-Liederhandschrift von 1646

A dark cloud is forming over the horizon,
I reckon it will bring rain,
Rain from the cloud
Falling into the green grass;
And if you, dear sun, won't shine soon
Then everything growing in the forest will decay
And all the tired flowers
Will die a slow death

(Song from the Thirty-Years War, 1646)

The *Sunday Morning Star* noted on May 14, 1905, "that from the reports of the immigration officers in New York … Germans are not so eager as in former years to emigrate to the United States. The reason for this falling off is that in Germany a person of good habits can now under new circumstances prosper and get along as well as in the new world." Slowly, the "demands of the people" had been heard, and this had improved the situation for workers in Germany. The Anti-Socialist Law had been repealed, social welfare laws had been passed, and health and accident insurance were available. Working hours had been shortened for women and children. Sunday work in factories was banned for children under age thirteen, and women could not work more than eleven hours a day. The Reichstag ratified the *Bürgerliches Gesetzbuch*, a new civil code that became effective on January 1, 1900.

These changes were noticeable enough to affect the earlier immigrants' societies. Without a new influx from Germany, German organizations everywhere grew concerned about the local *Nachwuchs*, the younger generation that would continue the traditions of their societies. In Wilmington, the Order of the Harugari was worried, because the younger generation was not joining "on account of the exclusive use of the German language." In fact, the German language had become a mixed blessing. The very language that once had provided German Americans with cohesiveness and distinctiveness had become a stumbling block against the continuance of their social organizations.

Churches also noticed a decline in attendance that was attributed to the language problem. St. Stephen's, established in 1888 as the first Lutheran church in Wilmington with English services, now drew in a large number of the younger families. In 1906, the German Baptist Church celebrated its 50th anniversary with two services, a service in German on Sunday, and an English service on Monday. On April 29, 1906, the *Sunday Morning Star* made this observation about the anniversary service: "It is gratifying to note that many American-born young Germans were present and took an active part in the celebrations. This goes to show conclusively that the religion taught them in the German language has fallen on good and fertile ground, and that there is yet little danger, at least for some time, of the Gospel not being preached in the German language."

But six years later, in 1912, Zion Lutheran Church voted English as the first language for services, alongside the German services. "Twenty years ago, it would have met with strong opposition, but times and ideas have changed," commented one church member. A Sunday school class in English was conducted parallel to one in German. A German *Samstagschule*—Saturday School—opened for the teaching of the German language. For a while four schools in Wilmington taught German: Sacred Heart Church School, Zion Lutheran Church School, the Wilmington Turners, and Wilmington High School. According to a report in the *Sunday Morning Star,* March 8, 1914, the Delaware Saengerbund donated the income of that year's spring concert to further the language programs at those four schools.

In a December 18, 1910, *Sunday Morning Star* column, the writer compared several nationalities in regard to their adherence to their first languages. He had noticed that in Italian and Polish neighborhoods the children still spoke the native language of their parents,

> but with German youth it is different. They only speak German when they are compelled, and English is their favorite conversation. The reporter as well as many other Germans think that this is wrong, not because of a dislike for the English language. On the contrary, every German should encourage the language of this country but he should also foster and cultivate his mother language because it is most useful. In nearly all departments of life, two languages

are invariably better than one. A person, who can read, write, and speak German as well as English, must be considered a person of education. Parents of children should therefore not neglect the teachings of German, although the English tongue is so much preferred by the younger folks.

Saengerbund member Dr. William Kleinstueber had seen the handwriting on the wall as early as 1904 when he invited young German Americans to a meeting, and seventy-five responded. Dr. Kleinstueber, a charter member of the *Germania Social Club* founded in 1888, helped organize the new *German American Society* along the lines of the older club. The purpose of the newly created society was "to further German ideals among those who otherwise would be lost to the older German societies and would not remain in close relationship to each other." This society met four times a year to unite the members in pleasant gatherings. From the beginning a charity board was instituted for the benefit of needy German Americans, and much good had been done at various times in a quiet and efficient manner. The society counted among its members some of the most influential and industrious citizens of Wilmington, and all were outspoken advocates of the principles that German Americans in general share. One of those principles, righteous living within the law of the country, was highlighted in a report in the *Sunday Morning Star* on April 1, 1906: "The reporter of this column does not generally follow up the criminal proceedings of the county court, but by investigating the work of the Grand Jury, he found that among all the accused persons not one of them was a German-American. This is very encouraging. The criminal docket for the September term is a very large one, but for all that Germans do not figure in any way in the proceedings, neither have they done so in the past few years. This speaks well for the 7,000 or 8,000 German-Americans of this county."

In addition to the language problem, the Wilmington Germans were beginning to lose contact with each other. Their residences now were dispersed throughout the city, instead of living in one, compact neighborhood. Many families moved to the west side of Wilmington. Even Zion Lutheran Church relocated to Sixth and Jackson Streets when the Stoeckle family made a parcel of land available there.

A third change was that news of German events now came to their doorsteps less frequently: In 1901,

Max Goetz had changed the name of the *Freie Presse* to *Wilmington Lokal=Anzeiger and Freie Presse*. At the time, it was published twice a week. After four years, on October 6, 1905, Goetz asked his subscribers for "the support and co-operation of the Germans in order to build up and maintain the only German publication in this city and State." But a year later, on April 1, 1906, an article in the *Sunday Morning Star* notified readers that, "After this week, the *Lokal=Anzeiger*, the only German paper in this State, will appear only once a week. This will be every Saturday morning. Max Goetz, the owner, informs the [*Sunday Morning*] *Star* reporter that he will have an up-to-date weekly issue with all the local and foreign news. The paper will be mailed to the subscribers, which he says will be a more prompt delivery as his readers are scattered in all parts of the city." Goetz made it his business to keep the Germans and their societies together, at least on paper. He published a directory of the German societies for several years after 1911. Unfortunately no copies have surfaced to date. To give an idea of the scope of the work, the *Sunday Morning Star* of August 1, 1915, informed its readers, "eighty-three advertisements are found in the directory. Each German society is listed separately with its meeting place and time … officers and the entire membership. Some interesting statistics may be gleaned from the pages. There are 28 German-American organizations in the city, comprising about 3,000 members in all. Pictures of the German balls are added, as well as photographs of the Zion Lutheran, Sacred Heart, and German Baptist churches where services are held in German."

Since 1905 the *Sunday Morning Star* had printed a weekly column compiled by A. J. Kooch, and later Sigmund von Bosse, entitled "News of the German-Americans." This not-so-subtle title is another indication that the Germans had become German Americans, different in many ways from the immigrants of twenty-five to fifty years earlier. On June 17, 1906, the *Star* observed:

"It is singular," said a prominent German the other day when a really creditable parade of Italians passed through the streets, "how little our German-Americans care any more for parades. In former years it was often the case that such parades preceded some of their festivals, but the custom has died out. The last German parade, I think … took place about nine years ago, when a celebration of some kind was held at Union Park. Since then our German friends have refrained from making any public show." The reason for this was asked, and … One said that parades were becoming out of date, and were altogether a waste of money. Another was of the opinion that some Germans in this city thought that parading in the public streets and for a public show was beneath their dignity, besides this parading was a very tiresome matter anyhow, and a third one expressed his idea as follows:

"Yes, it is true that 25 years ago parades were often held and some very good ones. I remember the peace parade in 1871. It was a grand affair. The industrial parades preceding the Volksfests then held at the former Schützen Park were very creditable, indeed also the turnouts given on the German Days, but in those days the Germans lived more as a unit, while now they are split up in many different organizations. Each organization is taking its own interest seriously to heart and attends only to its own affairs, and therefore it is really impossible to arouse any interest of a general nature among us any more. Here we have the Turners, the singers, the labor organizations, and other social societies. Each of them works only for their own benefit."

Nationwide, German societies had seen membership decline. To remedy the situation, the *Deutschamerikanischer Nationalbund*—the German American Alliance—was founded in Philadelphia on October 6, 1901, as a central body for German societies in all states of the Union and was chartered by an act of Congress. The society, whose motto was "Pro Bono Publico," was created "not for political purposes, but to consolidate the enormous forces of the German-Americans for the promotion of everything of value in German character and civilization for the benefit and welfare of the whole American people." According to an article in the *Sunday Morning Star* on September 19, 1915, the organization's constitution proposed adding German language courses and physical education to the curriculum in all public schools. It advised all Germans to become citizens as soon as they were entitled to their papers, to take an active part in public life, and to practice their civic duties fearlessly and vote according to their own judgment at the polls,

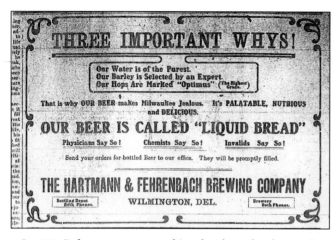

In 1907 Delaware was engaged in a legislative battle over the sale of liquor. (Courtesy of UD)

but it refrained from taking a position on politics or religious issues.

Wilmington's German societies saw no need to join this national organization until 1907 when a matter of great consequence stirred them into action. Governor Lea had signed the local option law in March, and it passed the state legislature. The next step was to decide by a special election in November if "License or no License" should be the law of the state. A letter of urgency went out to nearly 4,000 Germans who were expected to vote, and a mass meeting was called for May 8 at the Turnhalle, with the result that a chapter of the German American Alliance was chartered here.

Of twenty-two incorporated German societies in Wilmington, eight claimed membership in the alliance: The German Library Association, the Delaware Saengerbund, Harugari Lodge, German American Society, Turngemeinde, Men's Lutheran Society, Liberty Lodge No.10, German Beneficial Society No. 2, and the Wilmington Labor Lyceum. Christoph Bauer, president, and William Schoenhaar, vice president, were the first Alliance officers. Gustav Ripka and clergyman Sigmund von Bosse became the Wilmington chapter's leaders. The Alliance refrained from all politics though, and had no intention of acting against this "no license" prohibition. The Wilmington Labor Lyceum then sided with the German Brewers Union and withdrew its membership. Even so, by 1915, the organization had over 2,500 members.

For a number of years, organizing German Day became the German American Alliance's main focus. It usually took place close to October 6th as a way of marking the landing of the thirteen German families from Krefeld who founded Germantown, Pennsylvania. For several years, this celebration brought German societies and citizens together for a much-needed show of unity and support.

In February 1913, literally out of the blue, the Saengerbund was fined $50 by Wilmington's police chief for serving alcohol to members at a ball. This matter was discussed at length at the club's next general meeting. Both languages were used. Many of the speakers argued that the police did not have the right to enter the property of a chartered club and enforce any rules as long as that club did not violate the law by disorder and gambling. According to the *Sunday Morning Star*, February 9, 1913, one member complained, "A chartered club is the same as a family and must be respected as such even by the chief of police." Another speaker favored a license law for clubs to end the muddle. "It is a shame," said another club member, "that a society like the Saengerbund with 1,000 respectable members should be singled out for such an insult when others can do as they please and are not molested."

The Saengerbund appealed the fine, but the lower court ruled against the club and made selling drinks to members illegal. The Saengerbund then called a meeting of delegates from the other twenty-two incorporated German societies and proposed the next steps to be undertaken. Delegates asked for a decision from the Delaware Supreme Court as to the rights and privileges of clubs of good standing. Months later the Supreme Court ruled in favor of the lower court and against the clubs. This was reported in the *Sunday Morning Star* of June 20, 1915: "In the Supreme Court last Tuesday the last decision handed down was that in the appeal of the Delaware Saengerbund, in which the right of a club to dispense drinks to its members was brought into question. Without reading any of the opinion, Chancellor Curtis simply stated that the Supreme Court agreed with the charge and opinion of the lower court and that the judgment of the lower court was affirmed." Thus, the lower court and the Supreme Court had ruled against all clubs.

During this upsetting time, Hermann Gossen was president of the Saengerbund. Born in Germany, he had come to Wilmington to join his uncle who owned a store that sold cigars, spices, coffee, and other imported articles. At the advice of a music expert in the city, the

Hermann Gossen

'Annie Laurie,' and 'Old Kentucky Home' which are invariably repeated at every concert.... The Saengerbund's aim and object is to cultivate music of German composers."

The critical writer of this 1913 editorial clearly chose to ignore the concert's purpose—to raise money to help Cincinnatians whose homes and businesses were damaged or destroyed when spring floods caused the Ohio River to overrun its banks in March 1913. And what he did not know was that in a very short time *what* the chorus was singing would not be as important as the fact that it *was able to continue* singing at all. By 1914, Germany was engulfed in war, and Wilmington's German American community felt the effect.

Throughout this period, the German American Alliance had been keeping its members informed about the war in Europe as a way of counterbalancing newspaper accounts that drew heavily on the propaganda image of German soldiers as Huns. Letters with news from the "Fatherland" were shared with Saengerbund members and other Wilmington Germans. Chorus rehearsals continued and the usual social events were well-attended. Although the society needed money to maintain the German Hall and the summer home, concert proceeds were given to relief organizations such as the Red Cross of Germany and Austria-Hungary. The entire profit from the annual masquerade ball was donated to the Irish Relief Fund. Individual Saengerbund members lent or gave their own money to the club when the treasury ebbed so low that it could not meet expenses. In October 1915, a small notice appeared in the *Sunday Morning Star*, "Due to unsettled conditions in Wilmington, several members of local German-American circles will leave the city for other homes. Their loss will be heavily felt in local circles." Among those leaving was Hermann Gossen.

April 6, 1917, the day the United States entered the war, was a dark day for German Americans. The Saengerbund wondered if rehearsals should be suspended. The slogan of the German American Alliance urged German Americans to "Keep quiet! Be loyal!" In this spirit, Saengerbund president William Kiepe pondered cancelling the spring concert. Instead he recommended that the Saengerbund present a benefit concert for the American Red Cross on June 24 as part of the Red Cross observance in Wilmington that

young Hermann Gossen was encouraged to develop his fine baritone voice. He sang with the Sacred Heart church choir and the Saengerbund chorus and became a leading baritone soloist of the city. He was in charge of a benefit concert which was noted in the *Sunday Morning Star*, March 30, 1913: "Through the auspices of the Delaware Saengerbund, an organization which always comes to the front in case of need, a delightful concert has been arranged for this evening to be given at the Garrick Theatre for the benefit of the western [Cincinnati] flood sufferers." The program included harmonies sung by the Saengerbund chorus, solos and duets by Hermann Gossen and Madame Gummert, a tenor solo by Arthur Heinel and a bass solo by Harry Schnepf. This concert prompted an unnamed critic to write a letter to the *Sunday Morning Star*, June 1, 1913: "Permit me to say that the rendition of the twelve numbers was excellent and almost without fault. It showed that real musical spirit is manifested by the Delaware Saengerbund, of which I had the honor of being a passive member for many years. But it seemed to me that the Saengerbund is devoting too much time on the English choruses such as the time honored

The Saengerbund gave a concert in the Queen Theater for the benefit of the Red Cross. (Courtesy of Balch Institute)

weekend. By that time, the well-known Hermann Gossen had returned to the city and was in charge of the program.

On July 1, 1917, the *Sunday Morning Star* reported: "The spring concert of the Delaware Saengerbund for the American Red Cross last Sunday evening will stand out prominently as one of the really big musical and philanthropic affairs in the city of Wilmington." Gossen, who had gathered together the guest artists and secured free quarters for them, was quoted as saying, "I have been a member of the Saengerbund for many years and have sung with it on numerous occasions. On last Sunday, I did not sing in the chorus on account of my solo work, but I must say that never have I heard the Saengerbund sing as well as it did in this concert." The audience was large and enthusiastic, responding well to the patriotic songs. The incredible amount of $625.00 raised that evening was turned over to the Red Cross.

In the fall of 1917, the United Singing Society of Philadelphia organized a great festival at Strawberry Mansion that brought together over 50,000 people for a community sing-a-long. In Wilmington, community singing took place each week in the high-school auditorium, and all the choral organizations participated. The *Sunday Morning Star's* columnist, in the February 3, 1918 edition, suggested that these gatherings provided a splendid opportunity for the men to practice English songs. The Saengerbund chorus was also invited to sing at the Zion Lutheran Church's Easter service, a tradition for both the congregation and the chorus. The 1918 spring concert benefitted the tobacco fund for soldiers.

As war continued, the mood in German American circles was heavy. Wilmington's Germans were required to register with the police. The 25th Sängerfest of the Nordoestlicher Saengerbund—planned for summer 1918 in Baltimore—was cancelled. Nevertheless, the regional singing societies remained in close contact and made it their mission to see that larger choruses helped the smaller ones if they needed financial assistance. The Saengerbund showed its support for the government by purchasing $100 Liberty Bonds and offering the summer home to the government for its use. The club received letters of thanks from Senator Saulsbury and Joseph Daniels, Secretary of the Navy. Local German Americans heeded the call to arms and signed up for military service. The German American Alliance asked each member organization to compile a list of members who had gone into military service. Also, the names of all members who served in the army or navy as volunteers or draftees were registered and openly displayed by the churches and the German societies.

In Wilmington, more and more familiar voices now were missing at rehearsal time. Too often the Saengerbund chorus was called together to sing the hymn *Stumm schläft der Sänger*—"Quietly the singer is sleeping"—at the graveside of one of the members. Frederick von Bourdon, Joseph Niedermaier, Andrew Wilhelm, and Charles Yetter were not there to celebrate the golden Stiftungsfest. Peter Ebner, Henry Feldmeier, Daniel Maier, and Harry Zimmermann were greatly missed at the mortgage-burning ceremony. Two close friends, J. P. T. Fuekel and Henry Miller, passed away within a week of each other in the summer of 1917. These Sangesbrüder, close friends in life, were buried near each other in Riverview Cemetery, as if they were waiting to assemble for a great Easter sunrise hymn.

J. P. T. Fuekel had been an incredibly active person. He owned a delicatessen, led the Saengerbund chorus, was Zion Lutheran Church's organist for over thirty years, and had been a charter member of many German organizations. From 1880 to 1892, he belonged to the Board of Education and initiated the custom of

The Riverview Cemetery is the resting place for many Delaware Saengerbund members.(Photos by Teipelke)

rewarding the best high-school scholars of German with a silver medal. In 1911, "Papa" Fuekel fell getting off a trolley car and injured his head. His physician advised him to take it easy that weekend, but he paid no attention. Instead, he continued with his busy schedule of attending to his store, having lunch at the summer home, visiting his wife's grave at Riverview, his daughter's home in New Castle, and presiding over the meeting for the German Day preparations. On Monday morning he appeared as one of a panel of petit jurors at the County Court House. "One must never believe oneself sick and must keep up one's spirits. I feel better after my accident than before," was his only comment when someone inquired about the accident. But the fall may have been the first sign that Fuekel's health was starting to fail. According to the obituary notice on August 15, 1917, the war dealt his spirit an even greater blow: "The hardest thing for him to bear was the world war, for he thought that one of his chief aims in life, the bringing about of a better understanding between the old and new home, had not been reached."Henry Miller followed his friend J. P. T. Fuekel within a week. Both had lost their eyesight and had been confined at home for some time but managed to send greetings to each other through their many friends who stopped to visit.

As leaders of the German societies, they had shaped the organizations they had started and cared about, and they knew how to combine love of homeland with the ability to serve their adopted country.

In November 1918, a parade marking the end of the First World War made its way down Market Street. Whereas a splendid carriage portraying German Emperor Wilhelm I had figured prominently in the 1871 procession that celebrated the end of the Franco-Prussian War, a coffin bearing a caricature of deposed Emperor Wilhelm II was the main attraction of this parade. German Americans stayed home. The cloud of prejudice they had experienced still hung heavily above them. The German language was frowned upon in schools and public places but remained the language of Saengerbund meetings. Some of the German societies, like the Red Men and Odd Fellows, had so few members that they were absorbed into larger organizations.

In spite of the gloom, action was required in response to disturbing news *von drüben,* from overseas. The Saengerbund responded by giving concerts to benefit the relief fund for the suffering children of Germany and Austria, and a lottery conducted by the German societies also raised a considerable amount of money for this cause. Concentrating on their music allowed the Saengerbund friends to stay together and maintain their morale, as another disturbing development wreaked havoc on their social club life.

-Prohibition-

Prohibition was an absolute disaster for dyed-in-the-beer Germans. The Eighteenth Amendment had been adopted by Congress in December 1917 and sent to the states for ratification. Many who supported it claimed German American brewers and their customers were disloyal. On June 30, 1918, the *Sunday Morning Star*'s headlines screamed, "Liquor Sale in Rural New Castle Now is Unlawful," and "Saloons Passed Out of Existence at Midnight Under New Dry Law—Wilmington Only Oasis in Little Delaware." Such headlines were devastating to brewers and brewery workers, and to the entire local hotel, inn, and tavern industry.

Twenty years earlier, a *Sunday Morning Star* report on Wilmington's industries dated March 6, 1898,

Advertisement in the Wilmington Lokal-Anzeiger on November 22, 1904. The largest breweries in Delaware were Stoeckle, Hartmann & Fehrenbach, and the Bavarian Brewing Co. first owned by Eisenmenger and later by Lengel. Peter Ebner bottled and distributed lager beer from all the breweries. (Courtesy of Balch Institute)

attested to the strength of the breweries just before the turn of the century: "In no city in the United States is less beer sold that is made out of the city. The beers made by the city's three great breweries, Joseph Stoeckle's Diamond State Brewery, The Hartmann & Fehrenbach Co., and John A. Lengel's Bavarian Brewery, are not surpassed in quality by the products of any brewery in the world. All three of the establishments have built up their great business from the smallest beginnings entirely by the force of the merit of their goods. About 150,000 barrels are produced annually, which supplies not only the local trade but also that of neighboring states." The capital then invested in breweries amounted to $1,000,000—the third largest

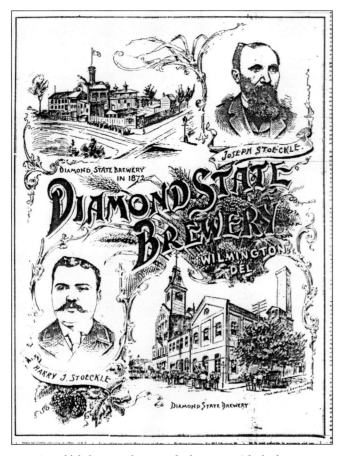

Stoeckle's brewery became the brewery with the largest output in barrels.

investment after cotton and yarn fabrics at $1,800,000 and the DuPont gunpowder manufacture at $4,000,000.

Now *Bier*—the liquid bread—was in jeopardy. United Brewery workmen facing the loss of their jobs circulated flyers and advertisements to alert people to the consequences of prohibition: "Prohibition does not prohibit! It breeds 'blind tigers,' 'speakeasies,' and 'low dives.' Prohibition increases your taxes by depriving the Government of millions of dollars paid as revenue and for licenses. Prohibition throws thousands of men out of work—their families are hungry and homeless, factories are shut down and stores are vacant. Think it over! You will be convinced that Prohibition is a Menace to our Country! Vote and work against prohibition!"

Wählt nass! "Vote wet!" became the battle cry of the anti-prohibitionists. The Saengerbund took its concerns over Prohibition to Senator Willard Saulsbury in Washington, sending him a telegram. He responded,

but the minutes did not report the content of his reply. Despite protests, Delaware was the ninth state to ratify Prohibition by a vote of forty to nine.

Saengerbund member John Fehl was just one of many directly affected. At the time he owned the Jefferson House in New Castle, a popular destination for members of the German societies who made excursions there to eat *Hasenpfeffer*, a seasonal stew made with marinated rabbit. The Saengerbund held some of its summer rehearsals on the Jefferson House's large porch to escape the city heat and, many beautiful songs floated off his porch and out over the river. The new law definitely affected John Fehl, but he planned to keep the hotel open because of the great need for "accommodations as the houses are all occupied and scores of men seek places." An amusing story Fehl liked to tell was included in the same article.

> A few years ago, a young woman book agent walked up to the owner of the hotel who was standing at the bar of the Jefferson House and addressed him:
>
> "Sir, I would like to sell you the latest Shakespeare and …."
>
> "Never mind, young woman," he replied, "we sell Stoeckle's beer here and I wouldn't sell Jake's beer."

The 1919 Volstead Act, which defined alcoholic beverages as one-half of one percent alcohol by volume and extended wartime prohibition, made matters worse. By 1920, Prohibition was the law of the land. Local breweries tried bottling soda water products, but this venture simply was not profitable. Three years later, Hartmann & Fehrenbach ceased brewing altogether. When the breweries closed, German societies lost their best supporters, and the struggle for survival was felt everywhere. The future looked dim.

-Delaware Saengerbund and Library Association-

Very few German immigrants entered the United States in the year 1919. With immigration so low, German American societies wondered how they could increase membership.

A German American Alliance directory published in Philadelphia in 1921 lists as German Societies of the First State the Delaware Saengerbund, Beneficial

Society No.2, Father Mayer Council No.256, *Feuerbestattungsverein* (the Crematorium Society), German Library Association, Germania Tempel No. 7—Ladies of the Golden Eagle, Harugari Lodge No. 349, Karl Marx Branch No. 1 of the Socialist Party, Labor Lyceum, Liberty Lodge No.10, Lutheran Men, St. Benedictus Beneficial Society, the Turner Association, and the Wilmington Skat Club. Wilmington had had a Skat club since 1908, and Saengerbund President Arthur Heinel was considered the best player. He often arranged tournaments with neighboring towns.

Men who enjoyed meeting regularly, but without any of the rules and regulations needed to run an organization successfully, favored the weekly Stammtisch as a way of staying in contact. The August 19, 1917, *Sunday Morning Star* explained a *Stammtisch*: "A number of the leading Americans of this community of German birth or descent have been imitating a custom, which is in vogue in almost every city or town of the Union where two or three Germans dwell. They have set aside several hours of a certain afternoon on which they meet, lunch together, and discuss various subjects of interest to the German Americans. Meeting informally as leaders in their respective circles, these men are in a position to speak for reforms and changes in general and to outline a course of action." Sometimes a regular society was born out of such meetings, as had been the case of the Saengerbund in 1853. Stammtisch conversations could become quite heated, but in the end all present would be friends again, looking forward to their next *Stammtischrunde*. Of course, there were also many Germans living in Wilmington not associated with any Verein; they pursued their interests in art or music or literature with their own circle of friends. They were the targets of all societies' membership drives, often without success. Most likely they would not have been members of any organization in Germany either. Some may have feared *Vereinsmeierei*, a term used to describe an organization that has lost its vision and whose members spend their time on petty issues and complaints. Vereinsmeierei will keep potential members away from any organization.

With its postwar membership now low, the Saengerbund resolved to form a committee to "wake up" the society and find ways to attract new members. A letter was sent out to the remaining German societies in the city urging their members with an interest in singing to join the Saengerbund, but this was not successful. When the Nordoestlicher Saengerbund held a Sängerfest in 1922, the Delaware Saengerbund could not participate. Not only were there not enough singers in the chorus, but also the Nordoestlicher Saengerbund dues had not been paid because there was not enough money in the treasury.

The financial situation was so severe after the war that the summer home had been rented out to families, but the rent did not cover expenses. Finally there was no choice but to sell. Treasurer Bernhard Kleitz was given power-of-attorney to sell it for not less than $12,000, but there were no buyers, not even at the reduced price of $8,000. Finally, on June 13, 1923, the sale was completed for $5,127.53. What happened to the house on the river after that was exactly what some had foreseen: it became notorious as Delaware's principal speakeasy. Called "The Whistling Buoy," it was operated by a group from Chester and "attracted many Wilmingtonians with its hot music, open sale of all kinds of liquor and its amiable hostesses," as the *News Journal* later commented in an article entitled "Life along the River," July 31,1965.

The money from the sale of the home was wisely invested in five $1,000 utility and railroad company bonds. From the interest, the treasurer could pay routine bills. Other fundraisers included evening entertainments featuring moving pictures that, at one time, netted $49.10 profit. But maintaining the German Hall was becoming more costly and there was talk of relocating to a new, less expensive hall for the first time. In 1923, committees of Delaware Saengerbund and the German Library Association met to consider ways to preserve both organizations.

The German Library Association owned nearly 6,000 books, about 5,000 German editions and 1,000 English. Following the team of Henry Miller and Frederick von Bourdon, it was George Kalmbacher, Lorenz Maucher, and Paul Steinke who dedicated their skills and time to the society and the library for many years. Now, however, almost no one was reading German books or attending lectures. For forty-nine years, the venerable Library Association had held an *Ostermontagtanz*, an Easter Monday ball, to celebrate its anniversary. Members knew that the fiftieth Stiftungsfest would be the last.

To simplify the management of the German Hall, the two societies decided to merge, mindful of the saying *Einigkeit macht stark*—unity builds strength. In

1924, the Delaware Saengerbund and the German Library Association were incorporated under the name *Delaware Saengerbund and Library Association, Inc.* The charter was amended and a new seal was approved. Hermann Gossen conducted the first meeting as president of the new organization. During this time, a core group of members served faithfully as officers or on committees: Christian Seidle, Albert Zuelke, Ernst Zuelke, William Kiepe, Arthur Heinel, Emil Dochter, Edward Gerres, and Max Goetz.

Edward Gerres was the house steward, an active singer, and a board member. As chairman of the House and Entertainment committee he initiated the custom of Friday night dances with a dance master and recorded music on the Saengerbund's Victrola. During this period the minutes dwindled down to no more than a financial account: The minutes of December 8, 1924 state, "Since only three members were present, business could not be transacted. Income: $319.25; Expenses: $495.66; Deficit: $176.41." One by one, the bonds purchased after the sale of the summerhouse had to be sold to pay the bills. A new mortgage was taken out on the German Hall.

Matters were so severe that Music Director Otto Wenzel offered several times to reduce his salary, and even worked without pay when the singers had no money at all. It was to his credit that the *Saengerbund* chorus survived these dark years. He was the music director with the longest service to the chorus until the present day, and he lived by the promise he had made in a letter to the *Saengerbund* in 1908: "*Ich mit Euch, Ihr mit mir, und Gott mit uns.*"—I with you, you with me, and God with us. On March 1, 1924, the *Delmarvia Leader* reviewed a concert he conducted:

> An audience of more than 2,000 persons, the largest that has attended the series of Sunday afternoon concerts this season … crowded into the Aldine Theater Sunday afternoon to hear the Delaware Saengerbund directed by Otto Wenzel and assisted by several prominent soloists of this city.
>
> The concert, judging from the applause accorded each number, which at times reached the proportions of an ovation, lived up to expectations. The Saengerbund in itself has always enjoyed an excellent reputation among music lovers of this city and, accompanied by such local talent as Miss Caroline Heinel, pianist; Herman Gossen, baritone; Arthur G.

Heinel, tenor; Carl Elmer, cello; and Kurt Florett, piano, it was a rare treat.

Chorus morale must have dropped after that, because members were asked in writing in January 1926 if they really wanted to continue singing in the chorus. They promised to do their part and attend rehearsals, and the situation improved. Otto Wenzel was made an honorary member of the society and retired after twenty-seven years of service.

After 1926, German immigration was still so low that the United States placed advertisements in German newspapers and broadsides in railroad stations to announce that skilled workmen were needed and welcome in America. Germany had just lived through a terrible inflation. A note in the local newspaper Delmarvia Leader from November 1923 records: "Golden Sausage" —Berlin, Nov. 22— German financiers of a statistical bend have figured out that it would require a freight train of 40 cars to haul enough 10 Mark notes to pay for a pound of sausages at the prevailing price, which is given at 2,000,000,000,000 Marks." People had been hoarding coins as the only valuable money. Cities had responded by printing *Notgeld* to be able to pay small change. The Notgeld was very attractive depicting landmarks of the cities, fairy tales, or historic figures and it too became a collector's item. New currency was issued at the end of November, and the young Weimar Republic fought strenuously to keep Germany on a democratic course. Motivated by the terrible postwar inflation in Germany, a new, though smaller, wave of German immigrants responded to the American invitation. Those who came to Wilmington and loved to sing immediately joined the Delaware Saengerbund. They were glad to have found a place where they could feel at home. New singers who joined in 1927 included Ludwig Schierl, Max Schilling, Peter Loch, George Kleiber, August Haase, Oscar Traeger (from Berlin); Henry Stuhmer, and Alfred Gilgenast (from Deutsch Eylau in West Prussia). In 1928, Paul Nake, Kurt Zeise (from Leipzig) and Paul Ulick joined the chorus. A year later Ernst Stoessel and John Winsel (from Altenbeken near Frankfurt) also joined. In 1930, membership applications were taken out by Paul Berger, Erich Kaeks (from Lindenberg near Berlin), Karl Kutterolf, Eugene Kachelmus, Paul and Louis Herold (from Leipzig), Francis Whiteside, Paul Witt, Richard and Fritz Steinke, Heinz Eschelweck (from Heilbronn), Joseph Stahl, and

Adolf Schroeder. Their youth, enthusiasm, and voices were what the Saengerbund needed. The minutes became longer, and the Saengerbund was singing again *"aus voller Kehle,"* with full voice!

-Seventy-fifth Stiftungsfest-

Das Leben ist ernst genug und zur Unterhaltung und Erheiterung gibt es kein besseres Vergnügen als den Gesang. "Life is serious enough and there is nothing better than singing to bring about joy and pleasure." So stated the chronicler in the booklet commemorating the 75th Stiftungsfest. The anniversary was celebrated on November 14, 1928 in conjunction with a Schubert concert. The booklet lists officers and committees, as well as chorus members and honorary members. The concert featured Rita Krapf, soprano; Arthur Heinel, tenor; Heinrich Habenicht, baritone, with Caroline Heinel at the piano. Refreshments and dancing followed the festive music.

Money was still scarce, and maintaining the German Hall was no less expensive. More than once, members and board wrestled with the thought of selling the building. A week after the seventy-fifth Stiftungsfest, during a meeting with the Turner Association, the discussion had centered on selling the building and looking together for a new location for a *Deutsches Haus*—German house—but the Turners were not interested. Several years earlier, in 1919, they had sold the Turnhalle on French Street and purchased a large house with an adjacent open field at 701 South Clayton Street, the corner of Clayton and Beech.

During the anniversary year, the Ladies of the Delaware Saengerbund decided to reorganize. Although they had continued to support the Saengerbund's social events, they had not had a slate of officers for some time. Now that there were younger women to help with preparations, the ladies were willing to get organized again. Their monthly sauerkraut suppers became well-known throughout the city and the German community. A typical dinner was served family style for 75 cents—and later for $1.50—per person. It included sauerkraut and pork, hot dogs, mashed potatoes and gravy, baked beans prepared by Eugene Kachelmus, who owned a German delicatessen at 4th and Madison Streets. Rye bread came from several local Jewish bakeries. Coffee with apple cake, baked by the German

bakers Paul Witt and Emil Kurzius, rounded out the meal. Often dancing followed the supper, and that made for a very *gemütlichen Abend*—a pleasant evening out. The Ladies also organized special events such as the popular bingo and card parties that featured attractive prizes. At times they donated their entire profit to the Saengerbund's treasury.

Yet the Saengerbund continued to struggle with expenses. President Ernst Stoessel called a special board meeting on March 21, 1932, attended by officers Paul Nake, Edward Gerres, Max Schilling, and Karl Kutterolf. The financial situation was so serious that the board recommended that all members be contacted. They also decided to inquire into the tax structure of the property, because it appeared to be too heavily taxed. As a last resort, they agreed to consider the library dead capital and try to sell it. The one happy outcome of this meeting was a letter from the tax office that the board received in June 1932 relating that the property valuation would be reduced to $12,000. That meant that the library could be saved. Debates about the German Hall's future continued in 1933, and finally it was resolved to sell if a suitable price could be obtained. The desired price was $10,000, but $8,000 would be accepted as a minimum. Ludwig Schierl and a passive member were authorized to consult a realtor and report on their findings, but no decisions were made at this time.

Picnics had been popular family outings for the club members throughout the years and were often held at a member's farm. The properties of Beste, Steinke, Bartsche, Robinson, and Zeitler were most often visited. There was always music, games for children, and lots of good food. Peter Zeitler had a farm near Elkton. Two picnics were held there in 1933, leaving enough profit that a beer box could be purchased for the use of the members. Finally, the prohibition years had come to an end! The Delaware Saengerbund could obtain a liquor license for the property at 205 East Sixth Street to buy and sell beer and alchol, posting their own strict house rules against abuses on Sundays.

Bernard Hessler Sr. was elected president in 1934. At the first meeting in January, he outlined his ideas for developing activities, programs, and membership drives. He was so enthusiastic that he addressed the members in English. Then he had to recess the meeting and reopen it, because the language for conducting a meeting was still German. Between ten and eighteen members attended the meetings regularly, discussing and resolving the issues brought forth. The singers decided to include more English-language music in their repertoire and to invite English-speaking singers to join the chorus, but only as participants in the musical opportunities; as stated in the society's bylaws, only German-speaking members had voting privileges.

At the same meeting Edward Gerres, who had been the house steward for many years, announced his retirement. The Board accepted his resignation with great dismay. A special committee consisting of Ernst Stoessel, Fritz Steinke, and Hans Schilling was named to prepare a farewell party and purchase a suitable gift for his years of service. In March 1934, Gerres was given a grandfather clock with a dedication plaque. He was deeply touched by the members' generosity. Confident that the Saengerbund would stay together *durch dick und dünn*—through good and bad times—Ed Gerres placed into the hands of the members the most valuable library books. He had kept them in his apartment for safekeeping during all the talk about selling the building. A year later he celebrated his 50th anniversary as an active singer and was invited to another party where old and young honored their oldest member and he was presented with flowers.

The evening was so enjoyable, that members decided to hold an *Alte Herren Abend*, an old gentlemen's evening, more frequently so the long-time members of the club would be able to get to know the younger members. They also realized that it was time to recognize those who had served the society so well for so many years: Conrad Heinekamp, Paul Hessler, Arthur Heinel, Albert Zuelke, Bernhard Feustel, Max Goetz, William Kurtz, and John Lengel were presented with honorary memberships. During a festive evening celebration, the secretary issued diplomas to all honorees.

Now that there were fewer German societies in the city, the *Delaware Saengerbund* became the stronghold of German language and traditions. Newspaper editor Max Goetz called on the German societies to revive the *Deutscher Tag*—German Day celebration of the early 1900's. Under Saengerbund auspices, a German Day was held on October 21, 1935. Paul Hessler, chairman of the festival, made it plain to the newspaper reporter covering the event that "the meeting of the citizens of German birth and descent is strictly a meeting of

entertainment … and has no political character whatsoever, as the German societies in this state are not concerned with politics in foreign lands." The program opened with the Sunday School orchestra playing *Kriegsmarsch der Priester*, "War March of the Priests," by Mendelssohn-Bartholdy. The program was printed in both languages, and program notes stated the purpose of the German Day celebration:

First it serves to bring together those citizens of Delaware who are of German birth or descent and remind them of their common heritage. Secondly, the Deutscher Tag has as its intent the perpetuation of all that is good and worthwhile in the fatherland in the minds and hearts of those who have come to this country, and to instill in them a love for the ideals and principles of America, their foster mother. Lastly, we desire to present an entertainment and evening of good fellowship which shall be in itself a salient event dedicated to hospitality, neighborly sharing of interests and amusements, and to that indefinable quality which the Germans call "*Gemütlichkeit.*"

German Day became an annual event for the next few years. Guests in 1936 included Governor C. Douglas Buck, Mayor Walter W. Bacon, Secretary of State W. Dent Smith, and the Rev. Kurt E. B. Malzahn. Students from four colleges—Haverford and Bryn Mawr (Pennsylvania), Washington College (Chestertown, Maryland), and the University of Delaware—participated in the program. They presented folk songs, pantomimes, folk dances and recitations. Each institution received a $25 prize for participating, and the school which, in the opinion of the judges, gave the best performance, received a silver plaque suitably engraved. After the program, there was dancing to the music of the Carl Elmer orchestra.

The Delaware Saengerbund was happy not to have sold the house. The burning of the second mortgage on May 1, 1936, was an exciting event for all present. In honor of the German Day celebrations, the German Hall was renamed *Deutsches Haus*, but for Wilmingtonians, it always remained the German Hall. Hermann Schweiger was the new house steward. When he married Elnora "Toots" Schweiger, the perfect *Hauseltern*—house parents—had found each other, and the club was in good hands again.

With its house in order, the Delaware Saengerbund reestablished ties with the Nordoestlicher Saengerbund.

A big change had taken place in that organization: at a Board of Directors meeting in January 1935, the Nordoestlicher Saengerbund authorized the admission of ladies' choruses that were auxiliaries of constituent societies. For the first time in eighty-five years, women's choruses could enter the Preissingen. The Delaware Saengerbund was so eager to participate in the 1938 Sängerfest in Baltimore that chorus members agreed to a fine of $10 for each rehearsal they missed.

After Otto Wenzel retired in 1935, Carl Elmer briefly led the chorus. Ludwig Schierl took over in 1936 and was paid $2 a week. He directed the chorus until 1939. Schierl was interested in starting a women's chorus, but the men were not in agreement. When the question of whether women could become active Saengerbund members was brought up in a meeting in 1936, the vote was a definite "NO." The society preferred to remain a men's club. So while fifteen to twenty active men attended monthly meetings downstairs, the Damenverein—the Ladies of the Delaware Saengerbund—held their meetings upstairs.

The year's activities followed the usual calendar, true to the old saying, *Man soll die Feste feiern wie sie fallen*—"One should celebrate the festivities as they occur"—New Year's Eve, the Fasching masquerade ball, Stiftungsfest, spring concert, Easter Monday ball, picnics, sauerkraut suppers, harvest ball, German Day, Christmas Tannenbaum-Abend. Invitations to attend other singing societies' concerts and anniversary celebrations were accepted frequently, and the chorus continued the tradition of surprising their Sanges-brüder with a *Ständchen*, a serenade at a special birthday celebration. When requested, they also assembled to sing at a member's funeral. Members' social lives still centered on family, friends, and evening rehearsals at the German Hall, even though dark clouds were forming again across the sea and casting shadows on this tranquil life.

-Dark Clouds-

The year 1937 began with another discussion about merging with the Wilmington Turners who had already moved from town to Clayton Street. The vote was fifteen for and nine against, but there were no further developments because the Saengerbund insisted that only German-speaking members could have voting rights. The Wilmington Turners, who had many American members, and who had used English as their business language and for gymnastic instruction for a long time, could not agree to such a clause. Further-more, the Turners viewed the political developments in Germany with great concern, because the Turner Asso-ciation there had become the target of political persecution. By 1938, the North American Turner Association had been renamed American Turners, a clear indication that members had distanced themselves from any national-socialist government in Germany and that they adhered to the American democratic principles they always had embraced. While the Turners put their German affiliations "on hold," the singing societies continued promoting German song and German ways.

A happy Saengerchor celebrated its 84th Stiftungsfest on March 18, 1937, and the spring concert a week later was a great success. Officers of a German vessel then at anchor in the Wilmington harbor stopped by at the club and presented to the Saenger-bund a new German *Reichsflagge*. When it was displayed, several members pulled it down. As members of a social club, they did not want to face any political questions. With the flag had come news from Germany that reminded older members of the dark days they had lived through twenty years earlier. They wondered what to think of the forces mobilizing overseas. But sentiments were strong in support of the homeland, so the Saengerbund sponsored a German Day in 1937 and again in 1938.

After the 1938 Sängerfest in Baltimore, the United Singing Societies of Baltimore decided to form a subgroup of the Nordoestlicher Saengerbund called the Gau Süd. The Delaware Saengerbund became part of this organization and hosted the first meeting of the delegates. Then the Nordoestlicher Saengerbund made plans to hold a Sängerfest in Washington, DC, in 1941. The Delaware Saengerbund chorus ordered the music, signed up to participate, and hired Arthur Lemke as director at an annual salary of $350, because the Gau Süd had not set a date for a festival of its member organizations. But change was on the way.

LeRoy Haitsch, elected president in 1940, was drafted in June of that year to serve in the National Guard. The Alien Registration Act, passed on August 27, 1940, required all non-citizens to register at the local post office. Anyone who wanted to travel out of the city had to obtain a special permit, even if the intent was only to visit friends or relatives a short distance away. Despite these restrictions, the club was unwilling to give up the German Day celebration, so they renamed the festival *Pastoriusfeier* in honor of Franz Daniel Pastorius, founder of Germantown, Pennsylvania.

The year 1941 brought more disturbing news. Fritz Steinke reported the difficulties Germans were encountering in the northeastern states. Then the Sängerfest in Washington, DC, was cancelled, as was the Pastorius Day celebration in Wilmington. In December, Germany declared war on the United States. The two countries were enemies, a terrible situation for German Americans. As during the First World War, "Keep quiet—Be loyal" were watchwords for all German Americans. Sangesbrüder were drafted. Each month, a letter signed by the "Singing Friends of Delaware" and cigarettes were sent to members who now served in the armed forces.

Even Wilmington became suspicious of its German citizens and the German club. Max Hamer was the president and Ludwig Schierl the recording secretary at this difficult time. Schierl resigned his office because he was under investigation by the government.

At the March 25, 1942, meeting, the question of changing the language to English was resolved: The business language would remain German, but members could speak English among themselves when club business was not being transacted. A second point of discussion was that *Alle Mitglieder müssen Bürger sein*—all resident members had to apply for American citizenship. The minutes give no indication as to whether this directive was enforced.

Attendance at meetings and rehearsals dropped. As a motivational device, the officers offered to give up their salaries, which were just token reimbursements, each time twenty members were present. After all, the Saengerbund had been in existence for ninety years! But, at the Stiftungsfest on March 26, 1943, those present wondered if the society would celebrate its 100th anniversary. During this same period, the club contributed the then-significant amount of $118.75 to the USO and received a thank-you note. Admission tickets for a dance with the Peter Puljer band and for a Washington's Birthday Dance were sold in the form of 75-cent United States defense stamps.

To maintain a low profile, Saengerbund members busied themselves making improvements to the German Hall. Just as problems resulted from an aging membership, so there were problems with an aging property. A new furnace was needed, the Ratskeller required remodeling, the roof needed repairs, the interior required periodic repainting, and the floors needed sanding. Much of this work was done by volunteer active and passive members, and Eugene Kachelmus provided them with lunches from his delicatessen.

In 1942, remodeling of the kitchen facilities was the priority. For years the Ladies had worked under difficult conditions in the small room, preparing oyster dinners and sauerkraut suppers. After David Dangel was awarded the contract and completed the work, the new kitchen, renovated at a cost of $2,455.14, afforded a more modern and practical operation. The Ladies themselves earned some of the money through their sauerkraut suppers. They charged only 75 cents per person for dinner and dancing, and at one time they showed a profit of $132.63. A few of the hardworking and enthusiastic ladies who prepared delicious dinners during this time included Emma Brustmann, Elly Gilgenast, Elnora Schweiger, Dorothy Kaeks, Margaret Richter, Frieda Schilling, and Martha Steinke. A special pig's-head supper was occasionally available at the bar, organized by Hermann Schweiger.

Hermann Steinke celebrated his 90th birthday in 1944 and, with a sense of humor, donated $50 to be used by the club members upon his demise. He invited everyone to attend his funeral and specified that it should not be a dry affair. The friends accepted with thanks and expressed the hope that he would be among them for many more years. Mr. Steinke died four years later at the age of 94. Another old-timer, Ernst Eckert, celebrated his fifty-year membership in the Saengerbund one year before his death. A new flag was now on display in the German Hall, a flag with a star for each member who had passed away.

That the 230 Saengerbund members stayed together during the Second World War is to the credit of their officers and faithful members—among them Max Hamer, Ludwig Schierl, Fritz Giesemann, William Schomburg, Alfred Gilgenast, Fritz Irion, Fred Fischer, Hermann Schweiger, Eugene Kachelmus, William Noell, Erich Kaeks, Joseph Maucher, Dr. Burton Meyer, Harry Schmidt, Fred Yaeger, Paul Nake, Ernst Stoessel, Otto and Fritz Steinke, and Music Director Arthur Lemke—and the Ladies of the Delaware Saengerbund as well.

"Those years were hard times, hard times at the Saengerbund," remembered Erich Kaeks, a past honorary president, but that was all he would say when asked about the Second World War years. No one spoke of the Vaterland. That word, with all its painful connotations, was buried with all who had died. Instead, *drüben*, over there, or *die alte Heimat*—the old homeland—where many had been born, gone to school, where the parents once lived—was relegated to memory or dreams. It was *die neue Heimat*, the new homeland, or *die zweite Heimat*, the second home, that required action and allegiance.

A forgotten aspect of the war was that, between 1943 and 1945, German prisoners were housed at Fort Delaware. Up to 1,000 men were there at a time, and among them was William Benecke who later became president of the Delaware Saengerbund. After repatriation to Germany, Benecke applied for immigration papers. He was sponsored by the family he had worked for during his time at Fort Delaware. Werner Sumpf, who also became a DSB president had a similar experience after being a prisoner of war in Fort Knox, Tennessee.

After 1945, the Nordoestlicher Saengerbund tabled plans for a Sängerfest. Instead the focus was *Wir wollen der anderen Seite helfen*—"We want to help the other side." News from the shattered German homeland spurred members to action. The Gau Süd was dissolved and the money in the treasury was added to the German Relief Fund. The Saengerbund collected gifts for a *Nothilfe Tanz*, a benefit dance, and gave a total of $748.10 to the relief fund. Additional concerts, activities, and out-of-pocket contributions to benefit this fund totaled $837.36. The American Friends Society of Philadelphia, which also served this project, received $200 from the Saengerbund's treasury. In November 1947, the Saengerbund officers bought canned and dried food and distributed it among the members so that they could prepare care packages. Forty of these care packages, which also included soap and clothing, needles, buttons, and thread, were shipped to Germany. The many thank-you letters the senders received expressed the gratitude of the recipients.

During this postwar period, the Saengerbund also showed the spirit of caring and concern to individual members and other local organizations. Mrs. Fritz Giesemann received a generous cash gift when her husband died, and Mrs. Fritz Steinke was helped when her husband was hospitalized. There were numerous collections for the Overseas Blind. The Elsmere Fire Company, Veterans of Foreign Wars Eagle Post 7006, and Chiefs of Police Children's Camp all received cash donations from the Saengerbund. Profits such as $207.65 from a sauerkraut supper and $188.16 from an *Ernteball*—a Thanksgiving dance—supported these benevolences.

Through all the hard times, singing in the chorus brought the members joy and held them together. When the clouds slowly began to lift, they were able to begin thinking about involving young people in Saengerbund activities. In 1948 Ralph Gilgenast, son of Alfred and Elly Gilgenast, represented the Saengerbund at the annual Pushmobile Derby in Newark. Members attended and cheered him on. Thinking of other endeavors that would involve the club members' children, Ludwig Schierl offered to give German language lessons and to look into the feasibility of a German school. Club members also started thinking about the new immigrants who were beginning to arrive.

The Delaware Saengerbund always opened its doors to those who left Germany because of a lack of work and educational opportunities. After the Second World War, many immigrants fell into this category. In 1950, New York's Ellis Island registered 128,592 Germans coming into the United States; in 1952 the number was still high, 104,236. Most were from West Germany, because the Iron Curtain divided East and West long before a concrete wall physically divided Berlin in 1961. In Wilmington, where most 19th century industries had disappeared, the newer chemical industries attracted many job seekers. When the West German *Wirtschaftswunder*—economic miracle—began to make employment more secure again, the number of immigrants declined accordingly, and some who had come right after the war even decided to return to Germany.

9

Farewell, Old House

So leb denn wohl, du stilles Haus!
Ich zieh betrübt von dir hinaus,
so leb denn wohl, denn ich muss fort,
noch unbestimmt, an welchen Ort.

-Raimund/Müller

Farewell, quiet house, farewell!
We leave you with a heavy heart,
Farewell, dear house, farewell.
We have to move, uncertain where,
Farewell, old house, farewell.

In 1948, Dr. Herbert Jenny was engaged as the new music director at an annual salary of $300. After he accepted, Secretary Fred Fischer happily exclaimed in the minutes: *Es blühe fort das deutsche Lied!*—"May the German song continue to bloom and blossom!" Singing, above all, had held the society together in so many circumstances for almost one hundred years.

Almost immediately the chorus began to prepare for the 31st Sängerfest of the Nordoestlicher Saengerbund, the first one since 1938. It was held in Philadelphia, June 16-18, 1950, in conjunction with the Nordoestlicher Saengerbund's Centennial celebration. President Walter Boehm proudly welcomed guests to the huge convention hall: "It is with genuine pride that I extend to all our friends and visitors from every part of America a sincere and hearty welcome. We are gathered on these festive days to commemorate the 100th Anniversary of the German American singers of the northeastern region of our country. May this city resound with the joy and jubilation that we feel over the part we have been privileged to play in the cultural development of America." That year, the Delaware Saengerbund returned home with a prize.

Having participated in the Nordoestlicher Saengerbund's Centennial celebration, the Delaware Saengerbund began looking forward to its own. As a first step, President Otto Steinke named a committee to begin the planning in 1951. Members assigned were Emil Dahnken, Alfred Gilgenast, John Hauck, Paul Heinemann, Erich Kaeks, Ludwig Schierl, and Richard Wolf. After months of preparation and hard work, the festivities took place on May 16 and 17, 1953, at the Wilmington Armory, Tenth and DuPont Streets. Dr. Herbert Jenny was the festival conductor, Miss Antonica Fairbanks the accompanist. The Color Guard of Delaware Post No. 1 under Commander Robert C. Donovan opened the ceremonies. Then, following the singing of the National Anthem by the full house, the Wilmington Symphony Orchestra, directed by Harry Stausebach, opened the festival concert with the overture to Rienzi by Richard Wagner. Three Wilmington choral groups, Choraliers, New Century Club Chorus, and the Orpheus Chorus, presented songs by Weinberger, Sibelius, and others. Four neighboring German choral societies added their voices to the program: the Fairmount Liedertafel and Liedertafel Saengerbund from Philadelphia, the Lancaster Liederkranz, and the Eichenkranz Gesangverein from Baltimore. Soloists Jean Deis, tenor, and Herbert Beard, baritone, rendered musical selections by Saint-Saens, Schubert and Ward-Syre. Honorary guests and speakers, Governor Caleb J. Boggs and Mayor James F. Hearn, delivered the congratulatory addresses. Walter Boehm, president of the Nordoestlicher Saengerbund, spoke about the Delaware Saengerbund's close relationship to the umbrella organization and concluded with his best wishes for a bright future of the 100-year-old singing society. The program closed with the anthem, "America the Beautiful," which had become a tradition of the festival concerts.

At the banquet, the oldest honorary members of the Delaware Saengerbund were introduced: Hermann Gossen, Michael Haitsch, Arthur Heinel, Lorenz Maucher, Charles Martin, and Ernest Stoessel. The "younger" honorary members in 1953 were Alfred Gilgenast, Max Hamer, Eugene Kachelmus, Emil Kurzius, Peter Loch, Paul Nake, William Noell, Max Schilling, Fritz Steinke, Richard Steinke, John Winsel, Paul Witt, and George Yaeger.

The 100th Stiftungsfest was such a financial success that the club was able to invest nearly $1,000 in U. S. Savings Bonds. Unfortunately, the hope that the celebration also would entice more German residents to join the singing society was not fulfilled. The Second World War had left too deep a wound. Not only had Germany lost the war, but also its image was further darkened as more information about the Jewish Holocaust and the vast number of other people who had been condemned to concentration camps was disclosed. For a considerable period, the only Germans willing to associate with a German club and venture into downtown Wilmington were those with a love for choral singing, a small number, since many new immigrants arriving after the war were more in tune with Rock 'n Roll and Jazz they had listened to on the Armed Forces Radio Network Stations in Germany than with old folksongs and romantic harmonies.

The group of people who contributed most to an increase in membership were the young Americans who had been stationed in Germany during or after the war. Those who returned home with German war brides quickly realized that the German Hall was the place to go. Their young wives welcomed the opportunity to speak German and form friendships through the Ladies' club and the women's chorus. The men enjoyed the atmosphere of Gemütlichkeit they had come to appreciate in Germany's pubs. On Sunday evenings, members and their guests enjoyed dancing to records, playing shuffleboard, and drinking beer. Delaware's "blue laws" prohibited the sale and consumption of alcoholic beverages on Sundays, but members could enjoy their "locker beer," which they purchased earlier in the week and then stashed in their lockers at the club. On the average, forty members now attended the monthly business meetings that were still conducted in German, which was not much help to new English-speaking members.

Despite the addition of some new members, the combination of a low treasury, low membership, and high expenses led club members to start looking for a new property. The men believed the German Hall could be sold for $35,000, so they first considered a property in Claymont listed at $42,500, but concluded it was inappropriate. Because the daily cash flow was low, many members continued to volunteer for work that needed to be done. Sunday evening guests kept the club going, but just barely. One month, the Ladies group paid the gas and electric bills from their own treasury, and more than once, when a bill had to be paid, the club treasurer made up the difference from his own pocket. Still, the members stayed together. A committee was named to visit the sick. Hospitalized and shut-in members looked forward to these visits by Richard Wolf, Max Schilling, Arthur Menk, Werner Hampel, and Alfred Gilgenast, because they provided an opportunity to hear club news and speak German. When Werner Hampel, an enthusiastic member and vice president of the club, and his wife were killed in an automobile accident while vacationing in Florida, members were deeply affected, and the chorus participated in their funeral service at Zion Lutheran Church.

In 1956 Otto J. Genhart became the new music director and continued until his retirement in 1971. Born in Lucerne, Switzerland, into a family of music teachers, he too chose music as his career. After engagements in Tilsit and Chemnitz, he spent ten years in Montreal as conductor of a radio program. In 1939, he came to the United States and began working with German American singing societies in New York State, New Jersey, Pennsylvania and Delaware. Under his leadership, the chorus continued the tradition of an annual spring concert and participating in the Nordoestlicher Saengerbund's Sängerfest, now held every three years. Through visits and excursions, close ties were formed with the societies of the United Singers of Philadelphia and with other northeastern choral groups.

Also at this time, a new flag was needed to replace the old one. The Ladies of the Delaware Saengerbund contributed funds to move things along, and the flag dedication took place in September 1959, attended by the president of the Nordoestlicher Saengerbund. A Festessen, or banquet, followed to mark the occasion. The flag was displayed a week later at its first official, public function, the von Steuben Parade in New York City, an annual event in honor of Baron von Steuben who trained George Washington's army.

Despite all the ups and downs of the postwar years, the Saengerbund prevailed and received a special honor on January 28, 1961, when it was awarded the Zelter Plaque. The plaque is presented to a singing society in existence for over 100 years, in recognition of its longtime commitment to German choral music and to nurturing the German folksong. It is named for Carl Friedrich Zelter, founder and leader of the Berlin Singing Academy. At the presentation, Dr. Edgar Reichel, German Consul in Philadelphia, congratulated the society and read the letter of honor from the president of the Federal Republic of Germany. Wilmington Mayor John E. Babiarz also gave a congratulatory address at the banquet held in the German Hall. That June, the singers, still under the baton of Otto Genhardt, chartered a flight to Germany where they participated in the German Saengerbund's Sängerfest in Essen.

-End of German Hall-

When the Singers returned from their excursion to Germany, they had to face reality again: bills, bills, bills. Long debates centered on the club's future, and members questioned whether raising of dues would help pay expenses. Dues were still just $3 per member for the active singers and $5 for passive members. Throughout 1962 the average monthly deficit was $100. A special committee looked into the possibility of selling the library, as there were some valuable books among the collection. Members were pleased when John Dawson of the University of Delaware expressed interest and accepted the books. The antique volumes were housed in the Special Collections Room of Morris Library, and the others were integrated into the library's open shelves where everyone with an interest in German literature would be able to use them.

Elections became chaotic, because no one wanted to accept an office. At the end of 1962, the election committee was unable to present a slate of officers. Consequently, in January 1963, the current officers were urged to remain in office for another two months. The financial committee presented several recommendations to alleviate the economic situation, including raising dues, cutting the steward's salary, saving on the director's salary by not paying him during the summer months, and proposing to form a committee that would plan the financial aspect of future activities. By March, the situation was worse. Four months had passed without an elected board. President Emil Dahnken announced that this was indeed a sad state of affairs: *Dies soll als ein trauriger Punkt allen Mitgliedern vor dem Gewissen stehen, dass ein Verein, der 110 Jahre besteht, keine Mitglieder hat, die den Ehrgeiz besitzen eine leitende Stellung im Saengerbund zu führen. Bestimmt ist es nicht angebracht noch einen Delaware Saengerbund zu haben!*—"This should be engraved as a sad time in the conscience of all members, that a society in existence for 110 years does not have members who have the ambition to take on a leadership role. It appears that the Delaware Saengerbund is unworthy of its existence!"

Secretary Alfred Escheu rose to the occasion and expressed two important points: first, that the constitution of 1903 was outdated and did not reflect current society as the Saengerbund was still a men's club; and second, that the language of business had to

DER SAENGERBUND SCHENKT BÜCHER AN DIE UNIVERSITÄT VON DELAWARE

TO DAS SCHULE

SAENGERBUND ÜBER ALLES

Jack Jurden, cartoonist for the News Journal, captured the exodus of the German Library books from the German Hall, 1962.

change to English. Up to this time, the idea of change had been met with strong opposition. Now a new wind was blowing. The officers called a special meeting and notified everyone of its importance by mail.

March 27, 1963, was an historic day for members of the Delaware Saengerbund. The fifty-six members present voted to accept women as equal partners in membership, including voting privileges. They also agreed that the constitution would be updated and that the language used in conducting meetings and in all other transactions would become English. A new Board of Directors was voted into office, and for the first time two women were elected: Elly Gilgenast became second vice president and Mary Ruth Morganstern recording secretary. The other officers at this crucial point were: Emil Dahnken, president; Helmut Hampel, first vice president; Alfred Escheu, corresponding secretary; Alfred Gilgenast, treasurer; and Simon Schock, financial secretary. Beginning on May 8, 1963, the minutes were recorded in English.

Another development was the Sunshine Fund. Its purpose was to bring "a ray of sunshine" to ill and bereaved members by sending flowers and cards. Dedicated members were getting older, and many deaths were being recorded. At the December meeting in 1963, a moment of silence was held for Fritz Steinke, Ludwig Schierl, Richard Kuhlmann, and the slain President of the United States, John F. Kennedy.

Although these changes in the Saengerbund's organizational structure were successful, the financial picture did not improve. As before, no one wanted to be saddled with the burden of accepting an office and managing the club business. Alfred Escheu saw no other choice than proposing that the doors of the German Hall be closed as of January 1, 1964, and that the current board remain in office until January 15 when a Board of Trustees would be nominated. But the doors remained open, acting officers were reelected, and Emil Dahnken and his faithful board of directors continued through the end of the year and through 1965 as well. As the society limped along, urban renewal plans for Wilmington provided a ray of hope: the prospect of selling the property to the city.

It is well-known that the structure of American cities changed after the Second World War. The GI Bill and an improving economy meant that families could fulfill their dreams of getting an education, owning a house surrounded by a spacious yard outside the city, and raising their children in the suburbs. Commuting to city jobs in Wilmington was easy, since almost everyone could afford one or two cars. Suburban living was the new way of life, and soon Wilmington became an office town. Ellen Rendle's book, *Ghosts of Market Street,* describes the way the stores followed the people out of town as the new concept of shopping malls took hold. Several stores opened branches along the major arteries and, after hanging on in downtown Wilmington for a few more years, decided to close their businesses there. The construction of Interstate 95 divided the city and allowed suburbanites and travelers to avoid downtown. Lower income families who stayed behind could not afford to care for the houses they lived in. Then the city government began to make plans for removing the decaying neighborhoods on Wilmington's east side. The Poplar Street Project led to the removal of 539 households. The area of Walnut, King and French Streets was designated a construction site for new high-rise buildings to house city, county, and state offices. The closely-knit German neighborhood of the late 1800s was gone.

The club property at 205 East 6th Street was sold on July 8, 1965, in the presence of Attorney Thomas Herlihy Jr., President Emil Dahnken, and Secretary

Alfred Escheu, for net total of $26,952.77. An additional $810 resulted from the sale of various club inventories. All monies were invested pending the club's locating another property. The *Delmarvia Monthly Review* reported in its German column in May 1965:

Letztes Hauskonzert der Delaware-Sänger—The last in-house concert of the Delaware Singers. The Delaware Saengerbund gave its 112th spring concert before a full house on May 8. A medley of Alpine folksongs arranged by music director Otto Genhart with soloists Sophia Kopec, Dorothy Dodds, Margaret Cyzyk, and tenor John Elliott was especially applauded. In his address, president Emil Dahnken had to inform the members and guests with a heavy heart that this concert was the last one in the German Hall. He thanked the chorus members for years of dedication to the "German Lied." He expressed hope that they would continue to sing, irregardless [sic] of where the Saengerbund might be, hopefully in its own house again soon.

The October 8, 1965, *Evening News Journal* also found the sale of the German Hall newsworthy: "Prosit Fades Out At The Saengerbund—1840s Hall Will Be Razed," was the somber title of an article describing the demise of the German Hall. Before the wrecking crew came in, Dale Fields, executive secretary of the Historical Society of Delaware, was able to retrieve some of the old record books and samples of old songbooks members had left behind.

For fifteen months, from July 1965 until October 1966, the Saengerbund moved into a temporary abode at the Officers' Club of the New Castle County Air Base. All rehearsals, meetings, dances and programs took place there. After that, the Saengerbund's belongings were moved to the Wil-

mington Turners clubhouse on South Clayton and Beech Streets in Wilmington, and meetings and activities were conducted there. The club's few treasures were placed in the hands of members who would take care of them until the club could find a home to call its own.

Last Concert in German Hall, 1965.

The chorus at one of their festivals around the turn of the 20th Century. The only singer identified is Henry Zimmermann, seated in the middle of the front row.

Plate 1

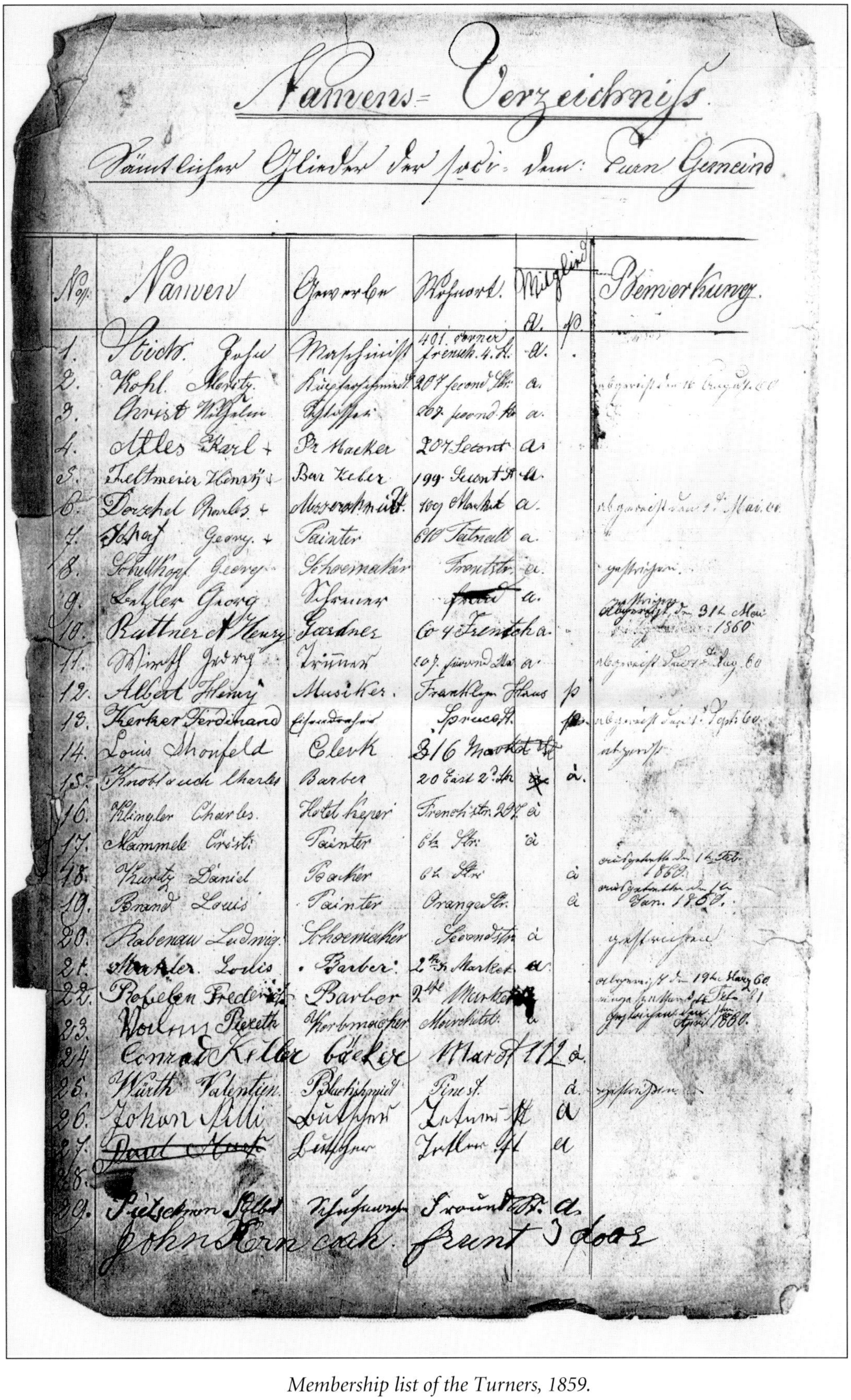

Membership list of the Turners, 1859.

Plate 2

Active Turners of 1913-1914
Front seated: Wm. Welch 2nd: H. Clodi, H. Smith, Joe Fidance, Charles Flickinger, instructor Henry Widdekind, L. Glick,
A. Pyne, B. Jockett, N. Wadley 3rd: Walter Murphy, Karl Holzhauser, Henry Roemer

Saengerbund members Frederick Kleitz, Peter Ebner, Henry Zimmermann, and Caspar Conrad formed the Tyrolean Quartet,
accompanied by Christoph Bauer and Harry Schnepf on the zither.

Plate 3

Festival edition of the Wilmington Lokal-Anzeiger *for the 1909 Volksfest with a picture of President Daniel Maier.*

Plate 4

The Ladies on an outing to Atlantic City, 1949
On horse: *Sophie Giesemann* **seated, 1st:** *Emma Brustman, nk, Eva Schwebler* **2nd:** *Edith Yaeger, Elly Gilgenast*

The Ladies in Atlantic City in summer of 1951
1st: *nk, Elly Gilgenast, Elsa Antoine, Frances Hauck, Dorothy Kaeks, Gretl Schierl* **2nd:** *Eva Schwebler, Frieda Schilling, Emma Brustman, Anna Hamer, Catherine Bergner, Sophie Giesemann, nk, nk, Elnora Schweiger, nk*

Plate 5

Delaware Saengerbund Männerchor , 1938
1st: *Ernst Eckert, Richard Steinke, Francis Whiteside, Conrad Heinekamp, Albert Zuelke, Harry Barker, Director Ludwig Schierl,*
2nd: *John Winsel, Eugene Kachelmus, Peter Loch, Max Hamer, Franz Rassman, Paul Nake, Alfred Gilgenast, William Noell*
3rd: *Dr. Burton Meyer, Arthur Bracken, Carl Elmer, Kurt Zeise, Fritz Giesemann, Fritz Steinke, Fred Yaeger*

Hermann Steinke's 93rd birthday party, 1948
1st: *nk, nk, Fritz Steinke, Hermann Steinke, Emil Dahnken, Dr. Herbert Jenny, nk, Emma Brustman* ***2nd:*** *Walter Hagelstein,*
Richard Wolf, Frances Noell , Mrs. Haas, Elnora Schweiger, Hermann Schweiger, nk ***On steps:*** *Ralph Gilgenast, Bill Noell*

Plate 6

Cooks and helpers of a turkey dinner in April 1956 in the German Hall Ratskeller Erich Kaeks, Dorothy Kaeks, Elly Gilgenast, Martha Steinke, Alfred Gilgenast, Emma Brustman, Elnora Schweiger, Margaret Richter, Max Schilling, Frieda Schilling

Ratskeller in German Hall

Plate 7

The Mixed Chorus of the Delaware Saengerbund in 1953

1st: Mary Loch, Catherine Bergner, Gretl Schierl, nk, Dr. Jenny, director, Margaret Cycyk, Hedwig Winsel, Elly Gilgenast Margaret Richter, Dorothy Kaeks
2nd: Mary Rotter, Johanna Hilsenrad, Elsa Antoine, Ernie Robinson, Frances Noell, Frances Hauck, Emma Brustman, Elnora Schweiger, Antonica Fairbanks, accompanist **3rd:** Walter Hagelstein, Erich Kaeks, Fritz Irion, Paul Bergner, Peter Loch, Dr. Burton Meyer, Fred Yaeger, Fritz Steinke, Joe Rotter, Hermann Boerstler, Mr. Wiedenman **4th:** nk, Max Borbe, Max Cycyk, Richard Wolf, Gus Hagenah, Alfred Gilgenast, Emil Dahnken, John Hauck, Ludwig Schierl

Plate 8

The Damen-Chor with Dr. Herbert Jenny in 1953

1st: *Catherine Sisofo, Gretl Schierl, Catherine Bergner, Margaret Cycyk, Rita Menk, Martha Heinemann, Sophie Giesemann, Elnora Schweiger, Dorothy Kaeks, Hedwig Winsel* **2nd:** *Ernie Robinson, Millie Frick, Martha Borbe, Frances Noell, Mary Loch, Emma Brustman, Frances Hauck, Elly Gilgenast, Mary Rotter* **3rd:** *Elisabeth Hampel, Rosemary Winsel, nk, Frieda Fischer, Elsa Antoine, nk, Johanna Hilsenrad, Margaret Richter*

Plate 9

Presentation of the Zelter Plaque
Mayor John E. Babiarz, Alfred Gilgenast, Emil Dahnken, German Consul Dr. Edgar Reichel

Joseph Sell was made honorary president in 1914. Saengerbund member Helga Schulz discoverd the framed diploma
at an antique sale in Wilmington. (Photo by Mike Ciosek)

Plate 10

The Kickers playing the elimination game at New Castle County Airport in 1961
1st: Siggi Geist, Werner Beyer, Victor Uro 2nd: Coach Sepp Hilsenrad, Captain Alfred Escheu, Schorsch Lang, nk, nk, nk,
Karl Schmidt, Siggi Fuchs, Albert Blind, nk, Hans Ulzhofer, Karl Heinz Schulz, Coach Paul Fuchs.

Rudy Schock (standing, second from right) organizer of the Delaware Saengerbund Friendship Tournament, and soccer team.

Plate 11

The Delaware Saengerbund Chorus in 1970 in the new clubhouse

1st: *Sophia Kopec, Maria Evans, Lilly Budzialek, Emmy Toman, Dorothy Kaeks, Vera Schock, Margaret Richter, Annalies Benecke, Martha Steinke, Margaret Cycyk,* **2nd:** *Martha Heinemann, Maria Wiedenman, nk, Elisabeth Hampel, Hilde Yaeger, Frieda Fischer, Brigitte Konrad, Emmy Paterniani, Dorothy Dodds, Johanna Hilsenrad, Elly Gilgenast, Elsa Antoine, Frances Hauck, Peggy Klabe, Eva Schwebler* **3rd:** *Gus Tuckmantel, Erich Kaeks, John Ellicott, Konrad Walter, Richard Wolf, Bill Klabe, director Otto Genhardt, Max Cycyk, Bill Benecke, Fred Yaeger, Helmuth Hampel, Joe Rotter, Bill Read, Herman Boerstler, Paul Heinemann, Alfred Gilgenast.*

Plate 12

10

The Delaware Saengerbund in Ogletown

Kein schöner Land in dieser Zeit
als hier das unsre weit und breit,
wo wir uns finden wohl unter Linden
zur Abendzeit, wo wir uns finden
wohl unter Linden zur Abendzeit.

-Zuccalmaglio, 1838

No land more beautiful at this time
Than ours here far and wide,
Where we are
Gathered under the linden tree
At eventide.

-49 Salem Church Road-

A building committee consisting of Erich Kaeks, Fred Holzhauser, William Benecke, and Sophia Kopek was charged with the search for a new home. Other members were also on the lookout for a suitable property. Paul Heinemann, a board member who knew that the club wanted a permanent home again, surveyed local real estate. He recalled looking at a property in Hockessin that was too wet, one on Route 273 that was nice but located on a very busy road, and a club on Churchman's Road that was too expensive. Then, driving through Ogletown one evening, he found something that seemed to be "just right." It was the Lydia Alcorn property on Salem Church Road. The 7.3-acre farm had a small brick house with a separate two-car garage and several farm buildings. The property, appraised at $45,000, was in the hands of the Delaware Trust Co., which had to sell in order to settle the estate. Heinemann immediately contacted attorney Bernard Hessler Jr. At the August 1966 membership meeting, Heinemann presented plans for the property, using charts to convey the past, the present, and the future of the Saengerbund. When he recommended that the club purchase the land, another special meeting was called so that everyone could participate in the decision. At that meeting, Heinemann presented three points in support of the purchase and moved that the club buy the land. The result of the roll call vote was fifty-three in favor and one against. Forty-eight members were absent. Thus, the Delaware Saengerbund had decided to relocate to Ogletown.

The stable on the Alcorn farm was converted into the Bauernstube

After the attorney entered a bid of $40,000, pledges by families and friends and other details were discussed and finalized. In May 1967, President William Benecke officially announced the purchase of the Salem Church Road property for $40,000 with a $15,000 mortgage. At that time, there were discussions about selling the house and part of the land to earn extra money. During a special meeting where sixty members were present, some spoke against selling the "heart" of the newly acquired property. Eugene Kachelmus gave several reasons for retaining the entire package, stating that now the club had something to offer to its members, something that had not been possible since the sale of the German Hall in 1965. Alfred Gilgenast moved that the club retain the entire property and set up a legal bond system in denominations of $100 with no interest rate and no specific expiration date. Karl Schmidt seconded the motion; the vote was forty-two in favor, three against, and fifteen abstentions.

What happened after that was nothing short of a miracle, according to Paul Heinemann. A loan for constructing the new clubhouse was obtained through Mr. Weis of the former Equitable Trust Bank of Delaware. Richard Trager, chair of the building committee, was in charge of the construction; John Sporay was appointed as temporary caretaker of the new property. The building committee sought volunteers to fix up the house as a rental property, and Wilhelm Schulz led the group of men to convert the barn into a *Bauernstube*, a little tavern with a bar.

The first picnic was held on the new home grounds on July 29, 1967, with pony rides, a merry-go-round, and an ice cream truck to keep the children happy. Paul Heinemann reflected: "Never in our or any older member's memory was there such a crowd. Kentucky Fried Chicken had nothing on us. Chicken went faster than we could fry it." The day ended with a very happy group of people who could envision their dream of a new clubhouse coming true.

During the early years at Ogletown, older members who had struggled valiantly to hold the club together continued giving their support, though less actively due to age and health. Fred Fischer, one of these dedicated members and frequent recording secretary whose clear and beautiful penmanship graced the pages of the older record books, passed away in 1967. As he so often wrote after the names of deceased members in the minutes, may he too "rest in peace. R. I. P."

New and younger families were attracted to the new grounds outside of the city. Attendance at meetings and functions mushroomed. Thirty-five new members were accepted in September of that year, mostly Americans of German descent and a few first-generation immigrants.

Delaware Saengerbund

The Singers performing under the direction of David Linton in Washington at the occasion of the German-American Day, October 6, 1988

Plate 1

Delaware Saengerbund

The Delaware Saengerbund Chorus with Music Director Robert Bunnell in 2002

1st: Edith Fischer-Berr, Anna Cowell, Simon Schock, Robert Bunnell, director, Hilmar Fricke, chair, MaryAnn Dowd, Sonja Ciresa **2nd:** Trudy Gilgenast, Margarete Hawkins, Ingeborg Keith, Marguerite Spittle, Mary Alice Nagle, Vicki Farmer, Ingrid Schober, Margot Kulp, Lilly Budzialek, Sophia Kopec **3rd:** Vera Schock, Helga Kissell, Kathryn Widdekind, Carol Fricke, Inge Thompson, Erika Schirm, Hermine Kuska, Erika Ambrosch, Norma Schroeder, Dawn Swartout, Barbara Menzian **4th:** John Marshall, Paul Hanke, Hans Schober, Werner Freyman, Richard Schechinger, Clyde Nafzinger, Richard Leaning, Erwin Grieb, Robert Picking, Otto Schwoegler

Plate 2

Delaware Saengerbund

The Ladies of the Delaware Saengerbund 2002
1st: Margaret Johnston, Marge Nagy, Doris Lang, Heidi Valiante, Margaret Sigmund
2nd: Sarah Viering, Connie Allen, Diene Grabner, Hilde Cox, Marilyn Downs, Anne Smith, Carmen Houseman, Karen Swank, Gary Huggler, Irmgard Sukalo, Annemarie McNeal

Board of Directors 2002
1st: 2nd Vice President Simon Schock, President Reinhold Kuska, 1st Vice President Robert Hawkins 2nd: Recording Secretary Samuel Simpson, Corresponding Secretary Henry Maier, Treasurer Hans Nafzinger, Membership Chair Clyde Nafzinger

Plate 3

Delaware Saengerbund

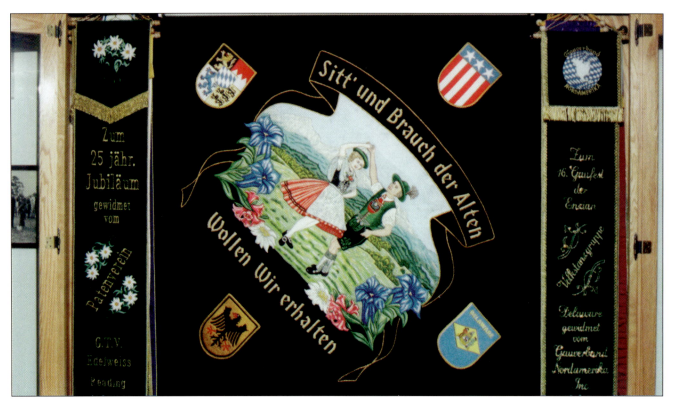

Embroidered flag of the EVTG

Preisplattler 1993
1st: *Hermine Kuska, Tina Stixrude, Stephanie Schulz, Jim Hall, Romie Kuska Lutz, Helga Schweiger, George Schweiger*
2nd: *Reinhold Kuska, Brian Schulz, Richard and Norma Grieb, Dieter Schulz, Joseph Ruff*

Plate 4

The winners of the Schafkopf Tournier at the Gaufest in St. Paul, MN, 1999.

Dancers at Oktoberfest

Plate 5

Delaware Saengerbund

The Enzian Volkstanzgruppe in their Tracht, 2002

1st: Eric Gonzalez, Wills Wagner, Jake Schneck, Emilie Grieb-Ginn, Drew Wagner, Alexander Lutz 2nd: Emma Marek, Abby Marek, Claudia Gonzalez, Charles Groff, Mary Cay Armstrong, Steve Armstrong, David Keith, Sarah Keith, Amber Kinney, Morgan Schulz 3rd: Margot Trager, Susan Vikari, Kerstin Vikari, Brook Winkleman, Julia Wagner, Matt Kinney, Sara Schreiber, Don Merritt, Allyssa Schulz, Stephanie Schneck, Traci Farmer, Helga Schweiger, Ingeborg Keith 4th: Vicki Farmer, Michelle Killian, Janette Merritt, Lizabeth Marek, Amy Smelgus, Stephanie Schulz, Norma Grieb, Lori Mauragas, Romie Lutz, Diana Winkleman 5th: Klaus Vikari, Joe Schreiber, George Schweiger, Alfred Escheu, Don Schneck, Steve Marek, Richard Grieb, Pete Mauragas,; Bill Winkleman, Bill Wagner 6th: Richard Trager, Tommy Keith, Brian Schulz Photo by Pouser

Plate 6

Delaware Saengerbund

The '88 Kickers team—2001 DELCO U-14 Champions
1st: Chris Burns, Kevin Feehery, John Delaney, Dany Alvarez, Kyle Fones, Leo Marianiello, Jeff Terkula, Andrew Riley,
Nathan Haas 2nd: Coach Alan Fones, Sean Delaney, Rob Kelly, Brian Thomas, Laura Shepherd, Stephan Schill, Bernie Sauppee,
Daniel Krantz, Jeremy MacMicking, Spencer Meltzer, Coach Doug Haas

The U 14 Girls team, Champions in 2000 and 2001
1st: Laura McCoy, Caitlin Mann, Colleen Dowd, Lindsay Wallace 2nd: Megan Watson, Ashley Fogelman, Amanda Davis,
Erika Roberts, Renae Patch 3rd: Mike McIver(coach), Diana Godwin, Jenn Piechowski, Jill Clark, Jen Montague, Cynthia Wray,
Heather Miller, Jerry Wegman(coach) Absent: Carla Durante

Plate 7

*The **Maibaum** representing the different groups of the Delaware Saengerbund*

***Maypole Dance at Old Town Hall exhibit** celebrating 300 years of German traditions in America*

Plate 8

-New Constitution-

As the Bauernstube began to take shape, work also progressed on the draft of a new constitution with Paul Heinemann as committee chair. The document was written in English, because this was now the society's official business language. The name Delaware Saengerbund and Library Association was retained, even though the library books were no longer part of it. However, the library's constitution became part of the Saengerbund's new constitution. The first of three required line-by-line readings took place on July 12, 1967. The objectives of the organization now were:

> To encourage, support and perpetuate the study and use of the German language, culture, traditions and customs, and German choral singing
>
> To share traditional sociability among the German community and extend it to the community at large
>
> To foster a better understanding of the contributions made by German immigrants to the American way of life
>
> To promote good citizenship

For the first time, membership was limited to a maximum of 800 members. Questioned as to the reason for this number, Paul Heinemann's answer was, "The new hall had room for 400 people. We could reasonably expect about fifty percent of the membership to be here at one time, so 800 seemed a good idea." Also, all groups using the club facilities had to be Saengerbund members.

As specified in earlier constitutions, the organization was to consist of voting and nonvoting members. Voting members were defined as active, associate and honorary. They had the right to vote, elect officers, hold office, and sponsor new members. Active status was granted to adults of German descent with full legal privileges for themselves and their spouses. Attendance at four regular general membership meetings was required. Nonvoting members could attend meetings, but could neither enter any motions nor vote. The organization was to be governed by an elected board of directors consisting of a president, first and second vice presidents, treasurer, recording secretary, corresponding secretary, and membership secretary. Board members had the additional responsibility of being chairpersons of the standing committees, and the president could call new standing committees or temporary committees as the need arose.

The first vice president was chair of the House Committee in charge of the operation of the facilities, a position that required knowledge of state and local laws. The second vice president headed the Entertainment Committee and was responsible for planning cultural and social events. Another board member was in charge of the Membership Committee, which processed membership applications and collected dues. The recording secretary had the awesome responsibility of accurately recording the business of both board and general membership meetings. (Up until 1963 the minutes were handwritten, but from that time on, they were typed. Today a computer makes maintaining all club records somewhat easier.)

Article 10 was dedicated to the eventual closing of the society: "When the number of enrolled voting members is less than seven, the Board of Directors shall move to disband the organization. In this event, the assets of the organization shall be liquidated and all outstanding debts paid. Any assets remaining shall be delivered to the University of Delaware to be used … for furthering the study of the German language and culture." At the meeting on November 8, 1967, the new constitution was approved in its entirety by a vote of forty-seven to two.

-House Committee-

The first vice president and the appointed House Committee were now in charge of the club's daily business. This included overseeing the use of the facilities, keeping the bar inventory up-to-date and, most importantly, knowing and adhering to the rules of Delaware's Alcohol and Beverage Commission. This information is passed on to the Saengerbund's bartenders who see to it that the guests in the Bauernstube or hall are well served and comfortable. Over the years, Adrian Olivier, Alfred Escheu, Richard Weis, Simon Schock, Fred Thompson, Horst Horn, Werner Reichert, George Schweiger, Wilhelm Schulz, Donald Smith, Gary Huggler, Robert Hawkins, and Teresa Escheu Lord have served as capable vice presidents.

Kris Thomassen, Werner Sumpf, and Joseph Pouser enjoying the accordion music played by Ted Antonelli and Bill Kux.

-Bauernstube-

On November 9, 1967, the Bauernstube was dedicated and officially opened. The names of all who had worked hard were inscribed on the stones placed throughout the walls: Frank Alberer, Bob Alcorn, Cecil Brown, C. Cool, Gerda Delagram, Alfred Escheu and son, Donald Deaven Fry, Fritz Goeckel, Paul Heinemann, Horst Horn, Michael Iwanuik, Eugene Kachelmus, F.C. Mayer, Merv, Tony Moosreiner, Adrien Olivier, Ralph Olivier, Anton Reder, Werner Reichert, Karl Schmidt, Norbert Schneider, Simon Schock Jr. and sons, Wilhelm Schulz, Karl Heinz Schulz, Brian Schulz, Hans Schwab, Karl Seitenbecher and son, Harold Snyder, Richard Stein, Werner Sumpf, Alex and Marion Sumpf, Frank Tempel, Richard Trager, Richard Wolf, and Woody Yaeger.

Werner Reichert's mother presented the new Bauernstube with a large Alpine cowbell. The tradition is that anyone who rings the bell buys a round of drinks for everyone sitting at the bar. Just as stopping in at the German Hall for a glass of beer had been a tradition in Wilmington, so it became one in Ogletown. From time to time, a group of Stammtisch regulars occupied the same table to play Schafkopf, Skat or other card games. Many trails followed by the Saengerbund's hiking group, Wandervögel, led to the Bauernstube. There the hikers enjoyed a refreshing glass of beer at the end of a long day.

During the 1990s, another popular event in the Bauernstube has been the Frühschoppen, a delicious meal served on a Sunday morning by the House Committee's breakfast gang. Translated as "an early pint," it grew out of the custom in some German towns that the men would stop after church for a glass of wine or beer in their favorite Gasthaus—Just so they wouldn't get underfoot, the men said!—while the women went home to prepare the main Sunday meal served at noon. Committee members and accomplished cooks who are part of the breakfast gang include Heinz and Erika Ambrosch, Fred and Linda Escheu, Teresa and Martin Lord, Don Merritt, Lois and Howard

Meyer, Andrea Nafzinger, Hans Nafzinger, Rolf and Alma Offschanka, Alex Piragow, Simon Schock, Cindi Spink, Irene Rice, and Bill and Sibylle Wansaw.

Often there is music in the Bauernstube. Talented members bring their instruments to play for the listening and dancing pleasure of members and guests. In past years, accordionists Horst Fischer and Charles Bowers encouraged everyone to join a sing-a-long, and the *Lustigen Musikanten* with Burkard Noack and Tom Yost played for dances. For over twenty-five years, the *Hauskapelle* played *Bauernstubenmusik* with George Keith, guitar, and Ted Antonelli, accordion. Other members with a talent for music were Bill Benecke, Walter von Ryik, Werner Vellrath, Elio Battista, and Wilhelm Schulz on the *Teufelsgeige*.

-Deutsche Halle-

A new era in the Saengerbund's history began on March 9, 1968, when the first meeting was held in the Bauernstube. Plans for building the large clubhouse were ready by late summer. Early in 1969, financial details concerning the mortgage and bonds were approved, and on May 10, 1969, the groundbreaking ceremony took place. The Ladies of the Delaware Saengerbund and Eugene Kachelmus prepared a gala luncheon for the guests and officers, and members enjoyed free beer and punch following the ceremony.

Local architect Ernest Lundgren and member Otto Koops drew the blueprints, and Richard Trager again chaired the Building Committee. Construction began in earnest and with great enthusiasm as well as some hard heads under the hard hats! The hall—like the Bauernstube—was built entirely by Saengerbund members who had expertise in many areas. Volunteer workers who spent countless hours on the building included Frank Alberer, Alfons Angel, Ted Antonelli, Hermann Boerstler, Georg B., John Cox, Tom Cic, Alfred Escheu, Horst Fischer, Alfred Gilgenast, Ralph Gilgenast, Fritz Goeckel, John Hauck, Horst Horn, Wolfgang Horn, George Keith, Otto Koops, Bill Marvel, Bill Maxwell, Arthur Mayer, Eric Mayer, Frank Mayer, Tony Moosreiner, Tom Nichols, Burkhard Noak, Franz Pilz, William Read, Bob Robertson, Joseph Rotter, Karl Schmidt, Simon Schock Sr., Simon Schock Jr., Wilhelm Schulz, Karl-Heinz Schulz, Werner Sumpf, Richard Trager, Gus Tuckmantel and son Ed, Hans Ulzhofer,

"Der erste Spatenstich" – Ground breaking ceremony for the new hall in Ogletown, May 10, 1969.
L-R: Wilhelm Schulz, State Senator W. Hart,
New Castle Co. Executive W. Connor.

Howard Wiedenman, Richard Wolf, and Charles Yenkowitz.

Construction progressed quickly. The traditional *Richtfest*—the roof raising ceremony—took place in September. In Germany it is customary to tie a small evergreen tree to the frame of the open roof and celebrate the work of the masons and carpenters with a blessing, speeches, and a keg of beer! The new hall was called Deutsche Halle to continue the tradition of the German Hall in Wilmington. The Ladies invited all workers to a builders' dinner, and all members enjoyed free beer and punch following the Richtfest.

-Property Committee-

When Alfred Escheu was elected president in 1971, he introduced a new standing committee, the Property Committee, to be chaired by the president. A cochair, Otto Koops, was designated to assist him. The committee's responsibility was to coordinate all building plans—including the future Phase II and Phase III—and to become familiar with local building codes, purchase all larger equipment, and oversee the general maintenance of the property. After Koops retired, Alfred Escheu and Richard Leaning took turns as chair and cochair, overseeing the never-ending work of this committee.

To take care of the large grassy area around the buildings, brothers Oskar and Walter Schmidt donated a farm tractor, still in use thirty years later! Hermann Rouwhorst designed a landscaping plan that included long-lasting trees and plants. Heinz Binsau donated shrubs and trees. More landscaping was needed after the completion of Phase I, the Bauernstube and Deutsche Halle, so Karl Grieshaber prepared a plan that would include evergreens, hemlocks, Norway spruces and blue Atlas cedars. President Werner Sumpf helped plant the trees, while members contributed flowers from their gardens. Ted Antonelli brought more evergreens from his tree farm in Pennsylvania. Not long ago, John Hauck imported horse chestnut seedlings from his hometown Bamberg and, with the help of Simon Schock, planted them around the pavilion. In time their stately bloom and shiny brown fruit will evoke memories of childhood play in Germany.

Schaffe, schaffe, Häusle baue! ("Work, work, and build your house!") is a Swabian saying. Not all Saengerbund members are from the Schwabenland, but the same energy shown by the founders and early members motivated everyone to put in long hours and work hard at Ogletown. When one project was completed, another was begun. Plans were drawn up for a building that would serve as a garage, a place to store equipment, and a workshop. When finished, it was named the Gus Tuckmantel Building for all the work that Gus had contributed to enhance the new property. His son Ed was the artist-in-residence who painted the Black Forest mural at the back of the stage and the picturesque Rhine landscape in the *Weinstube*. The Saengerbund's new emblem, the Saengerbund Kickers' insignia, the sign at the entrance gate, and the flag of the Enzian Volkstanzgruppe were also his designs.

Between 1967 and 1971, the club grew from just 100 members to over 500. Many worked constantly in an unassuming manner, expecting no applause. One such member, William Marvel, better known as "Uncle Bill" was honored at the society's 1972 inaugural ball.

He was presented with a German beer stein bearing the inscription "Member of the Year Award—1971." There were no other recipients of this award until 1979, when Simon Schock requested that the award be revived. The following members were then named as recipients: 1972, Fred Yaeger; 1973, Frank Temple; 1974, Wally Alberer; 1975, Otto Koops; 1976 and 1979, Alfred Escheu; 1977, Don Smith; 1978, Hilde Schwoegler. After 1979, It became too difficult to choose among the many hard-working members who all deserved recognition, so the Member of the Year award was no longer presented. After so many years of work, it was time for everyone to celebrate.

-125th Stiftungsfest-

According to the minutes, members were asked to vote on the kind of celebration they wanted for the 125th Stiftungsfest in 1978. The overwhelming response was to hold a BIG affair in May rather than on the anniversary date, March 17, to assure warmer weather. This gala event was combined with the 10th anniversary of the Enzian Volkstanzgruppe. Preparations by the planning committee headed by Helmut Hoeschel began a year and a half before the event. William Klabe took on this responsibility when Hoeschel was transferred to New York State. The anniversary celebration was covered thoroughly by the May 17, 1978, *Newark Weekly Post* and the *Delawarean*, the *Philadelphia Inquirer*'s Sunday supplement for May 14–20, 1978. Articles from both newspapers are part of the Saengerbund's records.

The celebration began on Friday with a *Bunter Abend*—an evening of entertainment—featuring performances by the Singers and dancing by both the Kindertanzgruppe and the Enzian Volkstanzgruppe. A birthday cake with 125 candles was enjoyed by everyone. A large tent behind the Deutsche Halle accommodated the guests invited to attend the festivities.

Saturday was designated as the *Festtag*, the festival day. Music and dancing continued throughout the day in the tent, while the children amused themselves playing all kinds of games on the lawn. On Saturday evening, the official ceremony opened with the singing of the German and American national anthems. Among the guests of honor were the Consul-General of the German Embassy, A. von Schmelling, Senator

Joseph Biden, County Executive Mary Jornlin; and Newark Mayor William Redd. Several dance groups, including the Patenverein Edelweiss from Reading and groups from Annapolis, Maryland; Richmond, Virginia; as well as the Ukrainian Dance Group of the University of Delaware, performed in colorful Tracht and received much applause.

For the *Ausklang*—conclusion—a *Bauernmesse* was celebrated on Sunday morning in the Deutsche Halle. Such a mass or religious service is a traditional part of all large celebrations in Germany. The 125th Stiftungsfest ecumenical service incorporated the music of the Bauernmesse prevalent in the Bavarian region. Alpine melodies were sung by the *Wandervögel*, under the direction of Beatrix Tannian and supported by the Saengerbund's chorus.

The remainder of the day was spent in *gemütlichem Beisammensein*, in friendly fellowship. The committee chairpersons who worked hard to make the weekend a success were: property, Richard Trager; art director, Edward Tuckmantel; program, Peter Schreier; communications, Clifford Weber; correspondence, Hilde Yaeger; and Ladies, Doris Ulrich. Dr. Allen C. Wooden, historian for the Delaware Saengerbund's souvenir booklet, brought the timeline up to date by adding the years' events since 1953, which already included ten years in Ogletown! To commemorate the 125th Stiftungsfest, board members donated a *Fahnenband*, an embroidered banner that is carried on the club's flag standard. This event demonstrated once again the pride and dedication of DSB members.

-Building Phase II-

In 1984 members looked into completing the plans drawn up in 1968. They voted on Phase II in May 1984 and planned an October ground-breaking. Since they would not be able to supply as much voluntary labor as

had been contributed during Phase I (the building of the Bauernstube, Deutsche Halle, and Tuckmantel Building), the club hired Hart Construction Co. of Newark to undertake the project. Bonds sold to DSB members financed the building. This was not a new idea. Treasurer William Sigmund gleaned from the minutes of the old Saengerbund that, in a meeting in December 1883, members voted to finance the purchase of the first German Hall by selling 600 certificates at $5 each to be paid back in six years at 6% interest. One hundred years later members responded well to this method of financing construction and invested in their club by also purchasing bonds.

The new complex was completed by July 1985. The clubhouse now had a new foyer, a balcony, rest rooms with handicapped access, and a *Nebenzimmer* with a beautiful stone fireplace built by Wilhelm Schulz. It was appropriate for banquets and smaller functions. When members were asked to suggest names for the room, they proposed Peter Minuit from Wesel who had commanded the *Kalmar Nyckel* from Sweden, and Baron Friedrich von Steuben, the officer who trained General Washington's army. Since the majority of the members were more familiar with the latter, the new Nebenzimmer was called the von Steuben Zimmer.

State and local dignitaries attended the dedication on September 8, 1985, which opened with ecumenical prayers led by the Reverend Russell Perkins and the

Newark Mayor Ron Gardener and Cultural Attache Dieter Murmann of the German Embassy assist Simon Schock at the ribbon cutting ceremony for the Phase II addition, congratulated by Representative Thomas Carper and Senator Joseph Biden.

Reverend Curtis Leins. President Simon Schock welcomed the guests. Hans Dieter Murmann, Cultural Attache of the Federal Republic of Germany in Washington, D.C., brought the congratulations of the German Embassy and a new German flag. Horst Fischer and the Frohe Klänge provided joyous music for dancing, and once again the Ladies prepared an elegant dinner.

Many members contributed to the enhancement of the new addition. Artist Lilly Budzialek donated a large painting of Castle Neuschwanstein and several smaller Alpine scenes; Walter Hagelstein donated an oil painting; Wilson (Bud) Swartout painted and donated a portrait of General von Steuben. Philip and Wilma Hoffecker provided funds for a solid oak table and chairs for the foyer. Alfred Pinehart built beautiful oak cabinets for the foyer and two large oak tables for the boardroom, and he and Phil Rice, Richard Schechinger, and Simon Schock handcrafted and installed the foyer staircase. Richard Schechinger added a bookcase in the boardroom. Andreas Dettling and Joseph Sell, the master carpenters in the time of the original

Saengerbund and the German Hall, would have been proud.

Landscaping in front and along the side of the building was taken care of by the club gardeners Elli and Rudi Beck, Mr. & Mrs. Mayer, Mr. & Mrs. Etter and Simon Schock. Alton and Ann Todd moved into the adjacent house. No better caretakers could have been found anywhere. Deliveries were made at all hours of the day, and Al was always the man with the key! In 1987, the club had the opportunity to purchase the adjoining property at 63 Salem Church Road. A positive decision by the board and members sealed the purchase, and 2.2 acres, including a house that is used as a rental property, were added to the Saengerbund's holdings.

-Entertainment Committee-

Under the 1968 constitution, the second vice president, who was also chair of the Entertainment Committee, was responsible for filling the calendar

The 1985 Board of Directors at the Phase II dinner party.
Seated: Carol Fricke, Linda Escheu, Jeanne Stanfield. Standing: Simon Schock, Werner Sumpf, Wilhelm Schulz, Erich Kaeks,
Alfred Escheu, Karl Schmidt, William Sigmund, William Klabe, who (except for Wm. Sigmund),
have all served as presidents of the DSB.

with events and the building with people. The early years' schedule included the Stiftungsfest, Easter Egg Hunt, Spring Concert, a May dance for teenagers, picnics for Pentecost and Father's Day, two Oktoberfests for the members, a *Bunter Abend* or evening entertainment, a children's Christmas party, and the members' *Tannenbaumabend.* A *Sylvester* (New Year's Eve) Ball closed the season and rang in the New Year. Because many of the younger immigrants missed the Fasching balls of their hometowns, one was added to the February calendar. This event became so popular that in subsequent years, two balls had to be scheduled. Joseph and Lee Pouser always took first prize as the best-costumed couple. Second vice presidents in charge of entertainment since the opening of the new hall in Ogletown include Tom Yost, Werner Sumpf, William Klabe, Joseph Pouser, Michael Zanfini, Eugene Ruff, Alida Cutts, George Keith, Ken Woodlin, Simon Schock, Wally Hansen, and Dieter Schulz. Their most important task is to hire the right band for the dances and Oktoberfest.

As news of the Saengerbund's beautiful clubhouse in Ogletown spread, visitors began arriving. The first guests from Germany, a band of eighty men from Saulgau, arrived in September 1972. Members hosted the guests in their homes overnight. In an article describing the group's tour, the *New York Staats Herold* reported that the Delaware Saengerbund's hospitality made a positive impression on the visitors. Tour arrangers Alfred Escheu, Peter Vassili, and Peter Degen told Saengerbund members that all German groups wanted to perform here! In subsequent years, choruses and bands from many German cities brought the newest dances and songs, but also knew that the old melodies would find an appreciative audience. All regions of Germany have been represented over the years, among them Duttenberg, Flensburg, Hamburg, Erfurt, Wendelstein, Moers, Pirmasens, Runkel, Göppingen, and Berlin. A visiting group from the Muscular Dystrophy Society of Berlin even enjoyed a wheelchair dance.

- Bundesverdienstkreuz-

The German Embassy occasionally recognizes the efforts of those who have dedicated themselves to the deepening of German American relations by awarding

them with the Federal Republic of Germany Friendship Award. Simon Schock was presented with the award in 1986 and Alfred Escheu in 1988 for their work in revitalizing the German singing society in Delaware.

The Federal Republic of Germany also awards the *Bundesverdienstkreuz,* or Distinguished Service Cross to individuals who have contributed in an extraordinary manner to the preservation of German culture. Few of these prestigious awards are presented in any year. However, at a memorable ceremony and reception at the German Embassy in Washington, D.C. on February 6, 1989, Karl Paschke, special representative of the *Bundespräsident,* presented the *Bundesverdienstkreuz* to Alfred Escheu and Simon Schock in recognition of their vision and determination to continue the work of a society that had been in existence in Delaware for over one hundred years when they joined. Although both men became citizens of their adopted country, they believed it was important to preserve the customs and culture of their homeland. The Saengerbund is indebted to both men for their years of dedication and recognizes with pride the high honor bestowed on them by the Federal Republic of Germany.

Alfred Escheu was born on January 29, 1933, in Neusäss near Augsburg. Upon completing school, he became an apprentice watchmaker and completed his

Simon Schock and Alfred Escheu received the
"Bundesverdienstkreuz" at the German Embassy in
Washington on February 6, 1989 for their commitment
to the growth of the Delaware Saengerbund.
(Photo by Andrea Escheu Haaz)

Meister Prüfung, or master craftsman exam, in 1951. In January 1955 he sailed from Bremerhaven to New York City on the *M. S. Berlin*, then traveled to Wilmington, where his sister Heidi Valiante lived. He was immediately employed at Allemann's jewelry store on Orange Street. He joined the Saengerbund, was called to serve in the Navy, and spent two years as a repairer of instruments on the *USS Sierra* and *USS Everglades*. After his honorable discharge, Escheu returned to Wilmington and became Allemann's partner, then sole owner of the business. He married Linda A. Gannon of Delaware City, and together they had four children, Alfred Jr., Andrea, Rainier, and Teresa.

Escheu has been a "mover and shaker" from the beginning; tatkräftiges Handeln is part of his Swabian Bavarian heritage. He has served on the board numerous times, played soccer, been an active dancer and president of the Enzian Volkstanzgruppe and, during the Ogletown years, has guided the Property Committee in its building projects. He has worked unselfishly for the good of the organization despite occasional opposition and differences of opinion. He believes that sacrifice on the part of the members is necessary for the good of the organization. Alfred Escheu displays great pride in his heritage. While upholding the Saengerbund's constitution, he has followed in the footsteps of the original Saengerbund members 150 years ago. His hope for the future is that "the younger generation will carry the torch forward, abide by this constitution, and continue to be proud of their heritage." He was made an honorary president of the Saengerbund in 2000.

Simon Schock was born on August 22, 1936 in Odessa, Ukraine. Growing up in a German diaspora, he was taught to speak German as a child by his parents. They also taught him love and respect for their German heritage. In 1945 his family arrived as refugees in Dachau, Bavaria. There, Schock finished school and trained as carpenter, staircase, and cabinetmaker. After his family immigrated to Wilmington in 1957, Schock immediately found work as carpenter and later was trained as machinist. He looked in at the Saengerbund, but had little interest in a club where "old people" met. That changed when he stopped by again one evening in 1965 and casually asked President Emil Dahnken: "What's there to do?" Dahnken replied, "Come by tomorrow morning and you'll see." He worked hard that day and chuckles, "I haven't stopped since!"

Schock soon became interested in the Saengerbund's history and salvaged many of the society's records before the building was razed. He married Vera Wacker and their wedding reception was the last one held in the old German Hall. Because he wanted to see his sons Rudolf and Robert play soccer, Simon did not rest until the Saengerbund offered a youth soccer program. He served on the board many times and, as frequent chair of the Entertainment Committee, made sure that the house was always full of life and people. Later, as Simon Schock himself became one of the "old people," he joined the chorus and enjoyed contact with the singing groups of Philadelphia and the Nordoestlicher Saengerbund. He was elected president of the Nordoestlicher Saengerbund for three terms.

Alfred Escheu and Simon Schock have both worked tirelessly to create an oasis where German culture and heritage can be nurtured. Both men have rolled up their sleeves and gone to work themselves before asking other members to help. This admirable attitude has made it easy for others to work with them, and many friendships have been the result. The Saengerbund is their life's work and their hobby, and they appreciate deeply the sacrifices their families had to make. Both families have been supportive and have taken active parts—as dancers in the Enzian Volkstanzgruppe, soccer players, coaches, singers, kitchen cochair of the Ladies, and board members.

Today neither man rests on his laurels. Both are involved with the building program and the calendar. Others follow their footsteps. Property chair Richard Leaning is often seen with clipboard in hand, making lists of repairs and needed improvements. When the main hall needed renovation, the Summer of '94 Gang undertook the task of paneling the walls in light oak. This gang included Escheu and Schock, Ralph Olivier, Ted Baumeister, Lois and Howard Meyer, Carl Renner, Andreas Wolf, Ed Brandenberger, and Bob Wamsher.

-Building Phase III-

President Carl Renner, who received the German American Friendship Award in 1994, called together an ad-hoc committee to work out a long-range plan for the society's changing needs and appointed as its members Edward Brandenberger, William Cox, Margaret Johnston, Richard Leaning, Irene Rice, Rudy Schock, Dieter Schulz, and Robert Spittle. Their report included a detailed financial analysis. Renner also supervised plans for the Phase III building program as it progressed throughout 1994. Architect Ralph Olivier drew up plans for an improved kitchen, a game room, a new office, and library. To finance the project, members again purchased bonds. Plans for a new pavilion were underway also, because hurricanes and high winds had damaged the first structure, built in 1970. To everyone's dismay, a tornado-like storm and rain in 1990 collapsed the roof of the new pavilion when it was about 80 percent complete, so that project had to start all over again.

Hart Construction Company began work in March 1995, and the clubhouse addition was finished by fall. The New Castle County building inspector approved the new kitchen one day before the opening of Oktoberfest! The Ladies of the Delaware Saengerbund took it in stride and were able to cook for thousands of festival guests using the new equipment. But nature was not cooperative. A tornado struck again and destroyed the second pavilion. This was Simon Schock's greatest disappointment and frustration—that the pavilion had to be rebuilt three times! May he take some comfort in the old German saying *Aller guten Dinge sind drei!*— "All good things (and some bad things) come in threes!" And may the new all-steel pavilion survive future storms so it can continue to be used for picnics and concerts—or just as a place for sitting outdoors. The old club members at 205 East 6th Street would have enjoyed just such a retreat.

Today the Saengerbund has the complicated task of accruing sufficient funds to maintain the property, continue the activities, and assure the society's future. So far the club has been fortunate in being able to rely on members with financial expertise who can steer it in the right direction. In fact, the record shows that Saengerbund officers, board, and standing committee members have led the organization so effectively that membership reached the ceiling of 800 several times. The members are the Saengerbund's greatest asset. Much work is done voluntarily and with great dedication. In turn, all members, active and passive, enjoy opportunities for friendship and learning when they participate in the Saengerbund's subgroups that are reported on in the chapters that follow.

The Clubhouse in Ogletown was built in three phases, mostly by the members themselves.

11

Delaware Saengerbund Chorus

Freude, schöner Götterfunken, Tochter aus Elysium!
Wir betreten feuertrunken,
*   Himmlische, dein Heilgtum.*
Deine Zauber binden wieder,
*   was die Mode streng geteilt;*
Alle Menschen werden Brüder,
*   wo dein sanfter Flügel weilt.*
Seid umschlungen, Millionen!
*   Seid umschlungen, Millionen!*
Diesen Kuss der ganzen Welt!
*   Brüder, überm Sternenzelt*
muss ein lieber Vater wohnen,
*   muss ein lieber Vater wohnen!*

Mortals join the mighty chorus,
   which the morning stars began;
Father love is reigning o'er us,
   brother love binds man to man.
Ever singing, march we onward,
   victors in the midst of strife.
Joyful music leads us sunward
   in the triumph song of life!

-Schiller/Beethoven

"The importance of music often grows as immigrants and their families live in another culture," wrote ethno-musicologist Matthew Shippee in an article on immigration in the *Portland Press Herald*, June 25, 2001. "Once you separate from home, the music and any other art form or tradition takes on more value for its symbolic importance and what it means to remember your heritage. Music is one of those fundamental characteristics of culture that instantly jogs nostalgic memories of a former life. Music makes a very strong bond."

For the Delaware Saengerbund, choral singing was—and still is—the bond that holds the club together. After the move to Ogletown, the DSB Chorus, now frequently referred to as the Singers, again had a place to rehearse, give concerts, and socialize. After Otto

Genhart retired from directing in 1971, Arthur Lemke was called out of retirement to take up the baton a second time. The mixed chorus was singing a wider variety of music, and more voices were needed. When Alfred Gilgenast became chair of the music committee in 1976, he urged members to break out of their lethargy. Paraphrasing John F. Kennedy, he exhorted them to "ask not what the club can do for you, but ask what you can do for your club!" Gilgenast lived by this principle for fifty years. Always diligent, just hours before the 1977 Spring concert, he arranged the tables, filled the flower vases, and checked one last time to see that everything was in order. Then he sat down in the Bauernstube for a well-deserved rest. At that moment he was called to join the heavenly chorus. In the evening the Singers, wearing black armbands in honor of their Sangesbruder who had dedicated his life to the continuation of the German song, sang their best.

Dorothy Dodds followed Alfred Gilgenast as chair of the Music Committee. The chair's important, behind-the-scenes job includes selecting the music and maintaining the music library, planning programs and coordinating events with other clubs. Charles Berr led the committee starting in 1981 and held the post faithfully for almost twenty years. The German Embassy honored his work behind the scenes with the Federal Republic of Germany Friendship Award in 1998.

Between 1978 and the present day, the DSB Chorus has had four directors. Betty Metz directed the Singers from 1978 to 1983. Under her leadership, the Singers cut their first record album, and William Klabe was elected vice president of the Nordoestlicher Saengerbund in 1979. He was the first Delaware Saengerbund member to serve as an officer of the umbrella organization.

Donald Rittenhouse, well known for his work with the Newark High School Madrigal Singers, followed Metz as director in 1983 and led the chorus in great style for two years. He then resigned due to the press of other obligations, and Betty Metz Demonic returned for one year. During this time, Betty Moudy was the accompanist.

David Linton, music teacher at William Penn High School, was engaged as the new music director in 1986, first with accompanists Sheila Gehrlein and Henry Chisholm and later with Keith Olivier, gifted tenor and accompanist. When Olivier resigned to pursue studies for the ministry in Philadelphia, Ruth Ann Chisholm was engaged as accompanist. For eighteen years, David Linton devoted his time and expertise to developing the rich sound that caused the Singers to stand out among all the societies of the Nordoestlicher Saengerbund.

In 1987, the Singers participated in the Saengerbund's first ecumenical *Erntedankfest-Gottesdienst*. Since Zion Lutheran Church and Sacred Heart Catholic Church had been linked closely to the Saengerbund's history, the services were held in these two churches in alternate years. They took place on the first Sunday in October, the traditional German Thanksgiving Sunday, instead of on American Thanksgiving Day when most singers preferred to be at home with their families or singing in their own church choirs. Church organists, the Johannes Brass ensemble, and the DSB chorus directed by David Linton provided the festive music. The annual Erntedankfest took on an even more special meaning in 1987 when President Ronald Reagan designated October 6, the date of the landing of the Krefelder families and the founding of Germantown, as German American Day. The following year, the Singers and board of directors were invited to participate in the German American Heritage Day, October 6, 1988, in Washington, D.C. They enjoyed lunch at the German Embassy, sang on the steps of the Capitol and in the Caucus Room of the House of Representatives, and attended an embassy reception in the evening. This was a joyous occasion, but it was surpassed by the absolute euphoria of November 9, 1989, when the Berlin Wall came tumbling down. Beethoven's "Ode to Joy" resounded around the world. Until that day, few Germans and Americans believed they would see the reunification of Germany in their lifetime. Several German clubs in the Philadelphia area spontaneously gathered at the Liberty Bell to celebrate this great event. On October 3, 1990, the world opened again for the people of the five new German states. With German unification a reality, they could travel, relocate to join relatives, or pursue careers outside of Germany.

The 44th Sängerfest of the Nordoestlicher Saengerbund took place in May 1991 with David Linton and Donald Winzer as festival conductors of the mass chorus. The Nordoestlicher Saengerbund had previously discontinued the practice of competitive prize singing in favor of a public concert presented by the combined voices for some time now. Without the pressure of having to compete for first, second, or third place, chorus members are able to enjoy the camaraderie of a Sängerfest weekend.

In October 1993, the Singers traveled to Washington, DC to participate in the first National Sängerfest. The evening program in Constitution Hall included performances by the combined chorus of the Nordoestlicher Saengerbund, the German American Singing Societies of New England, the Pacific Saengerbund, two choirs from Germany, and the North American Singers Union. Festival music director was Klaus Evert, director of music at the German School of Washington, DC.

The Nordoestlicher Saengerbund's 45th Sängerfest took place in 1994 on Long Island. Delaware's leadership in the organization was recognized when Simon Schock was elected president, and Sonja Ciresa, secretary. This special honor also carried a heavy responsibility, because the new officers needed to address the problem of how to increase membership in the struggling member choruses.

Sonja Ciresa, who joined the Delaware Saengerbund in 1988, brought with her a great knowledge of German choral music and skill as a pianist. Born in Wangen, Württemberg, she first immigrated to Potomac, Illinois, in 1947. She then moved to West New York, New Jersey in 1952 and joined the Frohsinn Damenchor, the Hudson County Singers, and the Schwäbische Saengerbund in Brooklyn. She also directed two men's choruses, the Patterson Saengerbund and the Saxonia, and served as vice president of the Hudson County Singers, a mixed chorus. In Ogletown, Ciresa formed the *Saengerbund Hausmusik*, a quartet of three violins and piano. These musical friends enhance numerous Saengerbund events with their festive music. They also entertain outside the society at weddings and special celebrations, including much-appreciated performances in nursing homes.

When the Singers were asked to form a *Kinderchor*, a children's chorus, Mary Ann Dowd offered to teach all interested children. Between 1995 and 1997, boys and girls, ages 4 through 12, learned the classic German children's songs and performed at spring concerts and Christmas parties, where they earned much applause from all present. Unfortunately the chorus dissolved, due perhaps to the broad range of voices and ages, but one day there may be another group of parents and children eager to spark a new Kinderchor!

The 1999 annual spring concert was the last one conducted by David Linton. As part of the program, Edith and Charles Berr received DSB service awards, and Dorothy Dodds, daughter of Honorary President Erich Kaeks, the golden needle, the fifty-year pin for active membership in the chorus. Ten years earlier, in 1989, Dorothy's father was awarded the sixty-year pin, another joyous note to ring through the society's history.

Despite the change in directors, the Singers did not miss a beat, for Robert E. Bunnell picked up the baton in September 1999. Rehearsals again were in full swing with Sharon Williams as the new accompanist, and Hilmar Fricke as the new music committee chair. Today the fifty-voice chorus presents a spring concert for club members and guests, but opens its annual Advent concert on the first Sunday of December to the public. Both programs, the latter with a selection of German and English carols and winter songs, are also presented to the residents of the Jeanne Jugan Home on Salem Church Road where senior citizens appreciate this Spring and Christmas cheer.

Guest choruses are also appreciative of the Saengerbund's hospitality. In November 2000, the tenth anniversary of the fall of the Berlin Wall, the *gropies*, a youth chorus from Berlin, presented a lively concert to a standing-room-only audience at the Saengerbund. The concert featured modern arrangements of folk songs with choreographed moves to match. All those who hosted the young people enjoyed sharing experiences, touring, and shopping with them. A highlight of their visit was the Berlin Airlift exhibit at the Dover Air Force Base Museum, arranged by DSB member, Brigadier General Thomas Lauppe. This was an especially poignant history lesson for young people whose parents had been children in Berlin during the time the Allied Airlift kept Berliners alive.

A high-school group from Goeppingen visited in 1999 and again in 2001, and wowed the full houses with their music. What made their programs so special was that the young people had learned German folksongs at the Saengerbund's request. By contemporary German standards, clubs such as the Delaware Saengerbund are considered old-fashioned, and folk songs are an unknown genre among German youth. Yet these students, who were taught by professional musicians Gabi and Peter Grabinger, took to the songs and liked them! Ray Lynch, dance master at a ballet school in Stuttgart, choreographed the songs so that the program was very professional and delighted the performers as much as the audience. Saengerbund members were astounded that their small request for traditional German songs had such an effect on this group from Württemberg, homeland of Friedrich Silcher. Interactions with international groups like these confirm that *Singen bringt Freude*—singing brings joy—and often a welcome celebration.

"Celebration" is a key word now that the Saengerbund has begun preparing for a very special double celebration in 2003. On May 23-25, 2003, the Nordoestlicher Saengerbund's 48th Sängerfest will coincide with the Delaware Saengerbund's 150th Stiftungsfest. This promises to be a special weekend for all singers, members, and guests. Robert E. Bunnell will serve as festival conductor and Johanna Teubner-

Prussak as coconductor of twenty-six choruses (nearly 700 voices). Sharon Williams will be the accompanist, and the Newark Symphony will provide orchestral music. The Delaware Saengerbund, the oldest and only German singing society in the state, is delighted and proud to be able to share its German musical heritage with members and the general public.

Special guest at the reception was the Minnesänger, the prize trophy won by the Philadelphia Männerchor in 1912. (Photo by Cox)

The Delaware Saengerbund celebrated the 150th anniversary of the Nordoestlicher Saengerbund at the 147th Stiftungsfest with a reception and exhibit. President Simon Schock and Secretary Sonja Ciresa of the NOSB with Bernard Freitag, president of the German Society of Pennsylvania.

12

Ladies of the Delaware Saengerbund

ESSEN IST DAS ALLERBEST

Kanon zu 3 Stimmen

Es - sen ist das Al - ler - best schon seit

vie - len hun - dert Jahr' ge - west, das

Al - ler - best, Al - ler - best, ja!

Worte und Weise: Helmut Bräutigam
Möseler Verlag, Wolfenbüttel / Voggenreiter Verlag, Bad Godesberg

Three picnics were held during the first summer in Ogletown. The women brought potato salad in the biggest bowls they could find at home and served it to accompany the chicken grilled by the men. Homemade cakes were eaten as fast as they appeared on the tables. Afterwards, Elnora "Toots" Schweiger and Kathryn Mayer invited the women to consider forming a ladies organization similar to the Damen-Verein at the old German Hall in Wilmington. Twenty-seven women attended the first meeting, and on October 28, 1968, the new auxiliary, Ladies of the Delaware Saengerbund, was officially organized. The first officers were Elnora Schweiger, president; Margot Trager, vice president; Valerie Hafeken, secretary; Käte

Angel, treasurer; and Wally Alberer, first kitchen chairperson.

The organization's purpose was to support the Delaware Saengerbund in all ways possible. Providing food at meetings and affairs was their main task. The Ladies' minutes for November 1968 recorded that they received a $100 loan from the Saengerbund treasury. By July 1969, the Ladies repaid the loan, and by December 1969 the records show a balance of $3,025.27 in the Ladies' treasury, enough to purchase new kitchen utensils.

By a decision of the Saengerbund's Board of Directors, the Ladies were in charge of the club kitchen. The rules of order taught in all German *Haushaltschulen*, or household academies, are put into effect for everyone's safety. The kitchen chairperson presides over the Kitchen Committee (a subcommittee), and the kitchen is run like a soccer team. Whatever the occasion, everyone plays a position, whether it is working at the preparation table, cooking, scrubbing pots and pans, decorating the hall, or serving. Afterwards, everyone cleans up, and no one leaves until the last dish is put away and the floor is swept. Of course there is always time to laugh and share memories of disasters or successes.

Not all women of the Ladies' organization belong to the kitchen committee, but those who do have made a commitment to work regularly for all kinds of club functions and catered affairs. They often take courses in food handling and food safety and are semi-professional at cooking and serving. For many years, Gabriel Sukalo, chef at the University of Delaware Dining Services, worked closely with the Ladies and taught them many skills.

Waltraud Alberer was the first kitchen chairperson. Born in Bad Lippspringe, Westphalia, she and her husband Frank emigrated from Austria to Wilmington in 1953. Wally had a unique talent for recruiting help; her sense of humor and persuasive manner enticed many formerly-reluctant helpers into the kitchen. The additional help made it possible for the Delaware Saengerbund to participate in the first Newark Community Day on the University of Delaware campus. The men carried tables, grills, water, ice, and all other necessities, while the women browned and sold sausages, Frikadellen, frankfurters, homemade cakes, and other German specialties.

Over the past thirty years, the Ladies of the Delaware Saengerbund have been fortunate to have had other outstanding women as kitchen chairpersons: Margaret Sporay followed Waltraud Alberer, then Hilde Schwoegler, Bertha Holsten, Mary Farver, Linda Escheu, and Annemarie McNeal. All have acknowledged that the help of the Ladies and the support of the Saengerbund members made their work easier.

Annemarie McNeal, kitchen chairperson since 1982, grew up in Wilhelmsdorf, Bavaria, and immigrated to the United States after marrying husband Willard in 1958. As an employee and later manager of Eckerd's Drug Store, she gained the valuable training and expertise needed to take on the demanding job of Oktoberfest food chair with its responsibility for feeding thousands of visitors. The

German Embassy awarded the Federal Republic of Germany Friendship Award to Annemarie in 1989.

Food is the most basic part of any ethnic culture and binds the generations together at mealtime while also preserving the group's heritage. Just as some members enjoy eating a meal that "tastes like home," others yearn for a meal they enjoyed while traveling in Germany. The Ladies have met this need and fulfilled these yearnings by preparing wonderful meals of *Rouladen, Sauerbraten, Schnitzel,* along with their well-known *Kartoffelsalat,* homemade cakes and buttercream *Torten,* a fitting end to any meal. So dedicated are they to preserving tradition that several years ago, when the WHYY camera crew was filming the German kitchen during Oktoberfest preparations, one lady noticed that the Kartoffelsalat recipe was lying on a counter. Fearing it might be filmed and therefore no longer a secret, she quickly tucked it into the *Ausschnitt* of her Dirndl blouse!

During a sabbatical semester in 1982, Professor Trudy Gilgenast made it her goal to collect customs and recipes from DSB members and the German American community of Delaware. That was not as easy as it sounds. Just as the Ladies of the Delaware Saengerbund are secretive about the ingredients and steps involved in making potato salad and herring salad, so other cooks were unwilling to disclose their recipes. When completed, *Das Mehl ist anders: The Flour is Different* brought together recipes from all parts of Germany. The title was chosen because, whenever a recipe didn't turn out the way it was expected, the frustrated immigrant housewife would sigh: *Kein Wunder, das Mehl ist anders*—"No wonder, the flour is different!"

As had been the custom at the old Saengerbund, the Ogletown Ladies also worked closely with the entertainment committee at parties for the members' children. Now that there was a big meadow to have an Easter egg hunt, it became an annual event like the Christmas party and the picnic. In addition, Bertha Holsten encouraged the Ladies to try catering weddings and other special celebrations for members. These endeavors soon became part of the Ladies' calendar and were so sought after that there were not enough weekends available in the year.

Oktoberfest and the annual Christmas bazaar are the year's most important events. At both the public is invited to enjoy the atmosphere of a German town celebration. All major cities of Germany and many smaller towns open the Christmas season with a *Christkindlmarkt* (Christ Child's Market) or *Weihnachtsmarkt* (Christmas Market), an outdoor market in the center of the city. There, the visitors warm themselves with *Glühwein*, or hot punch, as they stroll along the colorful stalls in the market square. At the Saengerbund's *Christkindlmarkt*, as the Ladies' bazaar is now called to evoke memories of visits to the great Christmas markets, many people arrive early in order to be sure of purchasing their favorite foods like the seasonal *Heringsalat* (herring salad) or homemade *Kartoffelsalat*, which is always in season. For many years, master baker Rudolf Beck prepared the traditional Christmas *Stollen*, and Elli Beck the butter-cream *Torten* for the festival. When Rudi Beck retired, Wally Hansen, Alex Piragow, and Sonja Ciresa took on the job of forming and baking over 400 Stollen each year.

Some of the women work all year making knitted garments, ornaments, and other handmade objects. Advent wreaths, greens, and door or table displays are creatively crafted with red ribbons, fir branches, pine cones, and candles. A Secret Santa workshop holds special delight for children. There they secretly purchase gifts for siblings, parents and friends and have them gift-wrapped. Of course, some children are so excited with their purchases that they can't wait until the magical day, and present their gifts immediately. White elephant treasures make unique gifts, as do the many books in both German and English. Imported candies, marzipan, chocolates filled with brandy, and imported linens, glass, toys, Advent calendars, and clothing offer an abundance of gift options. The children's dance group of the Enzian Volkstanzgruppe entertains with traditional dances, and the Saengerbund Hausmusik plays festive carols as Santa Claus's arrival at the Christkindlmarkt comes closer and closer.

On both sides of the ocean, *Weihnacht* customs and traditions evoke memories as dear as those shared by long-time Saengerbund member Johanna Hilsenrad in *Das Mehl ist anders*:

Sometimes a special recipe brings memories of a special time or place in your life. … and I would like to share [my] memories with you.

Saxony, in the southeastern section of Germany, is where I was born. I spent my childhood in Chemnitz, known today as Karl-Marx-Stadt. It was then and still is today a large industrial center, situated in the foothills of the Erzgebirge, or Ore Mountains. … It was a silver mining center, but more important and sheer magic for children, it was the cottage-industry center for the manufacture of toys and Christmas decorations that were sent thoughout the world.

Perhaps that's why the pre-Christmas season was so special for us children at home. Advent! At night by candlelight … we shared stories … sang and played music together. The children, there were four of us, were allowed to stay up longer than usual, and the special preparations for the holiday baking season began. First the cookies! My mother rolled out the dough and we children cut out all the fancy forms that were later to hang on our tree. Then the Stollen! The special recipes native to the area and jealously guarded by each family . . . are sometimes known as Dresdener Christstollen, after the capital of Saxony. … They were a family affair. We children would blanch and peel sweet and bitter almonds and clean and pick over raisins of three different varieties. Each of us watched closely that not too much was detoured into the other three mouths! We watched and learned as the grownups cut citron and prepared all the other ingredients for this once a year delicacy, the traditional Weihnachtsstollen!

Now I have lived in the United States for thirty years, but I still keep house the way I learned to do so long ago at home, and the special customs have never lost their meanings. My daughter and her family celebrate Advent and Christmas in much the same way, having learned in my house when she was little, and I hope that someday my only granddaughter will

The Christmas Stollen, drawing by Kathryn S. Dodson.

continue and carry on the customs and bakery of this loveliest time of the year.

In 1970, mindful of those who would continue the traditions they too had grown up with, the Ladies of the Delaware Saengerbund decided to take their teenage daughters under their wings and teach them the ways of their heritage. Over the years, regular mother and daughter teams developed, including Elnora and Suzanne Schweiger (Grzybowski), Wally and Diana Alberer (Levering), Marge and Lori Nagy (Maliszewski), Jeanne and Hannah Stanfield (Genoese), Irmgard, Monika, and Karen Sukalo (Swank), Mary Ann and Stephanie Bobik, Margaret Sigmund and daughter-in-law Heidi Sigmund. All remember the special events like the May Queen dance and the Mother and Daughter dinners that were held in the 1970s.

The 20th anniversary of the Ladies was dedicated to Toots Schweiger. Her love of children—she was the mother of five—inspired her to become president of the P.T.A. at Mary C. I. Williams School in Wilmington, where she started the first free breakfast program for underprivileged children. At the Saengerbund, she served as the president of the Ladies from 1968 to 1970, and again from 1972 to 1975. Daughter Suzanne Grzybowski followed in her mother's footsteps, becoming president from 1992 to 1998.

The 25th anniversary in 1993 was dedicated to Waltraud Alberer and Bertha Holsten in recognition of their contributions: Wally for her many hours of craft work for the annual Christkindlmarkt and as kitchen chairperson, and Bertha for starting the catering service for weddings and club functions. All presidents have been skillful leaders of a diverse women's group. They were from different regions in Germany and America, and no two cooked or did anything the same way. Heidi Valiante, Margaret Sporay, Margaret Johnston, Mary Ann Bobik, Joan Wooden, Ann Smith, Margaret Sigmund, and Doris Lang have all held the important position of president. Each one has treasured the joyous moment when the current president of the Ladies presents a sizable check to the president of the Delaware Saengerbund, the result of another year's hard work for the well-being of the club.

"We work for the club, that's our purpose. We don't entertain the members, we feed them," says Joan Wooden, who at age 83 is still active as Ladies vice president. "But most important for a well-run society is a good leadership, women who understand the requirements of the constitution and see to it that they are followed. Then you'll have continuity." For a Ladies group that has kept German traditions since 1896, that continuity includes the tradition of serving *Kaffee und Kuchen*—coffee and cake—at the end of each business meeting. *Ja, die Liebe geht durch den Magen!* "Love is a happy stomach!"

-Teen-Age Group-

When it became apparent that other teenagers were interested in participating, a coed group known as TAG was formed. The group has its own officers so that the young people learn to conduct the group in an efficient and democratic manner. They choose activities that interest them such as camping trips, dances and hayrides, roller-skating parties, and trips to the beach, ski slopes, Great Adventure, Williamsburg, and Busch Gardens. During DSB functions, they help by directing parking and checking coats. Participating in TAG helps young people who do not see each other during the week form close bonds.

TAG members also hold fundraisers to pay their expenses. They have manned the soda booth at the annual picnic and at soccer games, kept exact records of bake sales and car washes, and sold homemade decorations at the Christmas Market. They also cook and serve an annual spaghetti dinner each year.

After several years under the aegis of the Ladies organization, the teen group became independent, but retained the help of an adult advisor. The first advisors were Anne Yenkevich and Helga Schulz, followed by Mary Ann Bobik, Renee Rice and Cindi Spink, Charles Schauber, and Klaus Vikari. Several current DSB adult members started by participating in TAG. Among them are Diana Alberer, Stephanie and Barbara Bobik, Freddy Escheu Jr., Tommy Keith; Joe Pouser, Brian Schulz, and Mark Yaeger. Each year new members join when the older members graduate from high school. Saengerbund members always appreciate the teenagers' friendly smiles when they help with club affairs and hope there will always be young people who are interested in their heritage.

13

Enzian Volkstanzgruppe

Tanzen und Springen,
Singen und Klingen,
Fa la la la, fa la la la la la la .
Lauten und Geigen
sollen nicht schweigen.
Zu musizieren und jubilieren
steht all zeit mein Sinn,
Fa la la la, fa la la la la la la.

Dancing and springing
Singing and ringing
Fa la la la, fa la la la la la la.
Lute and fiddle
Shall not be silent.
Music to make and celebrate
Sets my spirit at a high state.
Fa la la la, fa la la la la la la.

-Hans Leo Hassler

Margot Trager came to Wilmington from Eckartshausen in Hesse in 1954. Her husband Richard Trager was already a member of the Delaware Saengerbund. When Margot joined the club, she dreamed of and talked about forming a German folk dancing group. Many years later—in 1968—she finally convinced Richard and three other couples to try it at least once! Her sister Ingeborg and brother-in-law George Keith, Helga and Karl-Heinz Schulz, and Gisela and Tom Yost responded and enjoyed themselves. And so the *Enzian Volks-tanzgruppe*, the Enzian Folk Dance Group (EVTG) was born.

The eight dancers learned their first steps from the *Bristoler Tanzbuch* and practiced in the Bauernstube. Their first public performance was in October 1968 at the Saengerbund's Oktoberfest, which was held that year at the Turners' Wilmington clubhouse. The *Gebirgskinder Ländler*—Dance of the Mountain Children—became their signature dance. However the dancers found that learning new steps from a book was

The blue Enzian Alpine flower is the emblem of the Enzian Volkstanzgruppe.

not ideal, so they were delighted to learn of a folk dance group in Reading, Pennsylvania, the *Gebirgstrachten-verein Edelweiss,* usually called Edelweiss dancers or GTV for short. The Edelweiss dancers agreed to teach the Enzian group original Bavarian dances if they were willing to travel to Reading every Friday evening. The GTV became the Enzian Volkstanzgruppe's *Patenverein,* the responsible godparents of the fledgling group. It was only natural that Enzian and Edelweiss, the best-loved flowers of the Alpine countries, soon developed a close friendship while practicing the figure dances and *Schuhplattler,* the shoe-slapping dance associated with Bavaria.

The Schuhplattler originated in the Bavarian Alps, and was originally performed as a pastime by isolated lumberjacks. The dance mimicked the Alpine *Auerhahn,* a fowl similar to a ruffed grouse that, during mating season, makes eccentric leg motions while dancing around the female bird. Figure dances like this one evolved as courting rituals where young men and women could secretly look for a partner for life.

The dancers' first *Dirndls* were sewn by hand, and the men wore *Lederhosen* purchased at a Bavarian clothing store in Germany. If they wanted to perform outside of the club, they knew they would need a *Tracht,* traditional Bavarian attire. The dancers chose the *Miesbacher Festtagstracht,* which is worn in Miesbach, a small village in Bavaria in the Tegernsee region, on Sundays, festival days, and outings. The woman's Tracht has six specific parts: white blouse, pleated skirt, bodice, apron, silk scarf, and hat. The simpler *Dirndl*-style dress may be worn for informal dances, and the dancers themselves have been able to make their own Dirndls. The men's costume replicates clothing worn by farmers in the mountains in the eighteenth and nineteenth centuries. Their clothing had

The founders of the Enzian Volkstanzgruppe, 1968
Front: Ingeborg Keith, Helga Schulz, Gisela Yost, Margot Trager
Back: George Keith, Karl-Heinz Schulz, Tom Yost, Richard Trager.

to last, so their shirts were made of sturdy linen, the jackets of felt and loden, and the pants and shoes of leather. Often decorative green embroidery was added to the pants. Wool or cotton stockings were knitted in two parts, the socks and the *Stutzen,* a piece covering the calf. A black, low-brimmed hat adorned with a *Gamsbart,* a brush made of mountain goat hair, completed the outfit. These pieces now comprise the Tracht worn by all Bavarian folk-dancing groups. A *Trachtenmutter* cares for the expensive outfits and makes sure that the clothing is worn properly. The terms used by the folk dance group are included in the Glossary.

In March 1969, the EVTG elected its first officers: George Keith, president; Karl-Heinz Schulz, *Vorplattler* and secretary; and Helga Schulz, treasurer. Also at this meeting, a *Kindertanzgruppe* was formed with these nine first members: Andrea Escheu, Gary Keith, Tommy Keith, Anne-Marie Schmidt, Brian Schulz, Christel

Andrea Escheu and Brian Schultz, 1971.

Trager, Jürgen Trager, John Washburn, and Heidi Yost. Accordionist Viola Palo accompanied the dancers at their practice sessions and performances, a *Liebesdienst*—service of love—that she carried out with

dedication and skill for the next three decades. Jim Hall and Stephen Armstrong learned to play the accordion and joined the group.

Since 1969 the Enzian Volkstanzgruppe has developed into a strong organization within the Delaware Saengerbund. It has its own constitution, officers, and treasury, but all members are also Saengerbund members, as required by the DSB's constitution. Working together harmoniously, the two groups have been able to present a positive image of the German culture in Delaware and elsewhere. EVTG members have danced in schools and nursing homes, at fairgrounds and festivals, wherever traditional German dancing was welcomed. The group has always attracted large, enthusiastic audiences and sometimes invited those watching to try some of the steps themselves. When the Ministry of Caring began serving international dinners to benefit Emmanuel Dining Room, the Enzian Volkstanzgruppe hosted the annual German Oktoberfest dinner, and for many years now all generations have helped in this fundraising effort. The city of Wilmington invited the Enzian Volkstanzgruppe to participate in the New Year's Eve First Night celebration in 1994, and EVTG has been a part of this celebration ever since.

In 1974, the Enzian Volkstanzgruppe joined the regional *Gauverband Nordamerika*—or North American Schuhplattler Association—an umbrella organization for dancers similar to the Nordoestlicher Saengerbund for singing societies. Every three years the Gauverband sponsors a festival for the member associations that includes a *Preisplatteln,* a dancing contest. The dancers have traveled widely throughout the United States to attend these festivals. As is the custom, each dance group carries a colorful flag in the opening ceremonies. The EVTG's beautifully embroidered flag was dedicated during a German *Bauernmesse* —a peasant-style mass held in Wilmington's St. Peter's Cathedral in 1979.

The Enzian Volktanzgruppe was delighted when the Delaware Saengerbund was chosen to host the 16th Gaufest of the *North American Schuhplattler Verband* in 1997. From July 3-6, this festival brought together sixty-two clubs with more than 2,000 dancers, among them 100 guests from Bavaria. The EVTG's Richard Grieb and William Sigmund from the Saengerbund served as cochairs and promised a "little bit of work and a lot of fun."… The executive committee included Brian and

Stephanie Schulz, Carl Renner, Alfred Escheu, and Norma Grieb.

Preparations for the July event included a three-day weekend at the Saengerbund in Ogletown where 170 dancers were trained as judges for the *Preisplatteln,* the dance competition. Tommy Keith, EVTG Vorplattler, was elected as Youth Administrator for all of North America.

For the occasion, the Saengerbund erected a beautiful white tent large enough to hold all 2,000 guests and decorated it with Bavarian white and blue banners. It was a cheerful place to be for special meals provided by the Ladies of the Delaware Saengerbund and for the times when the dance groups assembled.

The highlight of every Gaufest is the dance competition. Each group wants to win the coveted *Wanderpreis* donated by Bavaria's Ministerpresident. In 1997, sixteen groups participated. Following the competition, the festival banquet in the tent was a first in North American Gaufest history. The evening began with a flag presentation by the U.S. Marine Corps Wilmington Training Center and the Newark Fife & Drum Corps. Guest groups processed in, wearing their colorful Trachten. Richard Grieb, EVTG president, greeted the guests, and American and German representatives delivered speeches. Wilmington Mayor James Sills made a surprise visit and was warmly greeted. Saengerbund member, restaurateur, and chef John Degenhardt and his staff catered the elegant banquet that ended with confectioner Heinz Ambrosch's classic *Apfelstrudel* with vanilla sauce. Jakob Titz and his band provided music for dancing until late into the evening.

On Sunday morning, the tent was clean and ready for the traditional *Bauernmesse.* Alfred and Linda Escheu prepared the liturgy. Reverend Christopher Kopec preached in English and German. The Philadelphia Zither Ensemble accompanied the Singers as they sang Bavarian folk hymns during the mass. The day continued with a picnic followed by the *Schornsteinfegerball,* the chimney sweep's ball, which provided everyone with one more chance to get together before saying goodbye. Children had fun playing games, and the nursery gave the little ones a place to rest. Rest was what everyone looked forward to on the last day of the festival. The three-day gathering had involved a tremendous effort by many, many people, but nobody would have wanted to miss it. "It's fun to be Bavarian for a weekend," was the comment heard most often.

In the days that followed, Richard Grieb and William Sigmund were overwhelmed with the weekend's success. It had been a " lot of fun"—and a lot more than "a little work". Saengerbund members were thrilled with the fact that the First State was no longer just a spot on the map, but a real place in the hearts of all who attended. Compliments on the Delaware group's hospitality and friendliness energized all who participated. Brian Schulz even had a three-volume video set prepared for all who wanted to experience the weekend *noch einmal,* again!

Two years later, in June 1999, the EVTG undertook a Kinderfest. Nine dance groups representing four states brought a total of 150 children to Newark for another memorable gathering.

Without a doubt the success of these endeavors is the result of dedicated leaders and members who consider the group a cohesive family. Richard Grieb was born in Neu-Arzis/Bessarabia and immigrated in 1956. He joined the dancers in 1973, has served as Vorplattler and, since 1979, as president. Both Richard and his wife Norma, who serves as Trachtenmutter, have dedicated countless hours to the success and growth of the group. Grieb sees his role as promoting the club to the younger generation: "As there are fewer German immigrants, I try to translate for members the meaning of the dances and the . . . importance of the heritage." In 1993 the German Embassy bestowed upon him the Federal Republic of Germany Friendship Award at the EVTG's 25th Stiftungsfest. The award recognizes his dedication to the life of the society. Now that daughter Heidi and granddaughter Emilie participate, the Grieb family is one of several with three generations of dancers.

Intergenerational involvement is unique, admirable, and important, for only through the participation of the young will the group survive. The Schulz family boasts four generations of club involvement. When queried about their favorite aspect of the club, Allyssa and Morgan Schulz beamed as they replied: "Dancing is fun and exciting and it's a family affair". They are the great-granddaughters of Wilhelm and Lieselotte Schulz, granddaughters of Karl-Heinz Schulz and Helga Schweiger, and daughters of Brian and Stephanie Schulz. All have been active in the club. Brian, whose mother immigrated from Darmstadt and father and grandparents from Wilhelmshaven, danced with the group from the beginning; his parents were one of the four founding couples. Today as secretary and second Vorplattler, Brian enjoys working with the children. He remembers how it feels to pass through the awkward teen years, and he also recognizes the rewards and pride that result from belonging to such a group: "You get through the peer pressure. This is my heritage, a part of my family, for I grew up in the club." He is proud of his daughters and hopes that they will continue their interest.

The Keiths are another three-generation dancing family. Ingeborg and George, a founding couple, passed their love for dancing on to son Tommy and his children David and Sarah. Gerda and Jim Hall are also active with son Jimmy and granddaughter Jenna. A fourth family, Amy and the late Carl Smelgus, along with daughter Susan Vikari, husband Klaus, and daughters Jennifer and Kirsten also boasts three generations of involvement. Alfred and Linda Escheu and Reinhold and Hermine Kuska are looking forward to the day when grandsons Hunter and Alexander, who were born just minutes apart in November 2000, are old enough to try their first Schuhplattler steps.

The success of the EVTG is due to the dedicated families and leaders who have seen to it that the dance group was a family affair. The children's participation bears out the words of Dr. Edmund Stoiber, Minister President of Bavaria, in a letter to the Trachten Vereine assembled at the 1995 Gaufest in Milwaukee:

> When children and grandchildren show their connectedness to the homeland of their parents and grandparents with such enthusiasm and devotion, this is not only a compliment for our Bavarian culture. It shows that customs and traditions will be well

received and admired when they come from the heart and express a real *Lebensgefühl* [love for life]. Members of Trachten and dance groups know this, and they will honor and respect customs of other countries. The Bavarian dance groups in America prove that preserving customs can be a sign of openness, tolerance, and the willingness for greater understanding among nations.

The partnership of the E.V.T.G. has proven invaluable to the growth and visability of the Delaware Saengerbund. The energetic officers who have led the Enzian Volkstanzgruppe since its inception are:

Presidents: George Keith, William Crouch, Karl-Heinz Schulz, Sylvia Sporay, Alfred Escheu, Richard Grieb.

Vorplattler: Karl-Heinz Schulz, Alex Piragow, Richard Trager, Reinhold Kuska, Richard Grieb, Tommy Keith.

Vortänzerinnen: Margot Trager, Anita Ruff-Walters, Norma Grieb, Hermine Kuska, Tina Stixrude, Stephanie Schulz.

Trachtenmutter: Margot Trager, Hilde Schwoegler, Norma Grieb.

Kindertanzgruppe: Brian and Stephanie Schulz, Tommy Keith.

Members of the Enzian Volkstanzgruppe treasure the close bonds they have formed over the years, while never losing sight of the motto embroidered on the society's flag: *Sitt und Brauch der Alten wollen wir erhalten!* We pledge to preserve the customs and traditions of our forefathers.

The Kindertanzgruppe performing at International Night at McVey School, 2002. Circle: Stephanie Schneck, Alyssa Schulz, Jessica Miller; Foreground: Charles Groff, Jake Schneck, David Keith; Background: Claudia Gonzales, Sarah Keith.

14

Delaware Saengerbund Kickers

Der Theodor, der Theodor, der steht bei uns im Fußballtor!

Theodore, Theodore! He is our goalie!

The Kickers' emblem in the German colors was designed by Ed Tuckmantel.

After 1952, when Theodor Heuss became Bundespräsident of Germany, soccer fans broke out into this chant wherever he went. He was known for his love of soccer and his knowledge of all the team standings. Secretary of State Henry Kissinger, another famous man of politics with a fondness for soccer, was spotted more than once sitting among the fans and rooting for his home team, *Spielvereinigung Fürth* in the town where he was born. *Fussball*—soccer—is a lifetime love for players and spectators. No wonder then, that in 1958, several Saengerbund members attended a *Fussballspiel*, a soccer match, between the 1. F. C. Kaiserslautern and Philadelphia's Ukranian team. The match brought back memories of games in Germany and sparked the idea of forming a team in Wilmington. On October 30, 1958, under the

aegis of President Emil Dahnken and Vice President Alfred Gilgenast, the DSB Kickers came into being. The team's purpose was "to achieve physical fitness by means of sport and recreation." They chose a black and white uniform, the colors of the German national team, and elected as officers Siegfried Geist, president; Alfred Escheu, secretary; Burkhard Noack, treasurer; Horst Horn, manager; and Richard Weis, coach.

Over the next seven years, the Kickers became well-known locally and brought greater visibility to soccer as a team sport. The team played in the Delaware Valley Soccer League and won the championship in 1961, 1962, and 1965. Members of the 1961 team were Alfred Escheu, captain; Sepp Hilsenrad and Paul Fuchs, coaches; Werner Bayer, goalie; Albert Blind and Hans Ulzhofer, defense; Victor Uro, Karl Schmidt, Siggi Geist, middle field; and Siggi Fuchs, Schorsch Lang and Karl-Heinz Schulz, offense.

Saengerbund members associated with the first Kickers were Sam Allen, Werner Bayer, Albert Blind, Jurgen Diekmann, Paul Fuchs, Siegfried Fuchs, Ed Garcia, Paul Heinemann, Fred Heytrak, Sepp Hilsenrad, Lou Ibarra, John Klootwyk, Lascio Krupanski, George Lang, Joe Miller, Milton Olazagasti, John Peterson, Kjell Ringoen, Rudi Rotter, Albert Schock, Simon Schock, Karl Schmidt, Karl-Heinz Schulz, Hans Ultzhoefer, and Stanley Wierzchowski. Although supported by the Saengerbund, the men organized dances and activities to raise funds for the team. The *Faschingsball*—masquerade ball—became the most popular event.

After the German Hall was sold in 1965, the Kickers stayed together through the transition years. In October 1968 they met in the Bauernstube with W. Goeckel and Tom Briggs as cocaptains. Practice sessions and games were held at Banning Park. In the ensuing years the players had children who were old enough to play soccer and so, in the spring of 1978, all teenagers of Saengerbund members were encouraged to sign up. Eighteen boys responded and two Junior Kickers teams were formed. Simon Schock became chair of the DSB Soccer Club, Rolf Offschanka coach of the teams. "Growth through Sportsmanship and Teamwork" was the new team's motto. Ed Tuckmantel designed the Kickers insignia, and George Mackay made a wood carving of it.

Both teams played in the Kirkwood Soccer League. After their first season, the Under 10 Team had a record of eight wins, one loss, and one tie. This team played for the Bicentennial Cup at Baynard Stadium against the Concord Bullets on June 17, 1979, in a game that will never be forgotten. The young Kickers won in a shoot-out by one goal after two overtime periods and a one-one tie after regulation play. The Under 12 Team, also had a fine record for the first season: seven wins and no losses. This was remarkable, since the players had no previous soccer experience. By the fall of 1979, the Delaware Saengerbund Youth Kickers had four teams, and by 1980 seven teams that played in the Delaware County, Pennsylvania League. In the winter season of 1979, two teams joined the Northern Delaware Soccer League. Three more Saengerbund teams played competitively in the spring of 1980.

The league initiated a different system of registering team members in 1980 when the players were organized by year of birth. This meant that a team could stay together for more than one season and the coaches would have a consistent group to work with from year to year. Club photographers Joseph Pouser and Richard Cutts documented the progress of the DSB teams and the exciting moments of their games.

The Property Committee and the Soccer Club worked together to build a soccer field on the club-owned meadow behind the building so the many Kickers teams could practice at home and invite other clubs to games on their field. The addition of floodlights made evening practices possible. At times there were not enough young players among the Delaware Saengerbund members. When that happened, the openings were filled with friends from school and neighborhood. In this way the Saengerbund served the larger community by providing a safe place where young people could spend time together, develop physical skills, and learn the basic rules of good sportsmanship. Governor Pete du Pont congratulated the Delaware Saengerbund Soccer Club for providing such a sports program in a January 1981 letter: "Teamwork and sportsmanship are not only good traits to develop while playing in athletic competition, but also are ones that should be applied to daily living. Working well with others can spell success in sports as well as in the world of business and government."

In 1983 when the Adult Kickers celebrated their 25th anniversary, the festivities were chaired by Irene Rice. Youth Soccer continued its full schedule with plans for the 1984 team to travel to England and Germany that summer. At the same time, Saengerbund members hosted visiting German teams from Regensburg and Mitterteich. These exchanges gave all the young players a wonderful opportunity to make new friends. Soccer is popular the world over and a language that everyone can understand. While in Turkey on a business trip, one *Fussballer* who had played with the Saengerbund Kickers as a youngster, walked past a field where a group of young Turks were playing. He stopped to watch. "Hans, spiel mit," they called out to him when they noticed his interest in their game, mistaking him for a German because of his blonde hair. He was only too happy to oblige. *"Einmal ein Fussballer, immer ein Fussballer"*—"Once a soccer player, always a soccer player!"

A Kinder-Kickers program for six-year-olds was started in the 1980s with Lou Townsend as coach. When girls were also accepted, Ina Cutts and Anne Cox were the first girls to play on a Kickers team. A full girls' team was registered in 1999. The 1988 (birth year) girls team went on to win the championship cup for the Saengerbund in 2000 and 2001.

Among the many Saengerbund Soccer Club members who work with the teams are Barbara Fones, Phil Rice, Charlie Schauber, William Sigmund, Don Sturmfels, Lou Townsend, and Ken Woodlin. The list of enthusiastic parents who volunteered as coaches is long. Most visibly involved in the soccer program in addition to Simon Schock were Rolf Offschanka, Milton Olazagasti, and Rudolf Schock.

Coach Rolf Offschanka came to the United States from Hamburg in 1954 and joined the Delaware Saengerbund in 1976. An avid soccer fan, he played soccer for over thirty years and coached many teams for over twenty years. He took the adult team to his hometown Hamburg in 1990 and the 1979 youth team to Austria in 1993. His love and concern for the players found a concrete expression in his support of the David Wellborn Foundation's fundraisers and silent auctions. David was a young player who died in a motorcycle accident.

Simon Schock, who played in the first Kickers team, did not rest until the Saengerbund had a youth soccer program. His sons Rudolf and Robert Schock played on the first youth soccer team. Both then stayed on to play on the adult team, and both became coaches for the younger Kickers. Rudy Schock organized the annual Friendship Tournament of the Delaware Saengerbund for adults. In 1991 it was renamed the DSB Kickers Annual Simon Schock Sr. Memorial Friendship Soccer Tournament in honor of his grandfather who had passed on his own love for the sport to his grandsons and was a faithful spectator at all their games.

Rudy has been associated with the sport for over 20 years. Among his many memories, two stand out: "The wonderful tour of northern Germany in 1990. I don't believe we won any games, but everyone had a memorable experience. The second was being a part of the team that won the NCC Summer Soccer League

Adult Championship in 1991. The title game was played on what would have been my Opa's 85th birthday. Unfortunately, our greatest fan had died earlier that season. We all know Opa was there in spirit and had a lot to do with our winning that title."

No soccer game can be played without the most important person, the referee. The Delaware Saengerbund was fortunate to have Milton Olazagasti who lives and breathes the sport. In 1962 he played on the DuPont team against the Delaware Saengerbund Kickers. Later he became a member of Kickers and has refereed many games and made fair sportsmanship a household word among players. Olazagasti was an active referee in the youth and professional leagues for over twenty-five years and a past president of the Amateur Soccer Association of Delaware. He also coached college-level soccer at Goldey-Beacom and Brandywine Colleges. He remains active in the sport as a National Referee Assessor, State Referee Instructor, and Emeritus State Referee.

State soccer referees affiliated with the United States Soccer Federation initiated the Milton Olazagasti Cup in recognition of his numerous contributions to the game. The cup is awarded to the winner of single-game elimination tournament between the B and C division teams of the New Castle Amateur Soccer Association, sponsored by New Castle County Parks and Recreation. The tournament takes place annually on the third weekend of July with between sixteen and twenty-four teams participating.

The Kickers have done well in competition and on several occasions reached the semi-final or final stage. Most recently the work of DSB soccer coaches and referees was honored when the 1988 boys team won the Fair Play Award at the Spring 2000 Diamond State Cup. Today the numerous trophies in DSB's game room attest to the outstanding success of the many teams. But the teams could not be successful without the coaches and referees and the steadily increasing interest, locally, nationally, and internationally, in the German national sport, soccer.

-Delaware Wandervögel-

Wer recht in Freuden wandern will,

der geh' der Sonn' entgegen!

Da ist der Wald so kirchenstill,

kein Lüftchen mag sich regen.

Noch sind nicht die Lerchen wach,

nur im hohen Gras der Bach

singt leise den Morgensegen

-Geibel/Klauer

Walk towards the morning rays

If you want to hike with joy

When the woods are quiet like a church,

Not even a breeze is stirring.

The lark is not awake yet,

The only sound drifts softly

From the creek hidden in the grass

As it murmurs its morning blessing.

The map of the first hike to the Pinnacle and Pulpit Rock in Pennsylvania has signatures of the Delaware Wandervögel.

Hiking is another extremely popular German *Fuss-Sport.* Anyone traveling in Germany will encounter individuals or groups of people dressed in comfortable clothes and sensible shoes walking at a good pace for miles and miles, just for the sheer enjoyment of being outdoors! In fact, *Wandern*—hiking—has been a favorite pastime as far back as when people still lived within the confines of walled cities with their narrow streets, unpleasant smells and day-long noise. Hiking became more widespread at the beginning of the 20th century. In Berlin, the youth movement called *Wandervogel* (Migratory Bird) formed after 1901 and soon spread to other regions. The movement was envisioned as an alternative to the stiffness of the uniform-wearing bureaucracy of the Prussian Empire. Dressed in shirts with soft collars and loose pants, carrying rucksacks and *Zupfgeigen,* or mandolins, young men and women enjoyed hiking through open fields and meadows, cooking simple meals over open fires, and sleeping in hay barns or tents along the way. Their songs, collected in the *Zupfgeigenhansl,* criticized or ridiculed any institution that hindered freedom of expression, but they had no formal political agenda.

The influence of the Wandervogel remained strong in Germany throughout the century, and hiking became almost a national sport. Advocacy for environmental protection and an appreciation for folk art and music also had their roots in this movement.

At the old German Hall, Saengerbund members often met at 6 o'clock in the morning in order to spend a day hiking in the country. Not long after the Delaware Saengerbund opened its doors in Ogletown, a small group decided to go hiking together. Not surprisingly they called themselves the Delaware Wandervögel. On October 14, 1973, just like their predecessors, they met at the Saengerbund at 6 o'clock in order to drive to the Reading area. It was a beautiful fall day, perfect for hiking the Appalachian Trail from Port Clinton to the Hamburg Reservoir and on to Pulpit Rock and the Pinnacle. Along the way, the walkers enjoyed beautiful vistas over the surrounding area. Members on this first hike were Wolfgang Conrad, Alida Cutts, Alfred Escheu, Richard Leaning, Andy Olivier, Elard Scharffenberg, Sandy Schreier, and younger members Freddy Escheu Jr. and Glenn Schwoegler. "We had such a good time in spite of our blisters and *Muskelkater* [muscle pains] the next day," remembered Alida Cutts, "that we decided to do monthly hikes." One member was usually responsible for selecting the trail, and those interested signed up in the Bauernstube. Destinations included the New Jersey Pine Barrens as well as St. Anthony's Wilderness, Hawk Mountain, French Creek State Park, and various sections of the Horseshoe Trail and Appalachian Trail in Pennsylvania. Whenever the hikes were near Reading, the hikers stopped at the Reading Liederkranz for a nice cool beer and dinner, and even stayed for a Fasching ball one night.

Sometimes overnight outings were planned, for example to the Adirondacks for hikes in snow and ice, to Virginia's Blue Ridge Mountain trails in the spring, or to Pennsylvania in early summer to hike among the mountain laurels. Two hikes became an annual tradition, to the Pinnacle in October and to French Creek State Park on New Year's Day. The hikers' children also discovered the joy of hiking and singing. Visiting relatives from Germany often joined the group and marveled at the beautiful wild countryside at Kelly's Run and the Susquehanna River Valley. When the Delaware Wandervögel celebrated the twentieth year of hiking together, a brass Sierra cup was engraved for each member to mark the occasion.

As the hikers grew older and busier, finding leaders became more difficult, so the Delaware Wandervögel have gone their own ways, managing only occasional, spontaneous hikes together. The group still meets each year for the traditional New Year's outing to French Creek State Park. There, in front of a warm fire in the shelter near the fire tower, they have time to reminisce about the many miles and adventures of past years. With thankful hearts and thoughts of the future, the little group intones the *Andachtsjodler*—the Solemn Alpine Yodel—before heading down the mountain. The trails are still there, and a new, younger group could reactivate the spirit of the Delaware Wandervögel at any time. After all, *Wandern macht froh*—Happiness is hiking! It only takes a good pair of hiking boots and a leader with a map!

Richard Leaning, leader of many hikes, is studying a trail map on top of Mount Jo in the Adirondacks.
(Photo by A. Olivier)

15

German Heritage

All mein Gedanken, die ich hab,
die sind bei dir.
Du auserwählter einger Trost,
bleib stets bei mir.
Du, du, du sollst an mich gedenken;
hätt ich aller Wünsch Gewalt,
von dir wollt ich nicht wanken.

All my thoughts I have
    Are with you.
You, my only comfort,
    Abide with me.
    You too remember me;
Had I the power of wishes,
I would never waver.

-Lochamer Liederbuch, 15th Century

- 300 Years of Germans in America -

The year 1983 brought international awareness of the history of German immigration to North America. Commemorations were held throughout Germany and the United States. Although individual immigrants from Germany had arrived on board many earlier ships, the year 1683 was marked by the first group of German settlers to come on shore. Franz Daniel Pastorius, a German Quaker and lawyer, worked for the Frankfurter Land-Compagnie as real estate agent. This company had acquired a piece of land in Pennsylvania from William Penn. Pastorius then found thirteen interested families, all Quakers and Mennonites who wanted to leave the town of Krefeld because of religious persecution. They were easily persuaded to move to a new world. On August 18th, 1683, Franz Daniel Pastorius sailed up the Delaware River, past New Castle to Philadelphia on the ship *America*. The thirteen families followed on the *Concord*, arriving in Philadelphia on October 6, where Pastorius welcomed them. The parcel of land they had been promised by Penn was further inland than expected, but the families worked with a will to clear it and build small houses. They named the settlement Germantown, and it was credited as being the first German immigrant colony in America.

The Historical Society of Delaware, the University of Delaware Department of Languages and Literatures, and the Delaware Saengerbund sponsored an exhibit in the Old Town Hall that was partly funded by the Delaware Humanities Forum, a state program of the

Exhibit at Old Town Hall featuring German traditions and heritage.

National Endowment for the Humanities. The exhibit was titled, *Old Ways in the New World: German Traditions in the Delaware Valley, 1683-1983*. Dr. Barbara Benson, executive director, and John Braunlein, archivist of the Historical Society of Delaware, worked closely with Trudy Gilgenast, director of the exhibit, and her staff. Hilde Cox, Ruth Olivier, Maria Smith, and Beatrix Tannian, collected memorabilia for the exhibit from Saengerbund members and German Americans residing in Wilmington. The exhibit opened in March 1983 with a festive reception catered by Wayne Wilberding and his culinary arts students from Hodgson Vocational-Technical High School.

The exhibit concentrated on German immigrants who arrived in Wilmington in the mid- to late 1800s and gave the German community an opportunity to share its heritage, one that has contributed in tangible ways to the American way of life. Six large glass cases contained displays that depicted the trades and professions that German immigrants followed, the societies and churches they founded, and the festivals they celebrated. The display also included a variety of

Authors Hilde Cox and Trudy Gilgenast with Alida Cutts at the 143rd Stiftungsfest celebrating the 100th anniversary of the Ladies of the Delaware Saengerbund. (Photo by A. Olivier)

personal belongings they had brought as remembrances of home. Volunteer guides explained what the various traditions meant and often added stories of their own experiences in a new world.

The German Embassy and the Delaware Saengerbund funded a student booklet to accompany the exhibit. It was written by Kathryn S. Dodson and Trudy Gilgenast, with illustrations by Kathryn S. Dodson and cultural assistance by Udda Anderson and Hilde Cox. Hans Gass and Lonnie Hearn of the University of Delaware prepared a fifteen-minute video documenting the exhibit that was made available to groups and schools. In the following months, a steady stream of visitors convinced the Historical Society to extend the exhibit into October, at which time it received a national award from the American Association for State and Local History for contributing to the history of Germans in the Delaware Valley.

While working on this project, members of the Culture Committee turned to Ruth Olivier who was able to decipher the old German script used in the Saengerbund's record books and, in subsequent years, the work of transliterating and translating the minutes was begun under her expertise. As the information contained in these old books became accessible, Trudy Gilgenast, Hilde Cox, and Alida Cutts were bitten by the "history bug." They used many of the newly discovered vignettes to mount small displays at the society's Stiftungsfest celebrations as a way of highlighting the hard work and accomplishments of the *Alte Herren,* the early members, as well as specific events in the club's history.

As an immigrant, author Hilde Cox wanted to learn from the experience of others and find an answer to the question, "How can an immigrant be happy and content living in a different country?" For many immigrants, the initial excitement of new surroundings quickly gives way to feelings of loss and regret. Too many dear people and familiar sights have been left behind. Too often there is no way to take part in family celebrations or tragedies, and the potential for sharing new experiences is limited. Aging parents and their care at home become a deep concern. Should one return; should one stay? The heart is drawn back and forth, the same conflict experienced so many years ago by Franz Daniel Pastorius who tried to persuade his aging father to follow him into the wilderness of Pennsylvania. But his father hid behind his doctor's advice, *Man kann einen alten Baum nicht verpflanzen*—One cannot transplant an old tree—as a way of letting his son know that he was too old to move. Neither could Pastorius return to Germany. He had found his life's work in the new world, and he realized that *Das Herz muss den Füssen folgen*—the heart must follow the feet. When he was no longer torn between the old and the new home, he experienced an inner peace that enabled him to lead a productive life in the service of his new *Mitbürger*—fellow citizens—in Germantown and beyond. This truth was confirmed more than once in the stories of the early German immigrants and in the stories of Saengerbund members as well.

Author Trudy Gilgenast, first generation German American, grew up in a bilingual, bicultural household with her brother Ralph. Both parents had emigrated from Germany and incorporated many traditions and customs in their home. Trudy's interest in the German language and traditions led her to a career as a German teacher at Conrad High School, P. S. du Pont High School, and the University of Delaware, while Ralph chose to teach the well-respected German trait of excellence in workmanship as contractor and carpentry teacher at Howard, Hodgson, and Delcastle Vocational-Technical High Schools. The entire Gilgenast family has been involved in all aspects of the Saengerbund. Realizing the society's role as guardian of German traditions, customs, and language, Trudy concluded that its history had to be documented and shared, and that was the germ of this book. She was awarded the German Embassy's Federal Republic of Germany Friendship Award in 1987 in recognition of her lifelong work in disseminating the German language and culture.

-German Language Classes-

The Saengerbund's constitution states that the organization will foster and encourage the study and use of the German language and culture. Once the club was established at Ogletown, many members who were second and third generation German Americans with little or no facility in the German language became interested in language classes. They wanted to be able to read the language of their parents and grandparents, keep in touch with relatives still in Germany, and be able to understand the spoken language so that they could travel in Germany with more confidence. The Saengerbund responded to this need by offering

German language classes for members. Since Delaware public schools offered no foreign language courses in the lower grades, there was a need for children's classes as well. After all, the earlier a child is exposed to another language, the better. A child's brain accepts the new language together with the birth language, and the child quickly learns the appropriate context for each. In contrast, languages acquired later in life are processed in a different part of the brain and retained less easily. "It is a positive fact that the young mind is far more susceptible to the study of languages than older ones," observed the wise columnist of the *Sunday Morning Star* on May 10, 1910. "Children who have emigrated with their parents to this country learn and speak the English language within a few months, while it requires years for their parents to become anything like familiar with it." The person at a disadvantage is the one who is not able to speak another language.

The availability of German classes at the Saengerbund attracted many new members, especially if long-time members like Eugene Kachelmus or Alfred Escheu or a member of the Singers or the EVTG personally invited them. Sepp Hilsenrad, already involved with the DSB's soccer program, and his wife Johanna began teaching German classes in 1971. Thirty adults and 46 children were enrolled the first year. Wolfgang and Brigitte Conrad taught the children, using books they had brought from Germany, and the little ones soon learned daily vocabulary, pronunciation and songs, since singing made learning easier and more fun. The children came together for many years, singing the songs and hearing the stories every German child knows: *Alle meine Entchen, Frau Holle, Struwwelpeter,* and *Max und Moritz.* They practiced ü's by chanting: *Ritze, ratze, voller Tücke in die Brücke eine Lücke!* With songs and skits, the children in the language classes entertained all the children at the Easter and Christmas parties. Once, they even dressed in costumes to look like Christmas decorations of the Erzgebirge—the Ore Mountain region—and sang traditional songs. This program was repeated at the University of Delaware's 1977 International Christmas Festival.

Years later, one young German American who had taken these classes realized their value when she was visiting in the Palatinate during the grape harvest. The women working in the vineyard began singing folksongs to pass the time, and the now grown-up German American Saengerbund member sang along with them. The women were amazed and pleased, and a bond of friendship was created more easily.

The dedicated teachers in charge of the German Language classes for children and adults at the Delaware Saengerbund over the years have included Iris and Stephanie Busch, Monica Coslow, Hilde Cox, Alida Cutts, Arlen Haag, Tina Haight, McCrea Harrison, Ingrid Hasselbach, Paul Heinemann Jr., Helga Hoeschel, Elisabeth Kottenhahn, Freia Lorimer, John Maiorano, Susan McMahon, Roswitha Morrissey, Erika Schirm, Susan Schwaneflügel, Moira Sheridan, Annegret Sides, Beatrix Tannian, and Helga Walters.

-Student Awards-

Although the reward for learning a language is inherent when the goal is reached, incentives and public recognition definitely have their place in a successful language program. In 1969, Paul Heinemann recommended presenting an award of $200 to an outstanding student of the German language at the University of Delaware. After Sepp Hilsenrad had passed away following a long illness, Wolfgang Conrad suggested that this award be named the Sepp Hilsenrad Memorial Award in honor of Sepp's contribution to the language program. Alida Cutts moved that this be done, and the motion was seconded and approved by the membership. The award was increased to $300 and later to $500. Each year the Department of Languages and Literatures selects one or two outstanding students as recipients, and the award is presented during the May Honor's Day program. When there are two recipients, the award is shared. The winner or winners visit the general membership meeting in May so that Saengerbund members have the opportunity to meet the students and learn about their future study plans. Members have always been impressed with the enthusiasm of the young students for German studies, and the students are pleased with the honor and the generosity of the society. When Werner Beyer received the award in 1984, it was especially significant, since Werner's father had been the goalie for the Saengerbund Kickers twenty-three years earlier.

The Saengerbund also recognizes the efforts of outstanding Delaware high school students by presenting monetary awards for their successful participation in a national writing competition organized by the American Association of Teachers of

German and in the local oral contest sponsored by the Delaware Council of Foreign Language Teachers. Both awards are given annually.

A new award, introduced in 1984 for the members' children, affords a summer language immersion experience at Concordia German Language Village in Moorhead, Minnesota. Students have to submit an essay that is reviewed by a committee, and the winner is awarded transportation and a two weeks' stay at Camp Waldsee. Sharra Taylor, the first recipient of this award, and all who followed, returned with great enthusiasm for the program and a greater appreciation for German culture.

-Culture Committee-

Culture—*Kultur*—is expressed in every aspect of daily life, and all groups of the Delaware Saengerbund represent the German culture. Realizing the important connection between culture and language, President Alfred Escheu saw the need for a new committee and established the Culture Committee as a standing committee in 1978. It was to be responsible for language classes and other events related to the German language at the Saengerbund. William Sigmund was named the first chair, succeeded by Trudy Gilgenast, Alida Cutts, Hilde Cox, Marguerite Spittle, Lloyd Maier, and Rod Meehan. The work of the committee was recognized when Hilde Cox received the Federal Republic of Germany Friendship award in 1993.

Over the years, the Culture Committee's responsibilities have increased, and members are interested in continually expanding the committee's offerings as long as curiosity is piqued and knowledge gained. Beer and wine tasting events have attracted an interested audience who felt the information they gained enhanced their appreciation of both. The committee also sponsors an Arts Festival—begun in 1985 by Dawn Swartout and Margaret Johnston—where talented members of the Saengerbund can showcase their works, hobbies, or collections. So far six festivals have been held. A. K. Kissell, his wife Helga, and son Arno organize a German auto display at the annual June picnic. Autos, motorcycles, trucks, and tractors attract car enthusiasts and other picnickers who browse as they enjoy their *Wurst* and favorite beverage.

A genealogy group led by Lyle Hartman and Ellis Schmidt is enthusiastic about learning how to access information about their roots. Looking into one's heritage has become more widely accepted since the 500th anniversary of Columbus's voyage to the new world.

-Community Visibility-

The 1992 Columbus Quincentenary had two purposes: to commemorate the 500th anniversary of Columbus' voyage to America, and to help Americans become more aware of the native and immigrant groups who have contributed to our national identity. The hope was that as Americans learned more about their own roots, they would also become more tolerant of the immigrants' need to identify with their heritage. Here in Delaware, Governor Mike Castle created the Columbus 500 Committee and appointed Justine Mataleno as chair. "We feel the whole purpose of this event is for people to look inward and see where we are today and why," stated Mataleno in a *News Journal* interview on October 6, 1991. Members of many nationalities participated in meetings, workshops, and a final grand parade in Wilmington. The Delaware Saengerbund was involved from the beginning to represent the German Americans, and several lectures, including one by Dr. Hoffecker on the Wilmington Germans, were held at the club.

Schools also celebrated the multicultural backgrounds of their students and included an International Day in the school year. Young students were asked to interview and learn from immigrants, and the resulting interest and understanding made it easier for immigrants to acknowledge their heritage instead of hiding it. This is an important step in coping in a healthy way with separation, culture shock, and new experiences. Only recently have some German immigrants felt comfortable enough to share their early feelings of homesickness, culture shock, and frequent rejection.

Sometimes—perhaps not often enough—the disconnect of culture shock can be rather amusing, as in the example of Dr. Iris Busch, instructor of German at the University of Delaware. She immigrated in 1991 and, at a visit to the Saengerbund's Oktoberfest, was amazed to encounter an adult wearing Lederhosen who spoke no German! Since she had grown up in Leipzig, behind the Iron Curtain, she had never had contact with Bavarians. At the Oktoberfest in Delaware she learned about the American love of Bavaria, folk dancing, and traditions. Dr. Busch joined the Delaware Saengerbund. "For me personally," she says, "the Saengerbund offers a Heimatgefühl. It reminds me of my Heimat and it is a link with my past. But the Saengerbund also has a mission: preserving the German language, guarding traditions and culture, reaching out to the community, and sharing the values of the German heritage."

The Delaware Saengerbund supports programs that offer the community a greater awareness of this heritage, and volunteers participate at international or multicultural days sponsored by local elementary and high schools. The dancers of the Enzian Volkstanzgruppe, with their many invitations to perform, are special ambassadors.

Another successful undertaking has been the *Treffpunkt Saengerbund*—Meeting Place Saengerbund. Local high school students of the German language and their teachers are invited to spend a day at the Delaware Saengerbund where they are immersed in a German American atmo-

The children's language class: 1st row: Sarah Gilgenast, Morgan Schulz, Jacob Gilgenast, Maria Renner; 2nd: Rebekah Gilgenast, Matt Kinney, Amber Kinney, Don Merritt, Carla Renner, Sara Schreiber; 3rd: Stefanie Busch, Alyssa Schulz, Dr. Iris Busch.

"Deutsch macht Spass"—Dr. Iris Busch and language teacher Alison Matsen at the Treffpunkt 2000.

sphere. The first *Treffpunkt* was organized with the help of Dr. Iris Busch and Saengerbund volunteers in the spring of 1994. Two more followed, in 1996 and 2000, and plans are underway for the next one in 2003. Approximately 200 students and their teachers have visited each time to participate in workshops, craft demonstrations, folk dancing, singing, maypole dancing, playing games, and other activities. This gives the students an opportunity to use their German skills and enhance their cultural understanding. Excitement and enthusiasm were the keywords of the day, as everyone tasted German food and tried out Bavarian dance steps. Hearing the songs the students had practiced in their schools made everyone realize *Deutsch macht Spass!*—German Language is fun!—and thank-you-notes from the students conveyed their wish to have a *Treffpunkt* every year.

Teachers also found these visits useful, because they had an opportunity to meet other teachers. The sad truth is that German language classes often finish last in terms of popularity among students and are often dropped from the curriculum because of the small enrollment. Too often teachers have to struggle to keep programs alive. However that may be changing. Due to the persistence of German language teachers, the German language may be losing part of its reputation for being hard to learn. "German has a reputation for being difficult because of all the adjective endings and variations of the 'the'," stated Alison Matsen, foreign language teacher at Middletown High School in an article printed in the *News Journal* in March 2002. She likes to explain to her students that even if they use the wrong *der, die,* or *das* for the article "the," they still will be understood in Germany, while in other languages such mistakes may change the meaning completely and lead to misunderstanding. Still, that should deter no one from traveling abroad or participating in an exchange program, which can provide a broad learning experience. When Wilmington and Fulda became Sister Cities in 1997, opportunities to travel to and study in Germany increased. A stipend was made available to a female University of Delaware student each year as part of a program funded by the two cities. The Saengerbund supports this program by contributing to the student's travel expenses. The student is sponsored by the German American Women's Club of Fulda and spends a month at the Fachhochschule Fulda studying German.

-Library-

Those who cannot travel abroad can still explore German life through films and books. At the Saengerbund, classic German movies and modern videos are presented on Sunday afternoons, hosted first by Ted Baumeister and more recently by Joe Kellner.

Because language and literacy go hand in hand, a German club would not be complete without a substantial library. The Saengerbund missed the books of the old Bibliothek Verein and was delighted when members and individuals of the German community in Wilmington donated books from their libraries to the club. When the bookcase in the Ogletown boardroom overflowed, it became the goal of the Culture Committee to establish a library in the new wing of the clubhouse. Simon Schock, with the help of Adrien Olivier, built shelves using some of the boards saved from the old German Hall library. The German Embassy generously donated new editions of the classics and current materials for students. The library was officially opened in 1999 at the 146th Stiftungsfest. It was especially rewarding that the descendants of Henry Miller and Frederick von Bourdon, founders of the German Library Association in 1873, were there to celebrate and cut the ribbon at the door. Today Adrien Olivier and Lloyd Maier are in charge of the new library, which includes a children's book and video section. Members are encouraged to browse among the familiar titles and immerse themselves in new adventures waiting on the shelves in this quiet study room.

Too quiet? Then step out and listen to the "Umpah" music. The Delaware Saengerbund has always loved to share its German culture and heritage by inviting everyone to its greatest festival. In the last century it was the Volksfest at Brandywine Springs Park; today it's the Oktoberfest in Ogletown!

Margaret Johnston, Edward Brandenberger, Andy Olivier and Dorothy Brandenberger check out the new library shelves filled with German and English classic books. (Photo by Pouser)

16

Oktoberfest

Ein Pro-sit, ein Pro-sit der Ge-müt-lich-keit, ein Pro-sit, ein Pro-sit der Ge-müt-lich-keit

The well-received 125th Stiftungsfest celebration in 1978 provided the impetus for holding the Saengerbund's Oktoberfest under a big tent in 1979. With more space available, the public again could be invited, and the overwhelming response showed that the right choice had been made. President William Klabe pursued the idea of a public Oktoberfest again in 1982 and convinced the membership to try it once more outdoors, under a big tent. That year 3,500 guests attended. Nine hundred pounds of potatoes were peeled for potato salad. Twenty-nine cases of sauerkraut and 4,500 Bratwurst were consumed, and 1,000 slices of cake disappeared. The second Oktoberfest was so successful that it became an annual event after 1982. The income from the one-weekend celebration was consistently higher than the expenses, and the extra funds helped the club maintain the property and support the many activities. In each of the following years, the Oktoberfest committee learned to improve the handling of food and drink for so many people and to avoid mistakes. As Oktoberfest chairs, Richard Weis, William Klabe, Alfred Escheu, and Simon Schock carried a heavy load of responsibility, but all have been ably supported by their cochairs.

The club chose the name *Oktoberfest*, rather than *Volksfest*, for the three-day festival, because *Oktoberfest* was almost a household word, especially for the many Americans who had enjoyed the atmosphere of the Munich Oktoberfest when they were stationed in Germany, or when they were tourists there. The Munich festival dates back to a wedding ceremony celebrated on October 12, 1810. On that day, Crown Prince Ludwig, later King Ludwig I, married Princess Therese von Sachsen-Hildburghausen. All the people of Munich and surrounding countryside were invited to celebrate the newlyweds at a horse race held five days later on the *Theresienwiese*, a large meadow named in honor of the princess. In succeeding years, the city of Munich used the commemoration of this day as the reason for mounting a large, annual Volksfest that opened with a great *Festzug*. Dressed in the colorful traditional clothing of Bavaria, group after group paraded through the streets to the sounds of *Trachtenkapellen*, in the same manner in which Munich residents had congratulated the wedding couple. The festival featured the entertainment then popular: hot-air balloon rides, gymnastic displays by the Turner societies, merry-go-rounds for children, and agricultural exhibits. Beer, of course, was the favorite drink in Munich, the city famous for its breweries.

This festival expanded in size and length over time. People from all over southern Germany poured into Munich. Since the original festival took place in October, it soon became known as Oktoberfest. Concern about cold weather and early snow caused the opening of the festival to be moved into September, but the closing fell on the first weekend in October and the name *Oktoberfest* was retained. It is now enjoyed by nearly seven million people each year.

The Saengerbund's connection with Bavaria was easily made. The Enzian Volkstanzgruppe had already decided to wear authentic Tracht and was experienced at entertaining an audience with Schuhplattler dances. White and blue banners, the colors of Bavaria, were sewn by Dawn and Bud Swartout and the members of the entertainment committee to make the atomosphere more authentic. As always, the food was cooked by the Ladies of the Delaware Saengerbund. Bands from Germany and from local towns were engaged to play *Blasmusik*, the loud, jolly brass music needed for outdoor celebrations. The "Happy Austrian Band" with Jakob Titz and his Alphorn became as much a tradition as the Ernst Licht Bavarian clothing factory that managed a booth where Bavarian souvenirs, hats, and clothing were sold. For the children, there were amusement rides and Midway games. The Saengerbund decided to charge a small admission fee that would cover the expense of renting the tent and paying the bands; in return the amusement rides were free. This

arrangement proved to be very satisfactory indeed. When you have happy children you have happy parents!

Ed Tuckmantel designed an Oktoberfest poster, and Ed Severe provided advice on how to advertise the event. The local newspapers did their best to report on the new festival in town. Gerry Kainz, publisher and editor of the German weekly newspaper *Washington Journal*, made the Oktoberfest known south of Delaware. Clifford Weber, publicity expert, made many trips to the *News Journal* and *Newark Post* offices, supplying new information, stories, and pictures. Over the years, he became the public voice of the Delaware Saengerbund. The German Embassy recognized his efforts and presented him with the Federal Republic of Germany Friendship Award at the 1989 Oktoberfest.

Each year, more and more people looked forward to the German festival, the potato salad, the sauerkraut, the *Zwetschgenkuchen*—plum cake—the music, dancing, and beer. It was not long before the third weekend in September became a fixture on their calendars. "Delaware's Saengerbund and Oktoberfest certainly offer the public a jubilee," writes Marjorie McNinch in her book *Festivals*. The Delaware Heritage Commission even endorsed Oktoberfest as an official bicentennial event.

The year 1989, when the Berlin Wall fell, was a jubilee year for Germans. German unification was proclaimed the following year on October 3, 1990. That certainly called for a celebration! The Delaware Saengerbund was overwhelmed by the number of people who came to show their happiness for the German people; approximately 15,000 people attended the 1990 Oktoberfest.

Richard Weis served as chair that year. In spite of Hurricane Hugo, the opening day brought good weather and volunteers to undo the damage of the storm that wreaked havoc and almost demolished the tent. German Ambassador Dr. Jürgen Ruhfus personally helped with the *Anstich*--the first draw from the keg. The Embassy of the Federal Republic of Germany recognizes Oktoberfest as a festival that cements the friendship between Germany and America at the grassroots level. To acknowledge the tremendous amount of work required to produce this festival each year, the German Embassy presented the Federal Republic of Germany Friendship Award to Lois and Howard Meyer in 1995 and to William Sigmund in 1998.

Also each year, a representative of the German Embassy brings greetings to the opening ceremony on Friday evening. The brass band leads the parade of dignitaries, officers of the Delaware Saengerbund, and Oktoberfest and kitchen chairpersons through the tent. Dancers of the Enzian Volkstanzgruppe follow, carrying the *Münchner Kindl*, one of the children from the Kindertanzgruppe dressed in monk's garb. The child holds a large radish in one hand and a beer stein in the other. They are the symbolic food and drink of the Munich Oktoberfest.

A highlight in 1998 was the visit of a special United States Army group whose members had been stationed at a base in Herzogenaurach, Germany, or *Herzo-Base* in short. The men had been looking for a place where they could hold their first reunion in forty years. DSB member Gus Viehmann happened to overhear the conversation and recommended that they meet at the Delaware Saengerbund's Oktoberfest. Two hundred former soldiers came to Ogletown and had such a wonderful time that they repeated their vistit the following year with twice as many people.

Oktoberfest has evolved into a popular gathering place where music and food bring back happy memories. For German Americans the festival is a reminder of small town fairs in the old country. Martin Schaller of Washington D.C. wrote about his impressions of Oktoberfest in a full page story for the *Washington Journal* in October 1998:

> The ambience, the feel and atmosphere, the spirit and festiveness is German, is Bavaria, is Munich—the sights, the sounds, the smells all tell you that you're about to encounter an Oktoberfest that is as genuine and as good as it gets on this side of the Atlantic! In the First State, the Delaware Saengerbund Oktoberfest is, in every respect, the "First Oktoberfest!" But what really sets this Oktoberfest apart from all others, I believe, is its uniquely and quite wonderfully down-home, small town America character, charm, and flavor. Here in Newark, Delaware, some 100 odd miles and two hours north of our Nation's Capital, at this Oktoberfest there were all the festive elements and neighborliness of the traditional county fair, combined with an old fashioned political atmosphere as prominent Delaware politicians and elected and appointed State officials comfortably "worked the crowd." There was no pretense, no show or phoniness, it was local, it was folksy, it was family. The dignitaries came, because they wanted to honor these Americans of German heritage, and to encourage them to continue to respect their cultural traditions, and undertake activities that promote, strengthen and enhance those traditions—and they said it publicly and with enthusiasm. It created a wonderful spirit that embraced patriotism, politicians at their best, and pride.

In 2000, Senator Joseph Biden said that the Delaware Saengerbund was still celebrating a wedding, the union of two countries who kept their promise of faithfulness to their friendship in good and bad times. Senator William Roth invited the Saengerbund to participate in the Library of Congress's Bicentennial Celebration. In 2000, the Library of Congress undertook a Local Legacies project that documented and collected folk traditions and ethnic heritage events in all fifty states. Oktoberfest was included as the German American heritage event from Delaware.

No one will ever forget the 2001 Oktoberfest. On September 11, just three days prior to the opening of the festival, terrorists demolished the Twin Towers of the World Trade Center in New York City and crashed a jet into the Pentagon, stunning the world. The Oktoberfest chairs wrestled with the decision of whether or not to cancel the festival. They decided to go ahead, to offer guests an opportunity to gather and share friendship in this crisis. President Reinhold Kuska spoke thoughtfully in his opening address: "I was hoping that this gathering would allow us some time with friends, not to celebrate, but perhaps to assure each other that we are all right, and if need be comfort each other as we try to continue our lives. The events that took place in our country this past week shall not be forgotten, but we must not allow them to destroy our freedom and way of life." In general, it was felt the decision to hold the festival was the right one, for over 17,000 guests attended, glad of an opportunity to break away from the numbing news of the tragedy. As everyone enjoyed the food and music, the Oktoberfest became a true Amerikafest. At the meeting following the festival, the board of directors recommended and the members voted in favor of making a sizable donation to the disaster relief fund of the Salvation Army in Wilmington.

From the beginning, Oktoberfest has been the one event that brings all the committees and groups within the Delaware Saengerbund together. Chairman Simon Schock, assisted by cochairs Lois and Howard Meyer, has organized Oktoberfest for more than ten years. They are aided by a group of dedicated workers who help with every detail from parking to pretzels, and even go so far as to recruit family members, friends, and coworkers to help. Aside from a few "short circuits" due to overtaxed nerves, the feeling of camaraderie, teamwork, and genuine esprit de corps prevails so that not even hurricanes can dowse nor terrorists destroy the event. Each year, the membership votes to hold another festival, and the proud Oktoberfest chairman is able to call out the famous opening greeting: *O'zapft is!*— "The beer is tapped!"

Behind the scenes at the Oktoberfest.

17

Maibaum

Ein tiefer Sinn wohnt in den alten Bräuchen;
man muss sie ehren.

Friedrich v. Schiller

A deep meaning is inherent in the old traditions;
one must honor them.

With this remark, Friedrich von Schiller touched on a German trait, the love of traditions and customs. In 2000, when the Enzian Volkstanzgruppe looked into other Bavarian customs, members were intrigued by the tradition of raising a *Maibaum*, or May pole, similar to those often seen in Bavarian towns and villages. Originally a tall pine tree, a symbol of new life, was stripped of its lower branches, so that only the upper ones remained. They were hung with long, colorful ribbons, and the Maibaum was then erected in the town or village square where it remained for several months. Out of this tradition grew a new one, the placing of a permanent Maibaum. Affixed to its trunk are the shields of the various local artisans or trades symbolizing the economic, social, religious, and cultural life of the community. Remembering the Maibaum of Wörth, where he lived before coming to the United States, Klaus Vikari, a member of the dance group, proposed to his friends that they create such a symbol for the Delaware Saengerbund. Klaus, Richard Grieb, Brian and Dieter Schulz, Simon Schock, Alfred Escheu, and Richard Trager undertook the leadership of the project.

A 35-foot tall pine tree was brought to the Saengerbund's property, stripped of its bark, and painted in white and blue, the colors of Bavaria. In place of the traditional artisans' shields, the Delaware Saengerbund committees and groups were invited to submit a design representing their work: The Singers, Ladies, Enzian Volkstanzgruppe, TAG, Property and Culture Committees, Kickers, and Stammtisch all submitted designs, and Klaus Vikari and Joe Kellner transferred

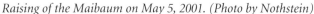

Raising of the Maibaum on May 5, 2001. (Photo by Nothstein)

them to wooden plaques. To stabilize the huge pole, Simon Schock designed a swing mechanism that was cemented into the ground by Brian and Dieter Schulz. A wreath of fresh greens and a small evergreen tree were hung from the top, as well as shields displaying the flags of Germany, Austria, Switzerland, and the United States. The beautiful Maibaum was raised on May 5, 2001, with much enthusiasm and excitement as well as sheer muscle! This Maibaum represents new life, hope, and rebirth, as well as the generational interconnectedness of all groups and committees toward a common goal—preservation of the German heritage.

The Delaware Saengerbund has been in existence for 150 years and is today vibrant and alive. One might ask, however, what the magic ingredient for the survival of such a society might be, since numerous similar groups across the country are declining or are close to extinction. If the society's history were to be graphed, the resulting chart would show that membership has ranged from as few as sixteen members to over one thousand, then dwindled down to only a handful before beginning to increase again. Similarly the Saengerbund has gone from meeting in homes to meeting in pubs before owning one and then two properties—only to have to sell both and literally start all over again. And it has swung from having a large corps of dedicated members to having only a few with any real interest in the society before a mere handful of *tatkräftige Leute* got things moving again. This

continuity in spite of setbacks is the result of the sacrifice and dedication of officers and members who are able to change with the times, cast off outdated rules, and expand programs. Adhering to the principles of the constitution and reworking the bylaws are skills that Saengerbund officers have shown to this day; the current constitution committee, headed by Membership Secretary Clyde Nafzinger, is scrutinizing the constitution, which was last revised in 1981, to accommodate the needs of a society that has moved into the twenty-first century.

-Connection-

By adhering to traditions, the Saengerbund has been a home away from home for many immigrants throughout its history. Today the Saengerbund continues to draw German immigrants looking for a connection to their roots. Heinz and Erika Ambrosch immigrated from Rosbach near Frankfurt am Main in 1990. Their only daughter Janette had married Donald Merritt II, an American soldier stationed in Germany, and moved with him to Newark, Delaware, in 1986. When their grandson, Donald III, was born they decided to relocate to Delaware so they could see him grow up and be closer to their only child's family. An introduction to the Delaware Saengerbund and visits to the Bauernstube helped them adjust, for this was a link with home. The whole family joined in March 1991 and became very active. The Merritt family joined the Enzian Volkstanzgruppe; Erika sings in the chorus and, in memory of her childhood, introduced St. Nikolaus to the children's Christmas party. Heinz's expertise as pastry chef is most welcome, as he bakes Apfelstrudel, Strietzel, and fruit tarts whenever needed for the various groups' programs and cooks for the Sunday morning Frühschoppen breakfasts. Because Heinz so enjoyed informal get-togethers in the Bauernstube, it wasn't long before a Stammtisch where he could converse in his native tongue was meeting regularly on Friday evenings.

On the average, 5,000 Germans have immigrated to the United States each year since 1990. In 1998 only twenty stated an intention to live in Delaware. Now that there are fewer immigrants, the Saengerbund's task of preserving German ways may lie with Americans of German heritage discovering their roots. Four current members stumbled over these roots—much to their surprise—when they traced their lineage directly to early members. Robert Spittle is the descendent of Henry Bleyer, Saengerbund president in 1853. Henry (Hank) Maier is the great-grandson of Daniel Maier, the popular and longtime Saengerbund president in the early 1890s. Some members' roots led to the Turners: Richard Schechinger is a grandson of Hermann Schechinger, steward of the Turners; Karl Widdekind is related to Henry Widdekind, gymnastic instructor of the Turners for over thirty years at the turn of the nineteenth century.

-Rooted in Delaware-

The Turners and the Saengerbund have shown by their very names—*Wilmington* Turners and *Delaware* Saengerbund—that they are *verwurzelt*, deeply rooted, in the local soil. This is one of the most important ingredients of a successful history. Just as an individual must become integrated into the new environment, so a society must grow within its *Wirkungsfeld*, or sphere of action. The German societies contributed to the city's intellectual heritage through their literary clubs and strong emphasis on education, which included physical education. The *Sunday Morning Star*'s prediction, cast in March 1901 for the new twentieth century, that physical exercise would become part of every school's

curriculum and even begin at home before school age, had its roots in the Turner movement that emphasized a sound mind in a sound body. The Saengerbund chorus participated in numerous events at the German Hall, the Aldine and Garrick, the Grand Opera House and even the Playhouse, adding to the cultural milieu of the city. Festivals the Saengerbund held at Rosendale, Schützen Park, Bavarian Park, Brandywine Springs Park, and the annual Oktoberfest in Ogletown certainly have brightened Wilmington's social calendar. The word *Fest* is now as common in the English language as Kindergarten and Gesundheit!

As the early immigrants settled down and reared families in Wilmington, the strong ethnic aspects they clung to in the early years were not always understood or upheld by their children, and soon evidence of the effect of this group upon the community became less visible. Nevertheless, the core values taught by the parents or *Meister* remained as the first, second, and third generations became integrated into local society. The outstanding and sought-after skills of their trades and professions were important factors in the industrial expansion of Wilmington and contributed to the overall development of the city. Thus the influence and effect of the Germans and their societies on the local community is indelible. As the German immigrants strengthened and enhanced the American way of life by their traditions and values, so have they in turn benefited from living in a more open society—and in the process of becoming an integral part of it, they themselves became more tolerant of other people's views and more generous in their ways.

-Interconnectedness-

Throughout its history, the Saengerbund has participated in regional, national, and international programs and festivals. Close contact with similar organizations often inspired members to carry on with more enthusiasm. Membership in a regional organization can be a further assurance of the continuation of any society. Through this type of support, an organization's lifespan can be extended, even if it has to face lack of interest of its members, financial hardship, or membership decline. Membership in the Nordoestlicher Saengerbund has helped the Delaware Saengerbund maintain its focus since the founding of the society: the nurture of the German song tradition, even in troubled times. The Enzian Volktanzgruppe, by joining the Nordamerikanisher Schuhplattler Verband, has the assurance of a similar experience.

-Family Affair-

The Delaware Saengerbund is a family-oriented society. Even during the early years when it was strictly a men's chorus, the members' families' needs figured prominently in the men's decisions. Dinners, dances, outings, and festivals were planned so that wives and children could attend. Every year there were special events for the children, and schools were opened for instruction in the German language. Children are important to the future of any organization, and the club has always kept this in mind. Today's members' children are active in the Enzian Volkstanzgruppe, the Kickers teams, and the Teen Age Group. The Easter egg hunt, St. Nikolaus celebration, the picnic, and Oktoberfest with its free amusement rides are occasions where members can spot the club leaders of the future among the children, as they see first-hand how happy they are in the Saengerbund family.

-Hospitality-

One other magic ingredient that has kept the society vibrant has been its open door. By reaching out into the community or inviting the community into its home, the society has garnered greater visibility and vitality. When you have an audience, you have to try harder!

As the Delaware Saengerbund looks forward to its 150th Stiftungsfest, it can reflect on a proud history as a German American society endowed with a unique role: it is the keeper of language, culture, and tradition. The Saengerbund also recognizes this country's freedom to experience its heritage and reciprocally honors this nation by concluding its festival concerts with the hymn, "America the Beautiful." That each generation may continue to honor and keep these traditions alive while remembering the Heimat is the challenge symbolized by the Maibaum at the entrance to the Saengerbund.

> O, beautiful for spacious skies
> For amber waves of grain,
> For purple mountain majesties
> Above the fruited plain.
> America, America!
> God shed his grace on thee,
> And crown they good with brotherhood
> From sea to shining sea.

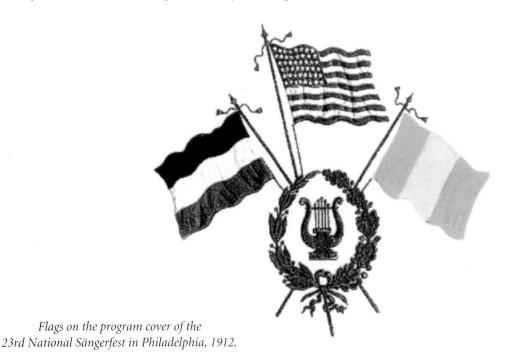

Flags on the program cover of the 23rd National Sängerfest in Philadelphia, 1912.

Music Directors of the Delaware Saengerbund

G. Anton	1853-1854	C. A. Hartmann	1895-1907
Henry Albert	1856-1858	Otto Wenzel	1908-1935
August Roebelen	1856-1857	Carl Elmer	1936
Max L. Lichtenstein	1857-1860	Ludwig Schierl	1936-1939
Henry Albert	1860-1865	Arthur Lemke	1940-1947
Max L. Lichtenstein	1863	Herbert J. Jenny	1948-1955
John Manz	1867-1869	Otto J. Genhart	1956-1971
J. P. T. Fuekel	1869-1870	Arthur Lemke	1971-1977
Frederick Becher	1871-1872	Betty Metz	1978-1983
J. P. T. Fuekel	1873-1874	Donald Rittenhouse	1983-1985
Julius Hess	1877-1879	Betty Metz DeMonic	1985-1986
J. P. T. Fuekel	1880-1882	David Linton	1986-1999
Calvin B. Rhoads	1882-1894	Robert Bunnell	since 1999
Gerhard Schirmer	1894		

DELAWARE SAENGERBUND CHORUS 2002

At the time of the writing of this book the chorus consisted of the following members:

Director: Robert Bunnell,
Accompanist: Sharon Williams
Chairperson of the Music Committee: Hilmar Fricke

First Soprano:
Lilly Budzialek
Sonja Ciresa
Elsie Schwertl Craig
Mary Ann Dowd
Edith Fischer-Berr
Alice Hanke
Sophia Kopec
Hermine Kuska
Mary McDonald
Barbara Prendergast
Erika Schirm
Phyllis Smoyer
Norma Schroeder
Dawn Swartout

Second Soprano:
Erika Ambrosch
Margarete Hawkins
Ingeborg Keith
Margot Kulp
Brigitte Moulson
Ingrid Schober

Alto:
Anne Bolduc
Patty Clay
Anna Cowell
Dorothy Dodds
Carol Foulke
Carol Fricke
Trudy Gilgenast
Helga Kissell
Mary Alice Nagle
Wilhelmine O'Shea
Valerie Reichenbach
Vera Schock
Marguerite Spittle
Inge Thompson

Tenor:
Vicki Farmer
Ron Fetterrolf
Erwin Grieb
Richard Leaning
Barbara Menzian
Robert Picking
Otto Schwoegler

First Bass:
Steve Bobik
Nils England
Keith Farmer
Werner Freymann
Paul Hanke
John Marshall
Richard B. Schechinger
Hans Schober
Simon Schock

Second Bass:
George Fisher
Hilmar Fricke
Clyde Nafzinger
Joseph Rotter

LADIES OF THE DELAWARE SAENGERBUND 2002

OFFICERS

President	Doris Lang
Vice-President	Joan Wooden
Secretary	Stephanie Bobik
Treasurer	Marge Nagy

Kitchen Committee

Waltraut Alberer
Stephanie Bobik
Diene Grabner
Suzanne Grzybowski
Doris Lang
Annemarie McNeal
Lois Meyer
Sophie Myers
Marge Nagy
Irmgard Sukalo
Karen Swank
Heidi Valiante

Members

Concetta Allen
Elli Beck
Anna Marie Cowell
Hilde Cox
Marilyn Downs
Dixie Gagon
Kathe Gass
Hannah Genoese
Reinfriede Houseman
Jan Huggler
Olga Jahn
Peg Johnston
Edith Langdon
Diana Levering
Ann Marie Markovchik

Lore Read
Irene Rice
Tilla Rotter
Jean Sedar
Joan Schmidt
Heidi Sigmund
Margaret Sigmund
Ann Smith
Jean Stanfield
Mildred Sunderland
Sarah Viering
Kathryn Widdekind
Marie Wiedenman
Emma Wipf
Joan Wooden

ENZIAN VOLKSTANZGRUPPE 2002

SENIOR ACTIVE

MaryCay Armstrong
Steve Armstrong
Alfred Escheu
Linda Escheu
Vicki Farmer
Andrea Fischer
Michael Fischer
Stephanie Gass
Norma Grieb
Richard Grieb
Heidi Grieb-Ginn
Andrea Haaz
James Hall
Gerda Hall
James Hall, Jr.
Jason Hall
Ingeborg Keith
Tommy Keith
Hermine Kuska
Reinhold Kuska
Gerhard Kuska
Jen Leszl
Teresa Lord
Romie Lutz
Melissa Mauragas
Mark Mauragas
Liz Merek
Steve Merek
Janett Merritt
Viola Palo

Alex Piragow
Donald Schneck
Joe Schreiber
Brian Schulz
Stephanie Schulz
George Schweiger
Helga Schweiger
Amy Smelgus
Margot Trager
Richard Trager
Klaus Vikari
Bill Wagner
Bill Winkelman
Diana Winkelman

SUPPORTING

Ann Fischer
Horst Fischer
Jeanette Hawks
Laurie Mauragus
Pete Mauragus
Lore Read
William Read
Ann Smith
Don Smith
Sue Vikari
Frank Wolf
Rose Wolf

CHILDREN

Tracy Farmer
Christopher Gass
Emily Ginn
Claudia Gonzalez
Erik Gonzalez
Charles Groff
Jenna Hall
David Keith
Sarah Keith
Matthew Kinney
Amber Kinney
Elizabeth Mauragus
Don Merritt
Ben Miller
Joel Miller
Jessica Miller
Jacob Schneck
Stephanie Schneck
Sara Schreiber
Alyssa Schulz
Morgan Schulz
Mattsy Stinson
Lidia Stlnson
Jennifer Vikari
Kirsten Vikari
Wills Wagner
Julia Wagner
Dominique Wansaw
Tori Widdekind
Brook Winkelman

SAENGERBUND MEMBER STATUS 1853

Saengerbund Member	Status	Trade and Profession	Residence
G. Anton	3/21/1853, active		
William Papemeyer	3/21/1853, active	draftsman	Railroad Depot
Ludwig Grieb	3/21/1853, active	tailor	504 Shipley Street, (1857) Tatnall Street
John H. Muehlhausen	3/21/1853, active	tailor	68 French Street, (1857) 210 East 5th Street
Henry Bleyer	3/21/1853, active	basket maker	51 West Front Street, (1862) 319 W Front St.
John Fehrenbach	3/21/1853, active	brewer	(1862) Hotel Franklin House, 115 E 4th St.
Christian Krauch	3/21/1853, honorary	saloon, hotel	70 King Street, (1862) 308 King St.
Solomon Prell	3/21/1853, active	tailor	92 Market or NE Corner of Knight & 3rd St.
Friedrich Rhein	3/25/1853, active		
Jakob Kienle	3/29/1853, active	baker	62 West Front St.
Robert Wagner	3/29/1853, active	gunlock smith	104 Shipley
Carl Schimminger	3/29/1853, active		
August Hilger	3/29/1853, active	machinist	211 East Front Street, (1862) 15 Walnut St.
Julius Krauch	3/29/1853, active		
Joseph Helmer	4/5/1853, active		
Valentin Walter	4/8, 1853, active	cordwain bootmaker	Seeds Alley, rear of 26 W 7th 32 Tatnall St. (1857)
Fred J. Freed	4/8/1853, passive		
Peter Robertus	4/12/1853, active		
Carl Braun	4/15/1853, active		
Heinrich Baker	4/19/1853, active	laborer	East 3rd St. n Pine
Loui Roder	4/22/1853, active		
Jakob Stuck	4/22/1853, active	baker	King & 7th Street
Reinhard Reinhold	4/26/1853, active		
Andreas Witz	4/26/1853, active	cooper	bds. Mill, betw. French & King St.
John Hess	4/26/1853, active		
Bernhard Loehr	4/26/1853, passive		
John Brodhag	5/3/1853, active	carriage trimmer	46 French Street
Matthäus Muehlheiser	5/3/1853, active	shoemaker	(1867) 203 W 2nd St.
George Hanson	5/3/1853, active	machinist	(1862) bds. 110 E 4th St.
Peter Emmert	5/3/1853, active	cooper	French betw. 14th & 15th St.
August Hiller	5/17/1853, active	dyer and scourer	(1845) 7th betw. Market & King (1853) 6 East 2nd Street
Charles Kaiser	5/31/1853, active	coachmaker	207 East 2nd Street
Peter Graf	6/7/1853, active	blindmaker	2nd & Washington St.
Peter Gross	6/7/1853	carpet weaver	57 King St.
Joseph Gulley	6/7/1853, passive	brewer	SE Corner French & 5th St.
Wilhelm Hirzel	6/21/1853, active	cabinet maker	NE Corner Pine & 4th St.
Friedrich Brodhag	6/21/1853, active		
William Kleinstüwer	7/12/1853, active		
Charles Grobe	7/17/1853, honorary	Prof. of music	145 Market St.
Hübner	7/17/1853, honorary		
Rudolph Wittig	7/19/1853, honorary		
John White	7/19/1853, honorary		

Jakob Beltz	7/26/1853, passive	baker	27th W 8th St.
John Betz	8/23/1853, passive	baker	251 Market St.
Joseph Falk	8/30/1853, passive		
William Wiggins	8/30/1853, honorary	Justice of the Peace	office at 154 Market r 136 King
Hampell Jones	8/30/1853, honorary		
John Fulmer	9/3/1853, honorary	cordwain	108 Market St.
Soles Hitz	10/21/1853, active		
August Hillger	11/23/1853, active	machinist	15 Walnut
Gott. Mammler	11/23/1853		
Gottlieb Bentz	12/14/1853, active	butcher	57 East 6th Street
Oswald Untz	12/28/1853, active	carriagemaker	(1866) 606 E 5th St.
Heinrich Höckler	12/28/1853, active		
John Betz	1/4/1854, active	baker	251 Market St.

SAENGERBUND MEMBER STATUS 1903

Active Singer	Trade and Profession	Residence
I TENOR		
Curran, J.A.		
DeLucca, Joseph	supt.	611 Tatnall St.
Fehl, John	wines and liquor	220 W 4th St.
Fuekel, Theodore J.P.	Fancy Grocer	806 W 5th St.
Gerres, Eduard		
Goenner, William	painter	320 E 4th St., h = 812 W 5th
Greiner, Frederick		
Hafner, Charles	tailor	506 Market St.
Heinekamp, Conrad	piano tuner	221 King St.
Heinel, Arthur	restaurant	1717 Delaware Avenue
Koenig, Carl	bartender	1009 Bennett St.
McCullen, Joseph		
Sell, Joseph	carpenter	1721 Delaware Avenue
Ward, J.		
II TENOR		
Adams, Joseph		
Bartram, F.G.	paper & bags	10 E 7th St., h=1222Tatnall
Bauer, Christopher	wines & liquor, Hotel Bauer	SW Corner 5th & Jackson Sts./ Home = 1000 W 5th St
Braunstein, John		
Eckert, Ernst	driver	1210 Conrad St.
Grigull, Otto		
Krastel, Frederick G.		
Lange, Gustav		
Maletzko, William	cooper	506 Madison St.
Neher, Harry	treasurer Stoeckle Brewing Co.	1123 W 5th St.
Sell, Charles	glazer	1717 Delaware Avenue
Snellenburg, Albert		
Solady, John	machinist	1013 Spruce St.
Wagner, Emil	baker	1126 E 13th St.
I BASS		
Beyerlein, Raymond	beamer	1617 Lincoln St.
Friedrich, Charles	ironworker	322 E 7th St.
Gillespie, James		
Gossen, Hermann	wholesale coffee, tea, cigars	12 E 4th St., h = 301 W 7th St.
Hauber, Anton	proprietor	1423 Harrison St.
Kleitz, Bernhard	jeweler	615 1/2 Market St.
Lacher, Frederick	tailor	303 E 6th St.
Loeber, William	provisions	
Maier, Daniel	baker	619 W Front St.
Michaelis, Joseph	lab	700 Tatnall St.

Omara, Michael
Scott, G.
Ullman, Victor   cooper   916 W 9th St.
Yaeger, Charles   machinist   1320 W 3rd St.
Zimmermann, Harry   caterer   209 Tatnall St.
Zuelke, Albert   cabinetmaker   211 W 2nd St.

II BASS
Brinkheide, Augustus   upholsterer   910 Shallcross Ave.
Grooms, William
Kiepe, William   carpenter   43 Lombard St.
Kleitz, Frederick   bartender   1214 French St.
Kleitz, Georg   jeweler   615 1/2 Market St.
Koerner, Louis   saloon   223&225 King St.
McCafferty, George   ironworker   1112 Pine St.
Preston, Louis   barber   1001 W 4th St., h=303 Rodney
Roach, Martin   sorter   217 Jefferson St.
Schnepf, Harry   saloon Atlantic Garden   224 King St.
Weil, Henry   plumber   2906 Market St.

HONORARY MEMBERS
Abberger, Kaspar
Braun, William
Clemens, G.
Ebner, Peter   bottler   4th & Union
Feldmaier, Henry   restaurant
Grotz, Andrew   cigars, tobacco   221 E 2nd St.
Dr. Hertel, Emil   physician, druggist   301 E 4th St.
Kurtz, Daniel   baker
Maier, Daniel   baker   619 W Front St.
Maier, John   baker
Maier Jr., John
Miller, Henry   baker
Schellkopf, George
Spoerl, Christian   saloonkeeper
Weil, Frederick   harnessmaker   211 W 2nd St.

PASSIVE AND CONTRIBUTING MEMBERS
Abberger, Kasimir   shoemaker   402 Madison St.
Abbott, Edward   clerk   451 S. Claymont
Alsentzer, William
Alexander, William
Blouth, Henry   Grand Union Hotel   NE Corner Front & French St.

OFFICERS OF THE DELAWARE SAENGERBUND

SAENGERBUND WILMINGTON

1853
First quarter:

Director	G. Anton
President	William Papemeyer
Vice President	Ludwig Grieb
Secretary	John H. Mühlhausen
Treasurer	Henry Bleyer
Music Librarian	John Fehrenbach

Second quarter:

Director	G. Anton
President	Henry Bleyer
Vice President	Ludwig Grieb
Secretary	John H. Mühlhausen
Treasurer	August Hiller
Music Librarian	Andreas Witz
Asst. Librarian	Reinhard Reinhold
Flag bearers	John Freed and August Hilger

1854
January: temporary officers

President	John Fehrenbach
Treasurer	John Betz
Music Librarian	Valentin Walter

April

President	John Fehrenbach
Vice President	Ludwig Grieb
Secretary	John Betz
Correspond. Sec.	Valentin Walter
Treasurer	Solomon Prell
Music Librarian	Matthaeus Mühlhausen

1855
October Election

President	Heinrich Albert
Vice President	Charles Mayer
Secretary	Friedrich Herzog
Treasurer	Friedrich Weil
Librarian	Valentin Walter

SAENGERBUND SAENGERBUND No. 1

1856
April election:

Music Director	Heinrich Albert
President	Ludwig Grieb
Secretary	A. Gnann

Treasurer	August Hilger

June election:

Correspond. Sec.	Xaver Scheuing
Music Librarian	Joseph Stoeckle

October election:

Music Director	Heinrich Albert	August Roebelen
President	Heinrich Albert	Henry Bleyer (November)
Vice President	Charles Mayer	Ernst Eylert/ Andreas Dettling
Secretary	Friedrich Herzog	Robert Wagner
Treasurer	Friedrich Weil	Jacob Stuck
Correspond. Sec.	Xaver Scheuing	Joseph Magg
Music Librarian	Valentin Walter	Sebastian Sparr/ August Hiller
Assistant Librarian		Joseph Fischer

1857
January election:

Music Director	Heinrich Albert
President	Charles Meier
Vice President	G. Bürkle
Secretary	Friedrich Herzog
Music Librarian	Andreas Krotz

April election:		March election:
President	Welke	Henry Bleyer
Vice President	Thielemann	Jacob Stuck
Secretary	Charles Meier	Ignaz Blank
Corresp. Secr.		Henry Haar
Treasurer	Friedrich Weil	Lorenz Lohner
Music Librarian		August Hiller
Asst. Librarian		Joseph Niedermaier

April election:

Music Director	Max L. Lichtenstein

July election:

President	Friedrich Herzog
Vice President	Jacob Pfeifer
Secretary	Charles Meyer
Treasurer	Friedrich Weil
Correspond. Sec.	Charles Noethen
Music Librarian	William Cloos

	October election:	September election:
President	Jacob Pfeifer	Ludwig Grieb
Vice President	William Cloos	August Hiller

Secretary	Friedrich Herzog	Joseph Kirn
Corresp. Sec.		Ignaz Blank
Treasurer	Friedrich Weil	Andreas Dettling
Music Librarian	George Schellkopf	Joseph Niedermaier
Asst. Librarian		Wiegand Kunz

1858
January election:

Music Director	Heinrich Albert
President	Friedrich Weil
Vice President	Jacob Pfeifer
Secretary	Friedrich Herzog
Treasurer	Charles Meier

	April election:	March election:
President	Jacob Pfeifer	Ludwig Grieb
Vice President	Christian Leineweber	August Hiller
Secretary	Friedrich Herzog	Adolf Kirn
Corresp. Sec.		Ignaz Blank
Treasurer	Charles Meier	Andreas Dettling
Music Librarian	William Cloos	Karl Hartmann
Asst. Librarian		Becker

DELAWARE SAENGERBUND

1858
May election:

President	Ludwig Grieb
Vice President	Jacob Pfeifer
Rec. Secretary	Friedrich Herzog
Financial Sec.	Adolf Kirn
Treasurer	Andreas Dettling
Music Librarian	Joseph Niedermaier/Wilhelm Cloos
Music Director	Max. L. Lichtenstein

November election:

President	Andreas Dettling
Vice President	Charles Meyer
Rec. Secretary	Adolph Kirn
Treasurer	Jakob Stuck
Music Librarian	Christian Spoerl/Gottfried Weil
Music Director	Heinrich Albert

1859
January election:

President	Gottfried Weil
Vice President	Christian Spoerl
Rec. Secretary	Ignaz Blank
Financial Sec.	Adolf Kir n
Treasurer	Joseph Niedermaier
Music Librarian	Hartmann/Banholzer
Music Director	

April election:

President	Heinrich Wagner
Vice President	Friedrich Franke
Rec. Secretary	Adolf Kirn
Financial Sec.	Ignaz Blank
Treasurer	Andreas Dettling
Music Librarian	Christian Spoerl/Wilhelm Cloos
Music Director	Heinrich Albert

July election:

President	Ludwig Grieb
Vice President	Andreas Dettling
Rec. Secretary	Friedrich Herzog
Financial Sec.	Adolf Kirn
Treasurer	Friedrich Weil
Music Librarian	Wilhelm Cloos/Gottfried Weil
Music Director	Heinrich Albert

October election:

President	Ludwig Grieb
Vice President	Heinrich Wagner
Rec. Secretary	Ignaz Blank
Financial Sec.	Adolf Kirn
Treasurer	August Hiller
Music Librarian	Wilhelm Cloos/Christian Spoerl
Music Director	Max L. Lichtenstein

1860
March election:

President	Charles Meyer
Vice President	Christian Hauser
Rec. Secretary	Friedrich Schwarz
Financial Sec.	Johann Stich
Treasurer	August Hiller
Music Librarian	Karl Herzel/Gottfried Weil
Music Director	Max L. Lichtenstein

June election:

President	Christian Hauser
Vice President	Andreas Dettling
Rec. Secretary	Friedrich Schwarz
Financial Sec.	Christian Spoerl
Treasurer	August Hiller
Music Librarian	Wilhelm Cloos/Andreas Grotz
Music Director	Max L. Lichtenstein

September election:

President	Charles Noethen
Vice President	Adolf Kirn
Rec. Secretary	Ignaz Blank
Financial Sec.	Heinrich Wagner
Treasurer	August Hiller
Music Librarian	W. Wagner/Manz
Music Director	

December election:

President	Charles Noethen
Vice President	Adolf Kirn
Rec. Secretary	Ignaz Blank
Financial Sec.	Heinrich Wagner
Treasurer	August Hiller
Music Librarian	Manz/Hiller
Music Director	Henry Albert

1861
June election:

President	Ludwig (Louis) Grieb
Secretary	Henry Wagner
Treasurer	Andreas Dettling
Music Director	Henry Albert

1862
First half of the year

President	Louis Grieb
Secretary	Henry Wagner
Treasurer	Andrew Dettling

Second half of the year

President	Louis Grieb
Vice President	Adolph Kirn
Secretary	Henry Wagner
Treasurer	Andrew Dettling
Music Librarian	Friedrich Hiller
Music Director	Henry Albert

1863
First half of the year

President	Carl Hartmann
Vice President	John Manz
Secretary	Ignaz Blank
Financial Sec.	Friedrich Hiller
Treasurer	August Hiller
Music Librarian	Friedrich Schulmeister
Music Director	Henry Albert

Second half of the year

President	John Manz
Vice President	Louis Grieb
Secretary	Adolph Kirn/Ferdinand Hiller
Financial Sec.	Henry Miller/August Hiller
Treasurer	Andreas Dettling
Music Librarian	Friedrich Schulmeister
Music Director	Henry Albert

1864
First half of the year

President	Louis Grieb
Vice President	Andreas Dettling
Secretary	John Manz

Financial Sec.	Ignaz Blank
Treasurer	August Hiller
Music Librarian	Friedrich Schulmeister
Music Director	

Second half of the year

President	Joseph Niedermaier
Vice President	Friedrich Schulmeister
Secretary	Adolph Kirn
Financial Sec.	W. Meier
Treasurer	August Hiller
Music Librarian	John Dörzbach
Music Director	Henry Albert

1865
First half of the year

President	Louis Grieb
Vice President	William Cloos
Secretary	John Manz
Financial Sec.	Wilhelm Wagner
Treasurer	Adolph Kirn
Music Librarian	Friedrich Schulmeister
Music Director	Henry Albert

Second half of the year

President	John Manz
Vice President	Andreas Dettling
Secretary	Otto Maurer
Financial Sec.	Franz Stuhlfeld
Treasurer	Spiegelhalter
Music Librarian	John Dörzbach
Music Director	Henry Albert

1866
First half of the year

President	John Manz
Vice President	John Dörzbach
Secretary	Andreas Dettling
Financial Sec.	Wilhelm Wagner
Treasurer	Joseph Niedermaier
Music Librarian	John Dörzbach
Music Director	Henry Albert

Second half of the year

President	John Manz
Vice President	Wilhelm Cloos
Secretary	Ferdinand Hiller
Financial Sec.	Wilhelm Wagner
Music Librarian	John Dörzbach
Music Director	John Manz

1867
First half of the year

President	Andreas Dettling

Vice President	John Manz/John Dörzbach
Secretary	Conrad Manz
Financial Sec.	Franz Stuhlfeld
Treasurer	Joseph Meier
Music Librarian	John Dörzbach
Music Director	John Manz

Second half of the year

President	John Manz
Vice President	Wilhelm Cloos
Secretary	Ferdinand Hiller
Financial Sec.	Wilhelm Wagner
Music Librarian	John Dörzbach
Music Director	John Manz

1868
First half of the year

President	Heinrich Müller
Vice President	John Dörzbach
Secretary	Ferdinand Hiller
Financial Sec.	Wilhelm Wagner
Treasurer	Andreas Dettling
Music Librarian	Christian Becker/Wilhelm Cloos
Music Director	John Manz

Second half of the year

President	Oskar Schwarz
Vice President	Wilhelm Cloos
Secretary	Ferdinand Hiller
Financial Sec.	Wilhelm Wagner
Music Librarian	John Dörzbach
Music Director	John Manz

1869
First half of the year

President	Heinrich Müller
Vice President	Christian Becker
Secretary	Arnold Zuppinger
Financial Sec.	Joseph Niedermaier
Treasurer	Andreas Dettling
Music Librarian	Franz Stuhlfeld
Music Director	John Manz

Second half of the year

President	Christian Becker
Vice President	Heinrich Müller
Secretary	A. Meyer
Financial Sec.	V. Schneider
Treasurer	Wilhelm Cloos
Music Director	J. P. T. Fuekel

1870
First half of the year

President	Heinrich Müller

Vice President	Dirhammer
Secretary	Wilhelm Wagner
Financial Sec.	V. Schneider
Treasurer	Wilhelm Cloos
Music Librarian	Franz Stuhlfeld
Music Director	J.P.T. Fuekel

Second half of the year

President	August Hiller
Vice President	Heinrich Müller
Secretary	Ferdinand Hiller
Treasurer	Wilhelm Cloos
Music Librarian	Franz Stuhlfeld
Music Director	J. P. T. Fuekel

DELAWARE HARMONIE

1871
First half of the year

President	Ignaz Blank
Vice President	Henry Miller
Secretary	Frederick von Bourdon
Financial Sec.	Leonhard Ritter
Treasurer	August Hiller
Music Librarian	Franz Stuhlfeld/Joseph Sell
Music Director	Friedrich Becher

Second half of the year

President	Julius Hess
Vice President	Conrad Manz
Secretary	Eberhard Freye
Financial Sec.	Anton Hauber
Treasurer	August Hiller
Music Librarian	Joseph Sell/C. Ochsner
Music Director	Friedrich Becher

1872
First half of the year

President	Henry Miller
Vice President	Cloberg
Secretary	Eberhard Freye
Financial Sec.	Chr. Bauer
Treasurer	W. Cloos
Music Librarian	Anton Hauber/Julius Hess
Music Director	Friedrich Becher

Second half of the year

President	Ignaz Blank
Vice President	Anton Hauber
Secretary	Frederick von Bourdon
Financial Sec.	Casimir Abberger
Treasurer	Joseph Niedermaier
Music Librarian	Franz Stuhlfeld/C. Moeves Jr.
Music Director	J.P.T. Fuekel

1873
First half of the year

President	Anton Hauber
Vice President	William Cloos
Secretary	Frederick von Bourdon
Treasurer	Joseph Niedermaier
Music Librarian	Franz Stuhlfeld
Music Director	J.P.T. Fuekel

Second half of the year

President	Henry Miller
Vice President	Ignaz Blank
Secretary	Frederick von Bourdon
Treasurer	William Cloos
Music Librarian	Franz Stuhlfeld
Music Director	J.P.T. Fuekel

1874
First half of the year

President	A. Cloberg
Vice President	John Reese
Secretary	Frederick von Bourdon
Treasurer	William Cloos
Music Librarian	Franz Stuhlfeld
Music Director	J.P.T. Fuekel

Second half of the year

President	Henry Miller
Vice President	William Cloos
Secretary	Frederick von Bourdon
Treasurer	Daniel Maier
Music Librarian	Franz Stuhlfeld
Music Director	J.P. T. Fuekel

No officers or minutes were recorded for 1875 and 1876

1877

President	Henry Miller
Vice President	William Cloos
Secretary	Frederick von Bourdon
Treasurer	Daniel Maier
Music Librarian	Franz Stuhlfeld
Music Director	J.P.T. Fuekel

DELAWARE SAENGERBUND

1877

President	Daniel Maier
Secretary	Francis Scheu
Treasurer	Joseph Sell

Second half of the year

President	Daniel Maier
Secretary	Conrad Manz
Financial Sec.	Christian Bacher

Treasurer	Joseph Sell
Music Librarian	Gottlieb Knittel
Music Director	Julius Hess

1878
First half of the year

President	Daniel Maier
Vice President	Charles Yetter
Secretary	Christian Reichard
Financial Sec.	John Maier
Treasurer	Joseph Sell
Music Librarian	Gottlieb Knittel
Music Director	Julius Hess

Second half of the year

President	Daniel Maier
Vice President	Francis Scheu
Secretary	Gustav Scheu
Financial Sec.	Gottlieb Knittel
Treasurer	Joseph Sell
Music Librarian	Gottlieb Knittel
Music Director	Julius Hess

1879
First half of the year

President	Daniel Maier
Vice President	Charles Yetter
Secretary	Christian Reichard
Financial Sec.	John Maier
Treasurer	Joseph Sell
Music Librarian	Gottlieb Knittel
Music Director	Julius Hess

Second half of the year

President	Daniel Maier
Vice President	Francis Scheu
Secretary	Gustav Scheu
Financial Sec.	Gottlieb Knittel
Treasurer	Joseph Sell
Music Librarian	Gottlieb Knittel
Music Director	Julius Hess

1880
First half of the year

President	Daniel Maier
Vice President	Charles Yetter
Secretary	Georg B. Metzner
Treasurer	Joseph Sell
Music Librarian	Franz Stuhlfeld
Music Director	J.P.T. Fuekel

Second half of the year

President	Daniel Maier

Vice President   Charles Yetter
Secretary   Georg B. Metzner
Treasurer   Georg Staib
Music Librarian   Franz Stuhlfeld
Music Director   J.P.T. Fuekel

1881
First half of the year

President   Christian Popp
Vice President   Charles Yetter
Secretary   Peter Ebner
Treasurer   Georg Staib
Music Librarian   Franz Stuhlfeld
Music Director   J.P.T. Fuekel

Second half of the year

President   Daniel Maier
Vice President   Conrad Manz
Secretary   Charles Yetter
Treasurer   Georg Staib
Music Librarian   Franz Stuhlfeld
Music Director   J.P.T. Fuekel

1882
First half of the year

President   Daniel Maier
Vice President   Conrad Manz
Secretary   Charles Yetter
Treasurer   Georg Staib
Music Librarian   Gustav Georgi
Music Director   Calvin B. Rhoads

Second half of the year

President   Peter Ebner
Vice President   Raymund Beyerlein
Secretary   Georg B. Metzner
Treasurer   Daniel Maier
Music Librarian   Gustav Georgi
Music Director   Calvin B. Rhoads

1883
First half of the year

President   Christian Popp
Vice President   August Kuhlmann
Secretary   Georg B. Metzner
Treasurer   Charles Yetter
Music Librarian   Gustav Georgi
Music Director   Calvin B. Rhoads

Second half of the year

President   Peter Ebner
Vice President   Raymund Beyerlein
Secretary   Georg B. Metzner

Treasurer   Daniel Maier
Music Librarian   Gustav Georgi
Music Director   Calvin B. Rhoads

1884
President   Daniel Maier
Vice President   Raymund Beyerlein
Secretary   Georg B. Metzner
Financial Sec.   G. Neumann
Treasurer   Charles Yetter
Music Librarian   Gustav Georgi
Music Director   Calvin B. Rhoads

1885
President   Anton Hauber
Vice President   Fred Weil
Secretary   Peter Ebner
Financial Sec.   Henry Schorr
Treasurer   Charles Yetter
Music Librarian   A. Steinke
Music Director   Calvin B. Rhoads

1886
President   Henry Zimmermann
Vice President   A. Steinke
Secretary   Peter Ebner
Financial Sec.   Georg B. Metzner
Treasurer   Charles Yetter
Music Librarian   Albert Armbruster
Music Director   Calvin B. Rhoads

1887
President   Daniel Maier
Vice President   Gustav Steinke
Secretary   Gustav Scheu
Financial Sec.   Henry Schorr
Treasurer   Henry Zimmermann
Music Librarian   Albert Armbruster
Music Director   Calvin B. Rhoads

1888
President   Daniel Maier
Vice President   Andrew Dettling
Secretary   Anton Hauber
Financial Sec.   Christoph Bauer
Treasurer   Charles Yetter
Music Librarian   Peter Ebner
Music Director   Calvin B. Rhoads

1889
President   Daniel Maier
Vice President   Gustav Steinke
Secretary   Gustav Scheu
Treasurer   Harry Zimmerman

1890
President   Daniel Maier

Vice President — Andrew Dettling
Secretary — Harry F.Schnepf
Treasurer — Harry Zlmmerman

1891
President — Daniel Maier
Vice President — Andrew Dettling
Secretary — Harry F. Schnepf
Treasurer — Harry Zimmerman

1892
President — Daniel Maier
Vice President — C. Clemens
Secretary — Harry F. Schnepf
Treasurer — Andrew Dettling

1893
President — Daniel Maier
Vice President — C. Clemens
Secretary — Harry F. Schnepf
Treasurer — Andrew Dettling

1894
President — Daniel Maier
Vice President — Anton Hauber
Secretary — Harry F. Schnepf
Treasurer — Frederick Kleitz

1895
President — Daniel Maier
Vice President — Joseph Sell
Secretary — Harry F. Schnepf
Treasurer — Frederick Kleitz

1896
President — Peter Ebner
Vice President — Joseph Sell
Secretary — Harry F. Schnepf
Treasurer — Charles Yetter

1897
President — Peter Ebner
Vice President — J.P.T. Fuekel
Recording Secretary — Christopher Bauer
Financial Secretary — Charles Jaeger
Treasurer — Charles Yetter
Librarian — Gustav Ripka

1898
President — Joseph Sell
Secretary — Henry F. Schnepf
Financial Secretary — Dr. Emil Hertel
Treasurer — Charles Yetter

1899
President — Joseph Sell
Secretary — Henry F. Schnepf
Financial Secretary — Dr. Emil Hertel

Treasurer — Charles Yetter

1900
President — Charles Yetter
Secretary — Harry F. Schnepf
Financial Secretary — Louis Koerner
Treasurer — Christopher Bauer

1901
President — Anton Hauber
Vice President — Christopher Bauer
Secretary — Louis Koerner
Treasurer — Bernard Kleitz

1902
President — Anton Hauber
Vice President — Christopher Bauer
Recording Secretary — Louis Koerner
Financial Secretary — Harry Neher
Treasurer — Theodore Fuekel
Librarian — Charles Hafner

1903
President — Harry Zimmerman
Vice President — Christopher Bauer
Recording Secretary — John Soladay
Financial Secretary — Joseph Adams
Treasurer — Bernard Kleitz
Librarian — Charles Hafner

1904
President — Christopher Bauer
Vice President- — J.P.T. Fuekel
Recording Secretary — A.J. Kooch
Financial Secretary — Joseph Adams
Treasurer — Anton Hauber
Librarian — Charles Hafner

1905
President — Harry S. Neher
Vice President — J.P.T. Fuekel
Recording Secretary — Harry F. Schnepf
Financial Secretary — B. Beste, Jr.
Treasurer — Anton Hauber
Librarian — George Bacher

1906
President — Joseph Sell
Vice President — J.P.T. Fuekel
Recording Secretary — Harry F. Schnepf
Financial Secretary — Joseph E. Adams
Treasurer — Bernard Kleitz
Librarian — Charles Hafner

1907
President — Joseph Sell
Vice President — J.P.T. Fuekel
Recording Secretary — Harry F. Schnepf

Financial Secretary	Albert Zuelke
Treasurer	Bernard Kleitz
Librarian	Ernst Zuelke

1908

President	Bernard Kleitz
Vice President	George Kleitz
Recording Secretary	Harry F. Schnepf
Financial Secretary	Frank Krastel
Treasurer	John Fehl
Librarian	Adolph Mueller

1909

President	Bernard Kleitz
Vice President	George Kleitz
Recording Secretary	Harry F. Schnepf
Financial Secretary	Frank Krastel
Treasurer	John Fehl
Librarian	Adolph Mueller

1910

President	Arthur Heinel
Vice President	Ernest Eckert
Recording Secretary	Conrad Heinekamp
Financial Secretary	Albert Zuelke
Treasurer	John Fehl
Librarian	Max Neumann

1911

President	Arthur Heinel
Vice President	Ernest Eckert
Recording Secretary	Conrad Heinekamp
Financial Secretary	Albert Zuelke
Treasurer	John Fehl
Librarian	Max Neumann

1912

President	Herman Gossen
Vice President	Gustav Lange
Recording Secretary	Conrad Heinekamp
Financial Secretary	Albert Zuelke
Treasurer	John Fehl
Librarian	Max Neumann

1913

President	Hermann Gossen
Vice President	Joseph Hess
Recording Secretary	Conrad Heinekamp
Treasurer	Frederick Kleitz
Financial Sec.	
Music Director	Otto Wenzel

1914

President	Hermann Gossen
Vice President	Christian Seidle
Secretary	Conrad Heinekamp
Financial Sec.	William Kiepe

Treasurer	Emil Wagner
Music Librarian	Joseph Graham
Music Director	Otto Wenzel

1915

President	Christian Seidle
Vice President	William Kiepe
Secretary	Conrad Heinekamp
Financial Sec.	Joseph Hagemann
Treasurer	Emil Wagner
Music Librarian	Joseph Graham
Music Director	Otto Wenzel

1916

President	William Kiepe
Vice President	Frank Krastel
Secretary	Conrad Heinekamp
Financial Sec.	Albert Zuelke
Treasurer	Ernst Eckert
Music Librarian	Eugen Basel
Music Director	Otto Wenzel

1917

President	William Kiepe
Vice President	Max Neumann
Secretary	Conrad Heinekamp
Financial Sec.	Albert Zuelke
Treasurer	Christian Seidle
Music Librarian	Eugen Basel
Music Director	Otto Wenzel

1918

President	William Kiepe
Vice President	Max Neumann
Secretary	Conrad Heinekamp
Financial Sec.	Albert Zuelke
Treasurer	Christian Seidle
Music Librarian	Eugen Basel
Music Director	Otto Wenzel

1919

President	Hermann Gossen
Vice President	Georg Kalmbacher
Secretary	Conrad Heinekamp
Financial Sec.	Moses zzz
Treasurer	Christian Seidle
Music Librarian	Karl Reineck
Music Director	Otto Wenzel

1920

President	William Kiepe
Vice President	Frank Hütwohl
Secretary	Conrad Heinekamp
Financial Sec.	Moses Weil
Treasurer	Christian Seidle
Music Librarian	Karl Reineck
Music Director	Otto Wenzel

1921

President	William Kiepe
Vice President	Frank Krastel
Secretary	Conrad Heinekamp
Financial Sec.	Albert Zuelke
Treasurer	Christian Seidle
Music Librarian	Frank Krastel
Music Director	Otto Wenzel

1922

President	William Kiepe
Vice President	Frank Krastel
Secretary	Conrad Heinekamp
Financial Sec.	Albert Zuelke
Treasurer	Christian Seidle
Music Librarian	Frank Krastel
Music Director	Otto Wenzel

1923

President	Ernst Eckert
Vice President	Joseph Hess
Secretary	Conrad Heinekamp
Financial Sec.	Albert Zuelke
Treasurer	Christian Seidle
Music Librarian	Edward Gerres
Music Director	Otto Wenzel

1924

President	Ernst Eckert
Vice President	Joseph Hess
Secretary	Conrad Heinekamp
Financial Sec.	Albert Zuelke
Treasurer	Christian Seidle
Music Librarian	Edward Gerres
Music Director	Otto Wenzel

1924

Incorporated as Delaware Saengerbund and Library Association

President	Hermann Gossen
Vice President	Bernhard Kleitz
Secretary	Conrad Heinekamp
Financial Sec.	Bernhard Feustel
Treasurer	Christian Seidle
Librarian	Georg Kalmbacher
Music Director	Otto Wenzel

1925

President	Ernst Zuelke
Vice President	Bernhard Kleitz
Secretary	Conrad Heinekamp
Financial Sec.	Bernhard Feustel
Treasurer	Christian Seidle
Librarian	Georg Kalmbacher
Music Director	Otto Wenzel

1926

President	Emil Dochter
Vice President	Bernhard Kleitz
Secretary	Conrad Heinekamp
Financial Secretary	Bernhard Feustel
Treasurer	Christian Seidle
Librarian	Georg Kalmbacher
Music Director	Otto Wenzel

1927

President	Emil Dochter/Albert Zuelke
Vice President	Bernhard Kleitz
Secretary	Conrad Heinekamp
Financial Sec.	Bernhard Feustel
Treasurer	Christian Seidle
Librarian	Georg Kalmbacher
Music Director	Otto Wenzel

1928

President	Albert Zuelke
Vice President	Bernhard Kleitz
Secretary	Conrad Heinekamp
Financial Sec.	Bernhard Feustel
Treasurer	Christian Seidle
Librarian	Georg Kalmbacher/Karl Kutterolf
Music Director	Otto Wenzel

1929

President	Albert Zuelke
Vice President	Eugene Kachelmus
Secretary	Conrad Heinekamp
Financial Sec.	Ludwig Schierl
Treasurer	Bernhard Kleitz
Librarian	Peter Loch
Music Director	Otto Wenzel

1930

President	Albert Zuelke
Vice President	Eugene Kachelmus
Secretary	Conrad Heinekamp
Financial Sec.	Ludwig Schierl
Treasurer	Bernhard Kleitz
Librarian	Peter Loch
Music Director	Otto Wenzel

1931

President	Albert Zuelke
Vice President	Eugene Kachelmus
Secretary	Conrad Heinekamp
Financial Sec.	Paul Nake
Treasurer	Bernhard Kleitz
Music Librarian	Karl Kutterolf
Library	Karl Klenk
Music Director	Otto Wenzel

1932

President	Ernst Stoessel

Vice President	Henry Stuhmer
Secretary	Edward Gerres
Financial Sec.	Paul Nake
Treasurer	Bernhard Kleitz
Music Librarian	Karl Kutterolf
Library	Hans Schilling
Music Director	Otto Wenzel

1933
President	Ernst Stoessel
Vice President	Henry Stuhmer
Secretary	Edward Gerres
Financial Sec.	Paul Nake
Treasurer	Bernhard Kleitz
Music Librarian	Karl Kutterolf
Library	Hans Schilling
Music Director	Otto Wenzel

1934
President	Bernard Hessler
Vice President	Fritz Steinke
Secretary	Ernst Stoessel/Hans Schilling
Financial Sec.	Albert Zuelke
Treasurer	Richard Steinke
Music Librarian	Karl Kutterolf
Library	Peter Loch
Music Director	Otto Wenzel

1935
President	Richard Steinke
Vice President	Karl Kutterolf
Secretary	Hans Schilling
Financial Sec.	Albert Zuelke
Treasurer	John Winsel
Music Librarian	
Library	Peter Loch
Music Director	Otto Wenzel

1936
President	Richard Steinke
Vice President	Edward Gerres
Secretary	Ludwig Schierl
Financial Sec.	Paul Nake
Treasurer	John Winsel
Music Librarian	Albert Zuelke
Library	Peter Loch
Music Director	Otto Wenzel

1937
President	Richard Steinke
Vice President	Franz Rassmann
Secretary	Ludwig Schierl
Financial Sec.	Paul Nake
Treasurer	John Winsel
Music Librarian	Albert Zuelke
Library	

Music Director	Ludwig Schierl

1938
President	Richard Steinke
Vice President	Franz Rassmann
Secretary	Ludwig Schierl
Financial Sec.	Paul Nake
Treasurer	John Winsel
Music Librarian	Albert Zuelke
Library	
Music Director	Ludwig Schierl

1939
President	Richard Steinke/Arthur Bracken
Vice President	Arthur Bracken
Recording Secretary	Peter Loch
Financial Secretary	Paul Nake
Treasurer	John Winsel
Librarian	Albert Zuelke
Music Director	Ludwig Schierl

1940
President	Roy Haitsch
Vice President	Fritz Steinke
Recording Secretary	Ludwig Schierl
Financial Secretary	Paul Nake
Treasurer	William Schomburg
Librarian	Josef Maucher
Music Director	Arthur Lemke

1941
President	Max Hamer
Vice President	Fritz Giesemann
Recording Secretary	Ludwig Schierl
Financial Secretary	Paul Nake
Treasurer	William Schomburg
Librarian	Josef Maucher
Music Director	Arthur Lemke

1942
President	Max Hamer
Vice President	Fritz Giesemann
Recording Secretary	Ludwig Schierl
Financial Secretary	Paul Nake
Treasurer	William Schomburg
Librarian	Phillip Schaal
Music Director	Arthur Lemke

1943
President	Max Hamer
Vice President	Fritz Giesemann
Recording Secretary	Ludwig Schierl
Financial Secretary	Paul Nake
Treasurer	William Schomburg
Librarian	Phillip Schaal
Music Director	Arthur Lemke

1944

President	Max Hamer
Vice President	Fritz Giesemann
Recording Secretary	Fred Fischer
Financial Secretary	Paul Nake
Treasurer	William Schomburg
Librarian	Joseph Maucher
Music Director	Arthur Lemke

1945

President	Max Hamer
Vice President	Fritz Giesemann
Recording Secretary	Fred Fischer
Financial Secretary	Paul Nake
Treasurer	William Schomburg
Librarian	Joseph Maucher
Music Director	Arthur Lemke
Music Librarian	

1946

President	Fritz Giesemann
Vice President	Otto Steinke
Recording Secretary	Ludwig Schierl
Financial Secretary	Bill Noell
Treasurer	Alfred Gilgenast
Librarian	Fritz Steinke
Music Director	Arthur Lemke

1947

President	Otto Steinke
Vice President	Emil Dahnken
Recording Secretary	Fred Fischer
Financial Secretary	Hermann Schweiger
Treasurer	Alfred Gilgenast
Librarian	Fritz Steinke
Music Director	Arthur Lemke

1948

President	Emil Dahnken
Vice President	Richard Wolf
Recording Secretary	Fred Fischer
Financial Secretary	Arthur Menk
Treasurer	Alfred Gilgenast
Librarian	Alfred Haase
Music Director	Dr. Herbert J. Jenny

1949

President	Emil Dahnken
Vice President	Richard Wolf
Recording Secretary	Fred Fischer
Financial Secretary	Arthur Menk
Treasurer	Alfred Gilgenast
Librarian	Joseph Maucher
Music Director	Dr. Herbert J. Jenny

1950

President	Max J. Hamer
Vice President	Erwin Faller
Recording Secretary	Fred Fischer
Financial Secretary	William Schomburg
Treasurer	Arthur Menk
Librarian	Joseph Maucher
Music Director	Dr. Herbert J. Jenny

1951

President	Otto Steinke
Vice President	Peter Loch
Recording Secretary	Fred Fischer
Financial Secretary	William Schomburg
Treasurer	Ludwig Schierl
Librarian	Joseph Maucher
Music Director	Dr. Herbert J. Jenny

1952

President	August Hagenah/Ludwig Schierl
Vice President	Max Schilling
Recording Secretary	Fred Fischer/Emil Dahnken
Financial Secretary	Paul Heinemann
Treasurer	Alfred Gilgenast
Librarian	Richard Wolf
Music Director	Dr. Herbert J. Jenny

1953

President	Ludwig Schierl
Vice President	Paul Bergner
Recording Secretary	Fred Fischer
Financial Secretary	Emil Kurzius
Treasurer	Paul Herold
Librarian	Fritz Steinke
Music Director	Dr. Herbert J. Jenny

1954

President	Ludwig Schierl
Vice President	Max Hamer
Recording Secretary	Alfred Haase
Financial Secretary	Walter Hagelstein
Treasurer	Hellmuth Czojor
Librarian	Fritz Steinke
Music Director	Dr. Herbert J. Jenny
Music Librarian	

1955

President	Erich Kaeks
Vice President	Paul Bergner
Recording Secretary	Robert H. Reineke
Financial Secretary	Werner Hampel
Treasurer	Alfred Gilgenast
Librarian	Peter Loch
Music Director	Dr. Herbert J. Jenny
Music Librarian	

1956

President	Erich Kaeks
Vice President	Alfred Gilgenast
Recording Secretary	Fred Fischer
Financial Secretary	Helmut Hampel
Treasurer	Werner Hampel
Librarian	Richard Traeger
Music Director	Otto Genhart
Music Librarian	

1957

President	Werner Hampel
Vice President	Arthur Menk
Recording Secretary	Fred Fischer
Financial Secretary	Helmut Hampel
Treasurer	Paul Heinemann
Librarian	Alfred Gilgenast
Music Director	Otto Genhart
Music Librarian	

1958

President	Emil Dahnken
Vice President	Werner Hampel/Alfred Gilgenast
Recording Secretary	Fred Fischer
Financial Secretary	Mike Venema/Paul Heinemann
Treasurer	Richard Wolf
Librarian	Otto Wedman
Music Director	Otto Genhart
MusicLibrarian	

1959

President	Emil Dahnken
Vice President	Alfred Gilgenast
Recording Secretary	Fred Fischer
Financial Secretary	Max Schilling
Treasurer	Richard Wolf
Librarian	Paul Herold
Music Director	Otto Genhart
MusicLibrarian	

1960

President	Emil Dahnken
Vice President	Alfred Gilgenast
Recording Secretary	Fred Fischer
Financial Secretary	Max Schilling
Treasurer	Richard Wolf
Librarian	Paul Herold
Music Director	Otto Genhart
Music Librarian	

1961

President	Emil Dahnken
Vice President	Alfred Gilgenast
Recording Secretary	Alfred Escheu
Financial Secretary	Max Schilling
Treasurer	Richard Wolf
Librarian	Paul Herold
Music Director	Otto Genhart
MusicLibrarian	

1962

President	Emil Dahnken
Vice President	Helmut Hampel
Recording Secretary	Paul Heinemann/Horst Zech/Helmut Hampel
Financial Secretary	Max Schilling
Treasurer	Richard Wolf
Librarian	Paul Herold
Music Director	Otto Genhart
MusicLibrarian	

1963

President	Emil Dahnken
First Vice President	Helmut Hampel
Second Vice President	Elly Gilgenast
Recording Secretary	Mary Ruth Morganstern
Corresponding Secretary	Alfred Escheu
Financial Secretary	Simon Schock
Treasurer	Alfred Gilgenast
Music Director	Otto Genhart

1964

President	Emil Dahnken
First Vice President	Helmut Hampel
Second Vice President	Elly Gilgenast
Recording Secretary	Mary Ruth Morganstern
Corresponding Secretary	Alfred Escheu
Financial Secretary	Simon Schock
Treasurer	Alfred Gilgenast
Music Director	Otto Genhart

1965

President	Emil Dahnken
First Vice President	Helmut Hampel
Second Vice President	Elly Gilgenast
Recording Secretary	Mary Ruth Morganstern
Corresponding Secretary	Alfred Escheu
Financial Secretary	Simon Schock
Treasurer	Alfred Gilgenast
Music Director	Otto Genhart

1966

President	William Benecke
First Vice President	Dorothy Dodds
Second Vice President	Elly Gilgenast
Recording Secretary	Helmut Hampel
Corresponding Secretary	Alfred Escheu
Financial Secretary	Simon Schock
Treasurer	Paul Heinemann
Music Director	Otto Genhart

1967

President	William Benecke

First Vice President   Dorothy Dodds
Second Vice President   Elly Gilgenast
Recording Secretary   Helmut Hampel
Corresponding Secretary   Alfred Escheu
Financial Secretary   Simon Schock
Treasurer   Paul Heinemann
Music Director   Otto Genhart

1968
President   William Benecke
First Vice President   Adrien Olivier
Second Vice President   Tom Yost
Recording Secretary   Helmut Hampel
Corresponding Secretary   Paul Heinemann
Membership Secretary   Dorothy Dodds
Treasurer   Werner Goeckel
Music Director   Otto Genhart

1969
President   Wilhelm Schulz
First Vice President   Richard Weis
Second Vice President   Werner Sumpf
Recording Secretary   John Cox
Corresponding Secretary   Siegfried Fuchs
Membership Secretary   Dorothy Dodds
Treasurer   Christa Coffey
Music Director   Otto Genhart

1970
President   Paul Heinemann
First Vice President   Simon Schock
Second Vice President   Werner Sumpf
Recording Secretary   John Cox
Corresponding Secretary   Valerie Hafeken
Membership Secretary   William Benecke
Treasurer   Helmut Hampel
Music Director   Otto Genhart

1971
President   Alfred Escheu
First Vice President   Simon Schock
Second Vice President   William Klabe
Recording Secretary   John Cox
Corresponding Secretary   Valerie Hafeken
Membership Secretary   William Benecke
Treasurer   Helmut Hampel
Music Director   Otto Genhart

1972
President   Alfred Escheu
First Vice President   Fred Thompson
Second Vice President   William Klabe
Recording Secretary   John Cox
Corresponding Secretary   Ann Smith
Membership Secretary   Wolfgang Conrad
Treasurer   Louis Valiante

Music Director   Arthur Lemke

1973
President   Alfred Escheu
First Vice President   Fred Thompson
Second Vice President   Joseph Pouser/Werner Sumpf
Recording Secretary   Peter Schreier
Corresponding Secretary   Ann Smith
Membership Secretary   Wolfgang Conrad
Treasurer   Louis Valiante
Music Director   Arthur Lemke

1974
President   Alfred Escheu
First Vice President   Fred Thompson
Second Vice President   Werner Sumpf
Recording Secretary   Peter Schreier
Corresponding Secretary   Ann Smith
Membership Secretary   Alida Cutts
Treasurer   Helmut Hoeschel
Music Director   Arthur Lemke

1975
President   Werner Sumpf
First Vice President   Fred Thompson
Second Vice President   Michael Zanfini/William Klabe
Recording Secretary   Christine Smith
Corresponding Secretary   Ann Smith
Membership Secretary   Alida Cutts
Treasurer   Helmut Hoeschel
Music Director   Arthur Lemke

1976
President   Werner Sumpf
First Vice-resident   Horst Horn
Second Vice President   William Klabe
Recording Secretary   Christine Smith
Corresponding Secretary   Hilde Yaeger
Membership Secretary   Erich Kaeks
Treasurer   Richard Grieb
Music Director   Arthur Lemke

1977
President   Karl Schmidt
First Vice President   Horst Horn
Second Vice President   Eugene Ruff/Alida Cutts
Recording Secretary   Virginia Swope
Corresponding Secretary   Hilde Yaeger
Membership Secretary   Erich Kaeks
Treasurer   Richard Grieb
Music Director   Arthur Lemke

1978
President   Karl Schmidt
First Vice President   Simon Schock
Second Vice President   William Klabe
Recording Secretary   Virginia Swope

Corresponding Secretary   Ann Smith
Membership Secretary   Lore Read
Treasurer   Christa Coffey
Music Director   Betty Metz

1979
President   William Klabe
First Vice President   Simon Schock
Second Vice President   George Keith
Recording Secretary   Clifford Weber
Corresponding Secretary   Ann Smith
Membership Secretary   Lore Read
Treasurer   Christa Coffey
Music Director   Betty Metz

1980
President   William Klabe
First Vice President   George Schweiger
Second Vice President   George Keith
Recording Secretary   Clifford Weber
Corresponding Secretary   Ann Smith
Membership Secretary   Lore Read
Treasurer   Christa Coffey
Music Director   Betty Metz

1981
President   William Klabe
First Vice President   George Schweiger
Second Vice President   Kenneth Woodlin
Recording Secretary   Charles Bowers Jr.
Corresponding Secretary   Ann Smith
Membership Secretary   Lore Read
Treasurer   Christa Coffey
Music Director   Betty Metz

1982
President   William Klabe
First Vice President   George Schweiger
Second Vice President   Kenneth Woodlin
Recording Secretary   Charles Bowers Jr.
Corresponding Secretary   Margaret Johnston
Membership Secretary   Anita Malanowicz
Treasurer   William Sigmund
Music Director   Betty Metz

1983
President   Simon Schock
First Vice President   George Schweiger
Second Vice President   Thomas Yost
Recording Secretary   Charles Bowers Jr./Linda Escheu
Corresponding Secretary   Margaret Johnston
Membership Secretary   Anita Malanowicz/Jeanne Stanfield
Treasurer   William Sigmund
Music Director   Betty Metz/Donald Rittenhouse

1984
President   Simon Schock

First Vice President   Wilhelm Schulz
Second Vice President   Thomas Yost
Recording Secretary   Linda Escheu
Corresponding Secretary   Carol Fricke
Membership Secretary   Jeanne Stanfield
Treasurer   William Sigmund
Music Director   Donald Rittenhouse

1985
President   Simon Schock
First Vice President   Wilhelm Schulz
Second Vice President   William Klabe
Recording Secretary   Linda Escheu
Corresponding Secretary   Carol Fricke
Membership Secretary   Jeanne Stanfield
Treasurer   William Sigmund
Music Director   Donald Rittenhouse/
                          Betty Metz-DeMonic

1986
President   Simon Schock
First Vice President   Gary Huggler
Second Vice President   William Klabe
Recording Secretary   Linda Escheu
Corresponding Secretary   Carol Fricke
Membership Secretary   Clifford Weber
Treasurer   Lawrence Glick Jr.
Music Director   Betty Metz-DeMonic/
                          David Linton

1987
President   Alfred Escheu
First Vice President   Gary Huggler
Second Vice President   Simon Schock
Recording Secretary   Carl Renner
Corresponding Secretary   Carol Fricke
Membership Secretary   Clifford Weber
Treasurer   Lawrence Glick Jr.
Music Director   David Linton

1988
President   Alfred Escheu
First Vice President   Gary Huggler
Second Vice President   Simon Schock
Recording Secretary   Carl Renner
Corresponding Secretary   Robert Spittle
Membership Secretary   Clifford Weber
Treasurer   Edward Brandenberger
Music Director   David Linton

1989
President   Alfred Escheu
First Vice President   Gary Huggler
Second Vice President   Simon Schock
Recording Secretary   Carl Renner
Corresponding Secretary   Robert Spittle

Membership Secretary	Clifford Weber
Treasurer	Edward Brandenberger
Music Director	David Linton

1990

President	Alfred Escheu
First Vice President	Donald Smith
Second Vice President	Simon Schock
Recording Secretary	Carl Renner
Corresponding Secretary	Robert Spittle
Membership Secretary	William Read
Treasurer	Heinz Beck
Music Director	David Linton

1991

President	Carl Renner
First Vice President	Donald Smith
Second Vice President	Wallace Hansen
Recording Secretary	Lois Meyer
Corresponding Secretary	Robert Spittle
Membership Secretary	William Read
Treasurer	Heinz Beck
Music Director	David Linton

1992

President	Carl Renner
First Vice President	Robert Hawkins
Second Vice President	Wallace Hansen
Recording Secretary	Lois Meyer
Corresponding Secretary	Hilde Cox
Membership Secretary	David Fricke
Treasurer	Heinz Beck
Music Director	David Linton

1993

President	Carl Renner
First Vice President	Robert Hawkins
Second Vice President	Dieter Schulz
Recording Secretary	Robert Spittle
Corresponding Secretary	Hilde Cox
Membership Secretary	David Fricke
Treasurer	Heinz Beck
Music Director	David Linton

1994

President	Carl Renner
First Vice President	Simon Schock
Second Vice President	Dieter Schulz
Recording Secretary	Robert Spittle
Corresponding Secretary	Hilde Cox
Membership Secretary	Reinhold Kuska
Treasurer	Richard Miller
Music Director	David Linton

1995

President	Alfred Escheu
First Vice President	Simon Schock
Second Vice President	Dieter Schulz
Recording Secretary	Robert Spittle
Corresponding Secretary	Hilde Cox
Membership Secretary	Reinhold Kuska
Treasurer	Richard Miller
Music Director	David Linton

1996

President	Alfred Escheu
First Vice President	Simon Schock
Second Vice President	Dieter Schulz
Recording Secretary	Robert Spittle
Corresponding Secretary	Ann Smith
Membership Secretary	Reinhold Kuska
Treasurer	Howard Meyer
Music Director	David Linton

1997

President	Alfred Escheu
First Vice President	Simon Schock
Second Vice President	Wallace Hansen
Recording Secretary	Irene Rice
Corresponding Secretary	Ann Smith
Membership Secretary	Reinhold Kuska
Treasurer	Howard Meyer
Music Director	David Linton

1998

President	Alfred Escheu
First Vice President	Robert Hawkins
Second Vice President	Wallace Hansen
Recording Secretary	Irene Rice
Corresponding Secretary	Trudy Gilgenast
Membership Secretary	Cynthia Spink
Treasurer	Howard Meyer
Music Director	David Linton

1999

President	Reinhold Kuska
First Vice President	Robert Hawkins
Second Vice President	Simon Schock
Recording Secretary	Irene Rice
Corresponding Secretary	Trudy Gilgenast
Membership Secretary	Cynthia Spink
Treasurer	Howard Meyer
Music Director	David Linton/Robert Bunnell

2000

President	Reinhold Kuska
First Vice President	Teresa Lord
Second Vice President	Simon Schock
Recording Secretary	Irene Rice
Corresponding Secretary	Marguerite Spittle
Membership Secretary	Adrien Olivier
Treasurer	Hans-Peter Nafzinger
Music Director	Robert Bunnell

2001

President	Reinhold Kuska
First Vice President	Teresa Lord
Second Vice President	Simon Schock
Recording Secretary	Irene Rice/Samuel Simpson
Corresponding Secretary	Marguerite Spittle
Membership Secretary	Clyde Nafzinger
Treasurer	Hans-Peter Nafzinger
Music Director	Robert Bunnell

2002

President	Reinhold Kuska
First Vice President	Robert Hawkins
Second Vice President	Simon Schock
Recording Secretary	Samuel Simpson
Corresponding Secretary	Henry Maier
Membership Secretary	Clyde Nafzinger
Treasurer	Hans-Peter Nafzinger
Music Director	Robert Bunnell

2003

President
First Vice President
Second Vice President
Recording Secretary
Corresponding Secretary
Membership Secretary
Treasurer
Music Director

Officers of the German Library Association 1873-1924

1873
President Heinrich Mueller
Vice President Clemens Moeves
Record. Sec. Fred v. Bourdon
Treasurer Andreas Wilhelm
Librarian Sebastian Burkhart

1874
President Heinrich Mueller
Vice President Anton Hauber
Record. Sec. Clemens Moeves
Treasurer Andreas Wilhelm
Librarian Frederick v. Bourdon

1875
President Heinrich Mueller
Vice President
Record. Sec. Clemens Moeves
Treasurer Andreas Wilhelm
Librarian Frederick v. Bourdon

1876
President Heinrich Mueller
Vice President
Record. Sec. Clemens Moeves
Treasurer Andreas Wilhelm
Librarian Frederick v. Bourdon

1877
President Heinrich Mueller
Vice President Casimir Abberger
Record. Sec. Clemens Moeves
Treasurer Andreas Wilhelm
Librarian Frederick v. Bourdon

1878
President Heinrich Mueller
Vice President Casimir Abberger
Record. Sec. Clemens Moeves
Treasurer Andreas Wilhelm
Librarian Frederick v. Bourdon

1879
President Heinrich Mueller
Vice President George Fink
Record. Sec. Charles Heinel
Treasurer Andreas Wilhelm
Librarian Frederick v. Bourdon

1880
President Anton Hauber
Vice President Casimir Abberger
Record. Secr. Charles Heinel
Treasurer Andreas Wilhelm
Librarian Frederick v. Bourdon

1881
President Christoph Bauer
Vice President Peter Ebner
Record. Sec. Frederick v. Bourdon
Financial Sec. Christ. Popp
Treasurer Eberhard. P. Freye
Librarian J.P.T. Fuekel

1882
President John Neuschel
Vice President William Cloos
Record. Sec. August Kuhlmann
Financial Sec. Charles Yetter
Treasurer William Alsentzer
Librarian Frederick v. Bourdon

1883
President A. Kuhlmann
Vice President Francis Scheu
Record. Sec. Eberhard P. Freye
Financial Sec. Charles Yetter
Treasurer William Alsentzer
Librarian Frederick v. Bourdon

1884
President Henry Miller
Vice President Francis Scheu
Record. Sec. Eberhard P. Freye
Financial Sec. Fritz Knapp
Treasurer William Alsentzer
Librarian Frederick v. Bourdon

1885
President Anton Hauber
Vice President Nicolas Herold
Record. Sec. Frederick v. Bourdon
Financial Sec. H. Schoor
Treasurer Henry Zimmermann
Librarian Frederick v. Bourdon

1886
President Franz Scheu
Vice President Matthias Nuernberg
Record. Sec. Frederick v. Bourdon

Financial Sec.	William Cloos
Treasurer	Henry Zimmermann
Librarian	Frederick v. Bourdon

1887

President	**William Cloos**
Vice President	H. Roesch
Record. Sec.	Dr. Emil Hertel
Financial Sec.	Daniel Maier
Treasurer	Henry Zimmermann
Librarian	Frederick v. Bourdon

1888

President	**Matthias Nuernberg**
Vice President	August Krienen
Record. Sec.	Dr. Emil Hertel
Financial Sec.	Josef Nuernberg
Treasurer	Henry Zimmermann
Librarian	Frederick v. Bourdon

1889

President	**Anton Hauber**
Vice President	Georg Kalmbacher
Record. Sec.	Dr. Emil Hertel
Financial Sec.	Josef Nuernberg
Treasurer	Heinrich Zimmermann
Librarian	Frederick v. Bourdon

1890

President	**Gotthold Yaeger**
Vice President	Albert Buehler
Record. Sec.	Dr. Emil Hertel
Financial Sec.	Joseph Nuernberg
Treasurer	Henry Zimmermann
Librarian	Frederick v. Bourdon

1891

President	**Ernest Hetzel**
Vice President	Georg Haas
Record. Sec.	August Faske
Financial Sec.	Josef Nuernberg
Treasurer	Fred Heiss
Librarian	Frederick v. Bourdon

1892

President	**Dr. Emil Hertel**
Vice President	Georg Haas
Record. Sec.	Albert Buehler
Financial Sec.	Josef Nuernberg
Treasurer	Fred Heiss
Librarian	Frederick v. Bourdon

1893

President	**Dr. Emil Hertel**
Vice President	Georg Haas
Record. Sec.	Henry Kleinstueber
Financial Sec.	Alfred Buehler
Treasurer	Fritz Heiss
Librarian	Frederick v. Bourdon

1894

President	**Alfred Buehler**
Vice President	Karl Oppenlaender
Record. Sec.	Ernst Hetzel
Financial Sec.	Kleinstueber
Treasurer	Fritz Heiss
Librarian	Frederick v. Bourdon

1895

President	**Alfred Buehler**
Vice President	Charles Oppenlaender
Record. Sec.	Ernst Hetzel
Financial Sec.	Edward Seidenberg
Treasurer	Fritz Heiss
Librarian	Frederick v. Bourdon

1896

President	**Charles Oppenlaender**
Vice President	Emil Hinderer
Record. Sec.	Ernst Hetzel
Financial Sec.	Edward Seidenberg
Treasurer	Fritz Heiss
Librarian	Frederick v. Bourdon

1897

President	**Louis Melchior**
Vice President	Max Koblinski
Record. Sec.	Ernst Hetzel
Financial Sec.	Edward Seidenberg
Treasurer	Fritz Heiss
Librarian	Frederick v. Bourdon

1898

President	**Ludwig Melchior**
Vice President	Gustav Steinke
Record. Sec.	Paul Steinke
Financial Sec.	Edward Seidenberg
Treasurer	Fred W. Heiss
Librarian	Frederick v. Bourdon

1899

President	**Ludwig Melchior**
Vice President	Ferdinand Grabowski
Record. Sec.	Paul Steinke
Financial Sec.	Edward Seidenberg
Treasurer	Fred Heiss

Librarian	Frederick v. Bourdon

1900
President	**Matthias Nuernberg**
Vice President	Max Koblinski
Record. Sec.	Gustav Steinke
Financial Sec.	Daniel Dohl
Treasurer	Fred Heiss
Librarian	Paul Steinke

1901
President	**Matthias Nuernberg**
Vice President	John G. Kalmbacher
Record. Sec.	Gustav Steinke
Financial Sec.	Daniel Dohl
Treasurer	Fred Heiss
Librarian	Paul Steinke

1902
President	**Georg Kalmbacher**
Vice President	John Wolf
Record. Sec.	Gustav Steinke
Financial Sec.	Daniel Dohl
Treasurer	Fred Heiss
Librarian	Paul Steinke

1903
President	**Georg Kalmbacher**
Vice President	Frank Hauck
Record. Sec.	Gustav Steinke
Financial Sec.	Frank Krastel
Treasurer	Fred Heiss
Librarian	Paul Steinke

1904
President	**Georg Kalmbacher**
Vice President	John Wolf
Record. Sec.	Gustav Steinke
Financial Sec.	Frank Krastel
Treasurer	Fred Heiss
Librarian	Paul Steinke

1905
President	**Georg Kalmbacher**
Vice President	Fred Greiner
Record. Sec.	Charles Hafner
Financial Sec.	Frank Krastel
Treasurer	Fred Heiss
Librarian	Paul Steinke

1906
President	**Georg Kalmbacher**
Vice President	Albert Zuelke
Record. Sec.	Charles Hafner
Financial Sec.	Frank Krastel
Treasurer	Fred Heiss
Librarian	Paul Steinke

1907
President	**Georg Kalmbacher**
Vice President	David Dangel
Record. Sec.	Charles Hafner
Financial Sec.	Frank Krastel
Treasurer	Fred Heiss
Librarian	Edward Seidenberg

1908
President	**Georg Kalmbacher**
Vice President	Wilhelm Woernle
Record. Sec.	Gustav Steinke
Financial Sec.	Frank Krastel
Treasurer	Fred Heiss
Librarian	Paul Steinke

1909
President	**Georg Kalmbacher**
Vice President	Lorenz Maucher
Record. Sec.	Edward Seidenberg
Financial Sec.	Frank Krastel
Treasurer	Fred Heiss
Librarian	Paul Steinke

1910
President	**Georg Kalmbacher**
Vice President	Lorenz Maucher
Record. Sec.	Edward Seidenberg
Financial Sec.	Frank Krastel
Treasurer	Fred Heiss
Librarian	Paul Steinke

1911
President	**Georg Kalmbacher**
Vice President	Joseph Hess
Record. Sec.	Edward Seidenberg
Financial Sec.	Frank Krastel
Treasurer	Fred Heiss
Librarian	Paul Steinke/Lorenz Maucher

1912
President	**Georg Kalmbacher**
Vice President	Christian Seidle
Record. Sec.	Paul Steinke
Financial Sec.	Frank Krastel
Treasurer	Fred Heiss
Librarian	Lorenz Maucher

1913
President   **Georg Kalmbacher**
Vice President   Joseph Hess
Record. Sec.   Paul Steinke
Financial Sec.   Alfred Bradford
Treasurer   Fred Heiss
Librarian   Lorenz Maucher

1914
President   **Georg Kalmbacher**
Vice President   Frank Krastel
Record. Sec.   Paul Steinke
Financial Sec.   Alfred Bradford
Treasurer   Fred Heiss
Librarian   Lorenz Maucher

1915
President   **Georg Kalmbacher**
Vice President   Joseph Hess
Record. Sec.   Paul Steinke
Financial Sec.   Alfred Bradford
Treasurer   Frank Krastel
Librarian   Lorenz Maucher

1916
President   **Georg Kalmbacher**
Vice President   Joseph Hess
Record. Sec.   Paul Steinke
Financial Sec.   Alfred Bradford
Treasurer   Frank Krastel
Librarian   Lorenz Maucher

1917
President   **Georg Kalmbacher**
Vice President   Joseph Hess
Record. Sec.   Paul Steinke
Financial Sec.   Alfred Bradford
Treasurer   Frank Krastel
Librarian   Lorenz Maucher

1918
President   **Georg Kalmbacher**
Vice President   Joseph Hess
Record. Sec.   Paul Steinke
Financial Sec.   Alfred Bradford
Treasurer   Frank Krastel
Librarian   Lorenz Maucher

1919
President   **Georg Kalmbacher**
Vice President   Joseph Hess
Record. Sec.   Paul Steinke
Financial Sec.   Alfred Bradford
Treasurer   Frank Krastel
Librarian   Lorenz Maucher

1920
President   **Oscar Doelze**
Vice President   Joseph Hess
Record. Sec.   Lorenz Maucher
Financial Sec.   Alfred Bradford
Treasurer   Frank Krastel
Librarian   Lorenz Maucher

1921
President   **Oscar Doelze**
Vice President   William Hoelle
Record. Sec.   Christian Seidle
Financial Sec.   Alfred Bradford
Treasurer   Frank Krastel
Librarian   Lorenz Maucher

1922
President   **Oscar Doelze**
Vice President   Gustav Steinke
Record. Sec.   Christian Seidle
Financial Sec.   William Hoelle
Treasurer   Frank Krastel
Librarian   Lorenz Maucher

1923
President   **Oscar Doelze**
Vice President   Gustav Steinke
Record. Sec.   Christian Seidle
Financial Sec.   William Hoelle
Treasurer   Frank Krastel
Librarian   Lorenz Maucher

1924 January and February
President   **Oscar Doelze**
Vice President   Gustav Steinke
Record. Sec.   Christian Seidle
Financial Sec.   William Hoelle
Treasurer   Frank Krastel
Librarian   Lorenz Maucher

From then on the German Library Association was incorporated with the Delaware Saengerbund as "Delaware Saengerbund and Library Association"

WILMINGTON TURNERS

No. Name	Gewerbe	Wohnort	Mitgl. a. p.	Bemerkung
1. Stich John	Maschinist	401 corner French 4th St.	a	
2. Kohl Moritz	Kupferschmied	207 Second st.	a	abgereist den 16. August 60
3. Christ Wilhelm	Schlosser	207 Second St.	a	
4. Atles Karl	Pr.Macker	207 Second St.	a	
5. Feldmeier Henry	Bar Keeper	199 Second St.	a	
6. Dorschel Charles	Messerschmied	109 Market St.	a	abgereist den 1. Mai 60
7. Scharf Georg	Painter	610 Tatnall	a	
8. Schellkopf Georg	Schoemaker	Front Str.	a	gestrichen
9. Betzler Georg	Schreiner		a	abgreist den 31. Mai 1860
10. Buettner A. Henry	Gardener	604 French St.	a	
11. Wirth Georg	Trimmer	207 Second St.	a	abgereist den 1. August 60
12. Albert Henry	Musiker	Franklin Haus	p	
13. Kerker Ferdinand	Eisendreher	Spruce St.	p	abgereist den 1. Sept. 60
14. Louis Shonfeld	Clerk	316 Market St.		abgereist
15. Knoblauch Charles	Barber	20 East 2nd St.	a	
16. Klingler Charles	Hotel Keeper	French St. 207	a	
17. Mammele Christ.	Painter	6th Str.	a	
18. Kurtz Daniel	Backer	6th Str.	a	ausgetreten den 1. Feb 1860
19. Brand Louis	Painter	Orange Str.	a	ausgetreten den 1. Jan. 1860
20. Rabenau Ludwig	Schoemaker	Second Str.	a	gestrichen
21. Mahler Louis	Barber	2nd St. Market	a	
22. Robelen Frederick	Barber	2nd Market		abgereist den 19. Mai 60 eingetreten den 4. Feb.61
23. Valen Piereth	Korbmacher	Market Str.	a	gestrichen den 1. April 1860
24. Conrad Keller	Baecker	Market St.112	a	
25. Wuerth Valentin	Blackshmidt	Pine St.	a	gestrichen
26. Johan Nilli	Butcher	?	a	
27. Paul Mack	Butcher	?	a	
28.				
29. Pietschman Albert	Schuhmacher	Front St.	a	
John Kern	coach	Front door		
30. John Schlegel	Barber	Market 118	p	abgereist
31. Barthel	Schneider	Second	a	
32. Gust. Fallscheer	Schlosser	Second 207	a	abgereist
33. Valentin Schneider	Schuhm.	Zweite	a	
34. Andreas J. Kaldt	Sattler	Walnut St.		
35. Gottlieb Rehfuss	Baecker			
36. Otto Maurer	Heizer			
37. John M. Staus	?	Poplar Str.	a	
38. Charles Heinl			a	
39. Georg Heinl	Baecker	Zoegling		
40. Nicklaus Jenny	Trimmer	Zoegling		
41. John Scherb	Baecker			
42. Leonhardt Weiss				
43. Carl Zehender				
44. Andreas Dettling				
45. Michael Boll				
46. Heinrich Kurz	Painter			

No. Name	Gewerbe	Wohnort	Mitgl.	Bemerkung
47. John Bolswald				
48. ? Koenig			p	
49. John Gosh			p	
50. ? ?				
Charles Kohl			a	
Albert Enderlein				
John Schuster	Baecker			
J. Jakob Bodamer	?			
Moritz Kohl	Kupferschmied			
Georg Schellkopf				
Michael Boll	Kleiderhandlung			
William Meier	Carpenter			
Frederick Blank	Baker			
John ?	Baker			
Louis Hammerer	Gerber			
Eduard Gustav Colin	Gerber			
Joh. Georg Riedel				
Christian Scheel	Carpenter			
John Kropp	Baker			
Joseph Miller	Machinist			
Christian Behringer	Schlosser			
Conrad Schmidt	Feilenhauer			
Martin Keller	Schlosser			
Christian Knittel	Baecker			
Benjamin Ferris	Machinist			
Wm. H. Evans	Tailor			
John ?	Schneider			
Friedrich Vogel	Baker			
Jacob Meyer	Metzger			
Charles Fehrenbach	Metzger			
Friedrich Egge	Schlosser			
Karl Combs	Baecker			
Julius Bacher	Buchbinder			
Ch. Hartmann	Butcher			
Heinrich Ulrich	Shuhmacher			
Theodore Allright	Machinist			
Kaspar Volk	Baecker			
Jacob Schneider	Cigarmaker			
Joseph H. Wiener	Tobacconist			
Adam Reinhard	Cigarmaker			
Charles Foell	Baecker			

Awards and Honors of the DSB

The society is and should be ever mindful of its purpose: to cultivate and preserve the German language and heritage. The various awards presented to members and students of local high schools and the University of Delaware are tangible aspects of this purpose and serve as an outreach and contribution to the community. As long as the treasury is able to afford these awards, they will be given. Future members and younger generations will hopefully carry the torch and continue this purpose as they take over as stewards of the society's resources. The following lists name the recipients of the respective award and the year in which it was presented.

Sepp Hilsenrad Memorial Award

Currently an award of $500 is presented to University of Delaware student(s) who demonstrates excellence in German. The faculty of the University of Delaware Department of Languages and Literatures selects the recipient(s) whose name appears in the Honors Day Program. The student receives the award at the DSB so that members may meet the individual.

Concordia Language Camp

This award is presented to a member's child to attend a two- week immersion German language camp at Waldsee in Morehead, Minnesota. The program is offered to ages 8–18. Interested children submit an application of interest and a written essay describing the reasons for attending this camp to the Culture Committee that selects the winner. The award includes camp fees and transportation for a total amount not exceeding $1,500.

Fulda Award

This is a recent award of $500, which came about with the visit of Mayor Hamberger of Fulda, Germany and his wife as guests sponsored by the Sister Cities program. Wilmington and Fulda became partner cities in 1997. Frau Hamberger was president of the German-American Women's Club, which offered a stipend to a female student of German at the University of Delaware to study for the month of August at the International Summer Course at the Fachhochschule Fulda. In this way the Women's Club which was founded in 1942 would like to provide one student every year the opportunity not only to improve her German skills but to enjoy the new sister city, Fulda in Hesse. The Women's Club provides the stipend abroad; however, the DSB, Sister Cities Wilmington, and the Department of Languages and Literatures provide stipends to cover airfare and other expenses. The DSB's contribution has been $500 and is awarded annually dependent upon financial status.

The Federal Republic Of Germany Friendship Award

This award is presented by the German Embassy in Washington, D.C. to members of the DSB whom they feel have contributed in an outreach manner. The award states that it is given in recognition of efforts on behalf of German-American relations, in recognition of endeavors in fostering and sustaining friendship between the Federal Republic of Germany and the United States of America.

Sepp Hilsenrad Memorial Award for Excellence In German Language Studies

1969	Louis A. Baer
1972	Linda Hale
1973	Diane Knight
1973	John Maiorano
1974	Maria Beyer
1974	Ruta Trieberg
1975	Nancy Barsch
1975	Paul Heinemann
1976	Sally Camper
1976	Seward Jones
1977	Peter Robinson
1977	James Flaherty
1978	Pamela Lynn Hause
1978	Kristine Connors

1979	Kathleen Cunningham	1990	Lisa Griesbach
1979	Linnie Swineford	1991	Teresa Escheu
1982	Joan Mitchell	1992	Robyn Spittle
1982	Michael T. Scott	1993	Andrea Fischer
1983	Angelica Honsberg		Geoffrey McCloskey
1983	David Fallick	1994	Erin Spittle
1984	Werner Beyer		Emily Beck
1985	Elizabeth Bell	1995	Stephanie Gass
1985	Susan Beyer		Dana St. John
1986	Lisa Chieffo	1996	Glenna Beth Pusey
1986	Lilliane Hammond		Eric B. Grzybowski
1987	Carolyn Handel	1997	Edward Schaeffer
1987	Fabian von Posern	1998	Stephan Schill
1988	Gerhard Kuska	2000	Stephen M. Nagle
1988	Ted Kitlila	2001	Michael Chaffin
1989	Jeffrey V. Comito	2002	Michael Chaffin
1989	Carol S. Gabyzon		
1990	Nanci Nusz		
1990	Tanya Paulson		
1991	Sandra Koebler		

Fulda Award

1991	Brent Weaver	1998	Kelli Barnes
1992	Tara McMartin	1999	Colleen Granger
1992	Catherine Saltern	2000	Amanda Sheldon
1993	Lauren Hill	2001	Dana Harrison
1993	Sheri Howe	2002	Sonia Hewitt
1994	Adrian Babler		
1994	Bart Sponseller		

Federal Republic of Germany Friendship Award

1995	Melinda Hayes		
1995	Kevin Kriebel		
1996	Susan Kight	1986	Simon Schock
1996	Aili Zheng	1987	Trudy Gilgenast
1997	Monika Ebi	1988	Alfred Escheu
1997	Antje Duvekot	1989	Annemarie McNeal
1998	Alys George	1989	Clifford Weber
1999	Gregory Knott	1993	Hilde Cox
2000	Elizabeth A. Mercante	1993	Richard Grieb
2000	Petra Rosenblatt	1994	Dr. Carl Renner
2001	Tammy Pasterick	1995	Howard Meyer
2002	Christine Wisowaty	1995	Lois Meyer
		1998	William Sigmund
		1998	Charles Berr

Concordia Language Camp Awards

1984	Sharra Taylor
1985	Tina Stixrude
1986	Robyn Spittle
1987	Robyn Spittle
1988	Teresa Escheu
1989	Erin Spittle

Delaware Saengerbund Timeline

1853	Saengerbund founded as all male chorus by German immigrants in Wilmington
1855	Saengerbund
1856	Saengerbund No.1
1858	Reunion and reorganization as Delaware Saengerbund
1861	Rehearsals suspended because of Civil War
1868 – 1870	Liederkranz and Delaware Saengerbund
1871	Both reunited under the name of Delaware Harmonie
1871	Membership in Nordoestlicher Saengerbund
1871	Formation of mixed chorus with children from the Singschule and interested women
1874	Reorganization under name "Saengerbund"
1877	Reunion of Saengerbund and Delaware Harmonie under the name "Delaware Saengerbund"
1883	Purchase of Wesleyan Female College at 205 East Sixth Street together with Deutscher Bibliothek-Verein, known as German Hall
1882	First Volksfest held by all German Societies in Schützen Park
1896	Damen-Verein founded – Ladies of the Delaware Saengerbund
1903	Golden anniversary
1911	Purchase of summer home at Grubb's Landing
1923	Sale of summer home
1924	Merger with German Library Association incorporated with new seal under the name Delaware Saengerbund and Library Association
1938	Damenverein reestablished
1948	Damenchor and mixed chorus founded
1953	100th Stiftungsfest — Centennial Celebration
1958	Soccer team Delaware Kickers; Siegfried Geist, first president

1962   Library books released to University of Delaware

1963   Joint meeting of Delaware Saengerbund men and women
                English becomes official business language

1965   German Hall sold to Wilmington Housing Authority for Urban Renewal Project, razed October 1965

1965 – 1967   Meetings at Officers' Club and Turners

1967   Property purchased in Ogletown at 49 Salem Church Road

1967   Bauernstube built, dedicated November 9, 1967

1968   Enzian Volkstanzgruppe (EVTG) founded, George Keith, first president

1968   The "Ladies of the Delaware Saengerbund" organized, Elnora (Toots) Schweiger, first president

1969   May 10, Groundbreaking for Deutsche Halle

1970   Language classes for adults and children

1972   Hiking group Wandervögel

1972   Teen Age Group founded by the LADIES

1978   Soccer Youth Teams –DSB Kickers, Rolf Offschanka, coach

1978   125th Stiftungsfest

1979   First public Oktoberfest held under the big tent

1983   Exhibit "Old Ways in the New World" - 300 Years of Germans in America in Old Town Hall,
                Wilmington sponsored by the Historical Society of Delaware

1985   Building Phase II: building of von Steuben Zimmer, Board of Directors room, foyer, larger kitchen

1989   Bundesverdienstkreuz awarded to Alfred Escheu, president and Simon Schock, vice president by the
                German Embassy

1991   Building of Pavilion

1995   Building Phase III, addition of library-lounge, game room, office, kitchen

1997   Sixteenth Gaufest of the Nord Amerikanischer Schuhplattler Verband held at the Delaware
                Saengerbund

2003   48th Sängerfest of the Nordoestlicher Saengerbund

2003   150th Stiftungsfest of the Delaware Saengerbund

SELECTED GLOSSARY

Abendschoppen	a glass of wine enjoyed in the evening
abgereist	departed from town
alte Heimat	old homeland
Altweibermühle	old women mill
Anstich	first tap of the keg
Ausklang	finale
Bauernmesse	peasant style mass
Bauernstube	little tavern with a bar
Bunter Abend	evening variety entertainment
Bürger	citizen
Christkindlmarkt	Christmas market/bazaar
Damen Verein	Ladies auxiliary
Deutscher Schulverein/Schulrat	German school board
Dirndl	traditional dress of a region
drüben	over there
durch dick und dünn	through thick and thin
Edelweiss	small white Alpine flower
Einigkeit macht stark	unity builds strength
Enzian	deep blue Alpine flower
Ernst und Scherz	serious and light-hearted
Erntedankfest	Thanksgiving festival
Erzgebirge	Ore Mountains
Fahne	flag
Fasching	the weeks after New Year ending with Ash Wednesday
Festzug	festival parade
Forty-Eighters	people who took part in the Revolution of March 18, 1848 in Germany and were forced to emigrate
Frikadelle	meat pattie
Frühschoppen	early pint
Gebirge	mountain range
Gemütlichkeit	good fellowship
Gesangverein	singing society
Glühwein	hot punch
Hausmusik	small music group
Herz Jesus Kirche	Sacred Heart Church
Indianer	North American Indian
Kartoffelsalat	potato salad
Katzenjammer	hangover
Kirmes/Kirchweih	festival to celebrate church's dedication
Kränzchen	small gathering with a dance
Ländler	figurative Alpine dance
Lied	song
Maibaum	May pole
Minnesänger	minnesinger/ minstrel
Muttersprache	mother tongue
Nachwuchs	next generation

Oktoberfest	annual festival held in Munich since 1810
	annual festival of the Delaware Saengerbund since 1982
Ostermontag	Easter Monday
platteln	Schuhplatteln – shoe slapping dance
Richtfest	roof raising ceremony
Sang und Klang	song and music
Sängerfest	singing festival
Sangesbruder	brother in song
Schafkopf	card game
Schatzmeister	treasurer
Schornsteinfegerball	chimney sweep ball
Schützenfest	shooting festival
Sportplatz	athletic field
Stammtisch	table reserved for a certain group
Ständchen	serenade
Stiftungsfest	anniversary festival
Sylvester	New Year's Eve
Tannenbaumabend	Christmas celebration
tatkräftiges Handeln	immediate/strong action
Tracht	the traditional attire of a region
Treffpunkt	meeting place
Turnfest	athletic festival
Überschuss	profit
Vaterland	fatherland
Verein	organization
Verwaltungsrat	board of trustees
Volksfest	folk festival
wählt nass	vote wet
Weihnachten	Christmas
Wirtschaftswunder	economic miracle
Wurstschnappen	contest to catch a sausage in teeth without using hands
Zwetschgenkuchen	plum cake

BIBLIOGRAPHY

Books

Abeles, J. Emil. The German Element in Wilmington from 1850-1914. Newark, DE: University of Delaware Master's Thesis, 1948.

Bacher Betty and Duane Conly. *Zion Lutheran Church 150th Anniversary.* Wilmington, DE: Zion Lutheran Church, 1998.

Beliebte Chöre fur vierstimmigen Männergesang. Leipzig: Gebrüder Hug & Co., 1903.

Bureau of the Census. *U. S. Census Records.* Washington, DC: Department of Commerce, various dates.

Delaware Saengerbund Records including Consititions and Bylaws, Minutes and Ledgers.

Fragen an die deutsche Geschichte. Bonn: Press und Informationszentrum, 1983.

Gilgenast, Trudy. *Das Mehl ist anders—The Flour is Different.* Wilmington, DE: North Light Studio, 1982; reprinted, Middle Atlantic Press, 1995.

Grier, A. O. H. *This Was Wilmington: A Veteran Journalist's Recollections of the "Good Old Days."* Wilmington, DE: News-Journal Company, 1945.

Hoffecker, Carol. *Wilmington: A Pictorial History.* Norfolk, VA: The Donning Company, 1982.

Kühlwein, Heinz. *Aufbruch in die Ferne: Die Auswanderung nach Amerika aus unserem Landkreis in der Zeit um 1850.* Neustadt an der Aisch: Schmidt, 1999.

Lawlor, Mark R. Brandywine Springs Amusement Park: Echoes of the Past, 1886-1923. Newark, DE: M & M Publishing, 1991; reprinted 1996.

McMahon, Virginia Stockhausen. *Bristoler Tanzbuch; die Tänze der deutschen Sommerschule von Middlebury College, mit Anleitungen der Tanzlehrer* Middlebury, VT. n.d.

McNinch, Marjorie. *Festivals.* Wilmington, DE: Cedar Tree Press, 1996.

Mück, Wolfgang. *Ein traditionsreiches Kapitel Stadtgeschichte: Die Kgl. Priv. Schutzengesellschaft 1471 Neustadt an der Aisch.* Neustadt/Aisch: 1996.

Mueller, Helmut M. *Schlaglichter der deutschen Geschichte.* Mannheim/Wien/Zurich: Meyers Lexikonverlag, Biographisches Institut, 1986.

Munroe, John A. *History of Delaware.* Newark, DE: University of Delaware Press, 1979.

Questions on German History : Deutscher Bundestag Herausgeber. Bonn: German Bundestag, 1998.

Rehs, Michael and Hans-Joachim Haager. *Wurzeln in fremder Erde: zur Geschichte der südwestdeutschen Auswanderung nach Amerika.* Stuttgart: DRW-Verlag, 1984.

Rendle, Ellen: *The Ghosts of Market Street: Merchants of Yesteryear.* Wilmington, DE: Cedar Tree Books, 1998.

Saengerfest-Almanach des Nordoestlichen Saengerbundes von Amerika. Philadelphia: 1912.

Scharf, J. Thomas. *History of Delaware, 1609-1888.* 2 volumes. Philadelphia: L. J. Richards & Company, 1888.

Schiek, Martha and Ray Hester, *Images of America: Claymont.* Charleston, SC: Arcadia Publishing, 2000.

Schrader, Frederick Franklin. *Handbook: Political, Statistical, and Sociological for German Americans and All Other Americans Who Have not Forgotten the History and Traditions of their Country, and Who Believe in the Principles of Washington, Jefferson and Lincoln.* New York: 1916.

Stolavik, Mark M. *Forgotten Doors.* Philadelphia: The Balch Institute Press, 1988.

Ueberhorst, Horst. *Turner unterm Sternenbanner: d. Kampf d. dt.-amerikan. Turner für Einheit, Freiheit u. soziale Gerechtigkeit, 1848-1918.* München: Moos, 1978.

Wilmington City Directories. Wilmington, DE: Eastern Directory Company, n.d.

Witter, C. *Deutsch-Englische Schreib-und Lese-Fibel.* Reprinted 1987.

Young, Toni. *Delaware Becoming American, Remaining Jewish: The Story of Wilmington, Delaware's First Jewish Community, 1879-1924.* Newark, DE: University of Delaware Press, 1999.

Recent Newspaper Articles

Kenney, Edward L. "Film Aims to Tap Fort's WWII History." *The News Journal,* 8 February 2002.

Matsen, Alison. " Learn a Foreign Language that Suits Real World" *The News Journal,* March 2002

Schaller, Martin. "Reflections on an Oktoberfest" *Washington Journal.* October 1998.

Redd, C. Kalimah. "Bridge to Countries Left Behind." *Portland Press Herald.* 25 June 2001.

Wilson, W. Emerson. "Prosit Fades Out At The Saengerbund—1840s Hall Will Be Razed." *Evening News Journal,* 8 October 1965.

The following older newspapers were also consulted:

Daily Gazette
Delmarvia Leader
Evening News
Every Evening
Freie Presse Philadelphia
Morning News
Newark Post
The Sunday Morning Star
Wilmington Freie Presse und Lokal=Anzeiger

<u>Interviews by the authors</u>

Ambrosh, Heinz und Erika. Ogletown, DE, 17 August 2001.

Busch, Iris. Ogletown, DE, 20 August 2001.

Escheu, Alfred. Ogletown, DE, 4 April 2001.

Grieb, Richard. Ogletown, DE, 4 February 2002.

Heinemann, Paul. Ogletown, DE, 22 February 1992.

Kaeks, Erich. Ogletown, DE, March 1992.

Olivier, Adrien. Ogletown, DE, March 1992.

Schock, Rudi. Ogletown, DE, 3 March 2002.

Schock, Simon. 4 April 2001.

Schulz, Brian. 17 February, 2002.

Index